The *Ontario*
CRAFT
BEER
GUIDE

Second Edition

The *Ontario* CRAFT BEER

Second Edition GUIDE

ROBIN LEBLANC
JORDAN ST. JOHN

DUNDURN
TORONTO

Insert photographs: © Robin LeBlanc
Cover Image: © pogonici | 123RF.com
Printer: Webcom

Library and Archives Canada Cataloguing in Publication

LeBlanc, Robin, 1984-, author
    The Ontario craft beer guide / Robin LeBlanc, Jordan St. John. -- Second edition.

Includes index.
Issued in print and electronic formats.
ISBN 978-1-4597-3929-1 (softcover).--ISBN 978-1-4597-3930-7 (PDF).--
ISBN 978-1-4597-3931-4 (EPUB)

    1. Microbreweries--Ontario--Guidebooks. 2. Breweries--Ontario--
Guidebooks. 3. Beer--Ontario. I. St. John, Jordan, author II. Title.

TP573.C3L43 2017   663'.4209713   C2017-901075-1
                                              C2017-901076-X

1   2   3   4   5   21   20   19   18   17

We acknowledge the support of the **Canada Council for the Arts** and the **Ontario Arts Council** for our publishing program. We also acknowledge the financial support of the **Government of Ontario**, through the **Ontario Book Publishing Tax Credit** and the **Ontario Media Development Corporation**, and the **Government of Canada**.

Care has been taken to trace the ownership of copyright material used in this book. The authors and the publisher welcome any information enabling them to rectify any references or credits in subsequent editions.

— *J. Kirk Howard, President*

The publisher is not responsible for websites or their content unless they are owned by the publisher.

Printed and bound in Canada.

VISIT US AT

dundurn.com | @dundurnpress | dundurnpress | dundurnpress

Dundurn
3 Church Street, Suite 500
Toronto, Ontario, Canada
M5E 1M2

CONTENTS

TOP BEERS AND BREWERIES

PREFACE

The Ontario beer landscape has changed remarkably in the last year, with more breweries opening up seemingly every week. For the second edition of the *Ontario Craft Beer Guide*, we have included all of the ones that have opened and released beer in that time. Additionally, a lot can happen in a year for an ever-evolving business, so we have revised the core list of breweries from the first edition, taking changes of staff, brewing direction, ownership, and closures into account and updating tasting notes where (frequently) necessary.

We have also included a section detailing the story of Ontario beer ingredients to add to the context set down by the chapter on Ontario's craft beer history. This allows us to further present the narrative of Ontario beer so you, the beer drinker, can see where we started, how far we've come, and where we stand now.

During the development of this edition, we have also greatly expanded on the recommended pubs list, from fifty listings to just over one hundred, providing a better range of options for you to explore on a night out.

Finally, we have included a photo section to provide a visual representation of the diversity and range found in Ontario beer.

INTRODUCTION

Until very recently, Ontario's craft beer scene was a fairly manageable affair. The explosion of small breweries that has taken place since 2007 means that it has become very difficult, even for beer writers covering the province, to keep track of what exists, let alone how everything fits together. While it is excellent to have an up-to-date list of breweries from across the province, it became apparent to us in mid-2014 that additional context and information was required if anyone was going to be able to navigate the huge amount of choice that currently exists in the marketplace.

So, in a climate where new breweries are popping up at a rate of one a week, the most frequent question we were asked when writing this book was, "How did you know when to stop?" We chose to make the cut-off point for inclusion three weeks before we had to hand in the manuscript for this book, approximately December 15, 2016. Such a cut-off was needed; otherwise, our editors would have suffered more headaches than they get now from emails requesting late additions.

The second most frequent question, and perhaps one of the more loaded ones, was, "How are you defining what makes a craft brewery?"

As many know, there are a lot of definitions out there, from making small amounts of beer to being independently owned to being community focused. In this book we have included just about any brewery that might be considered "craft," which means breweries, brewpubs, and contract breweries. In all cases, we have denoted the difference in types of business for the sake of clarity. Because contracting is sometimes used as a first step for a brewery before moving into its own facility, some are listed as transitional.

In cases in which a brewery has been purchased at some point in the past by a large multinational company, we have included them but made a note of the ownership. The historical context that breweries like Creemore and Mill Street have provided for the craft beer scene in Ontario cannot and should not be ignored.

The purpose of this guide is to assist you in navigating Ontario's craft beer market and finding something that you might like to drink. Each brewery's entry is composed of its contact information and coordinates, a brief biography to help give a sense of the brewery's identity, and a series of tasting notes and ratings for the beers that it has on offer.

In producing tasting notes and ratings, we have strived for fairness. That being said, we have offered brewers every opportunity to put their best foot forward by directly consulting with them to see which beers (usually capped at eight examples) they feel best celebrate who they are. In the majority of the entries, we've used samples directly from the brewery itself, avoiding any potential problems that might arise from tasting the beer from dirty tap lines in a bar or pub or from bottles or cans that have gone stale as a result of languishing too long on the shelves of a retail establishment.

A WORD ABOUT THE RATING SYSTEM IN THIS BOOK

In producing ratings, we have been mostly interested in three things: whether the beer has objective flaws, how well the flavour profile works, and how well the beer accomplishes what it sets out to do, i.e., the extent to which it is what the brewers claim it to be.

Beer preference is subjective. You may like a certain style of beer more than another for just about any reason, and you're not wrong to feel that way. Brewing quality is not subjective. Beer frequently has technical flaws or undesirable qualities that can leave an unpleasant impression. In the case of flavour defects, these might include the presence of diacetyl (which smells like buttered popcorn, leaves a slick, butterscotchy mouthfeel, and causes hangovers), dimethyl sulfide (an aroma of creamed corn, canned vegetables, or tomato sauce), acetaldehyde (overwhelming green apple), butyric character (blue cheese or baby vomit), inappropriate phenolic character (smoke, burnt plastic, or Band-Aid), or just a lack of conditioning resulting in rough, unpleasant mouthfeel. The beer may be inappropriately carbonated or under-attenuated (containing residual sugars that ought to have been fermented).

We have taken into account stylistic convention. The Beer Judge Certification Program style guidelines are a helpful tool in doing exactly that, and, combined with context, experience, and the knowledge that it is possible to push the envelope a little, they have helped form the backbone of our rating system.

We have been pleased to reward brewers for balance of flavours. A frequent criticism of websites for beer geeks is that they tend to reward the extreme, favouring beers with higher alcohol and in-your-face flavours. We've tried to eliminate this bias from our thinking, focusing on how balanced a beer is, its progression of flavours, and the overall impression that it leaves. Whether considering a beer with a simple style done well or a complex behemoth that somehow manages to attain balance, we've done our best to treat them similarly.

Finally, writing this book has given us an appreciation for how much the art of brewing has to do with expectation management. When deciding how to market a beer, brewers must decide exactly what that beer is in order to communicate its qualities effectively. If a brewer refers to something as a blonde ale and it has pronounced notes of chocolate and mint, something is seriously wrong. If a brewer has referred to something as "Belgian-style" and it shows no trace of Belgian influence, that's a real problem. If a "kölsch" is more like a blonde ale or a "cream ale" is more like a pale ale, we've taken that into account.

That said, there are always new styles of beer emerging. We have taken seriously the description of the beer provided. To give an example, the term *breakfast stout* may not be widely enough known to connote an actual style of beer, but it conveys the impression that it will contain oats, coffee, and chocolate. It lets you know what you're getting, which is of ultimate importance to the consumer.

The rating system is a simple five-star system that includes half stars for emphasis and versatility. The ratings describe the following properties:

1-POOR

A deeply flawed beer. Likely contains off flavours or does not seem to be well-made from a technical perspective. May be off style or poorly conceived. Not recommended.

2-FAIR

Beer may contain noticeable flaws in terms of flavour or technical elements. Beer approaches stylistic guidelines. Beer may not quite work from a conceptual standpoint.

3-GOOD

Stylistically accurate. Beer does not contain off flavours. Beer may have issues with balance in its flavour profile. Technical proficiency is not an issue.

4-VERY GOOD

A memorable example of the style. Very much in balance. Flavours are appropriate, and the beer has managed a distinct character that sets it apart from other examples.

5-EXCELLENT

A beer of quality such that it would hold its own against the best examples of its style in the world.

In a few cases we've been unable to get a hold of tasting notes for a brewery due to problems that vary from brewing schedule conflicts to travel issues. We have not provided ratings for those beers, but rather a simple description followed by **(NR)**, meaning "not reviewed."

LEGEND

In each brewery entry the contact information uses these symbols:

 ADDRESS   WEBSITE

 PHONE NUMBER   VISITING HOURS

 TWITTER   RETAIL STORE HOURS

ONTARIO'S CRAFT BEER HISTORY

The renaissance of brewing in Ontario has taken place in approximately the same timeframe during which the rest of North America's brewing industry has blossomed again. All across the continent, there has been immense growth in the number of breweries operating and the number and types of beers available.

For the most part, however, the history of the brewing industry in North America during the twentieth century had been about the consolidation and shuttering of various plants under larger banners. In Canada, throughout the middle of the twentieth century, one of our most successful business-men, E.P. Taylor, built Canadian Breweries, an empire that thrived on this model, reducing the number of players in the market and the selection of products available to beer drinkers. His empire was not limited solely to North America. In the United Kingdom, Taylor's consolidation of breweries and their tied houses led to a situation in which Carling Lager was served in over eleven thousand pubs by 1967.

By the end of the 1970s, the number of players in the Ontario beer market was the smallest since the advent of industrialized brewing in the province. Molson, Labatt, Carling O'Keefe, Northern Breweries, and Henninger were all that was left of an industry that a hundred years earlier had boasted nearly two hundred companies. The lack of selection in the marketplace briefly created a boom in sales. The late 1970s represent the historical high point of beer sales across North America.

An indirect effect of E.P. Taylor's empire building was the founding in 1971 of England's Campaign for Real Ale (CAMRA). Concerned about the shrinking amount of diversity in brewing, CAMRA strived to preserve traditional brewing methods and more flavourful ale styles. CAMRA in turn inspired many of the microbrewery start-ups in Ontario. Germany had similarly been a bastion for quality and full-flavoured beer because of the protections of the *Reinheitsgebot*, or beer purity law, which limited the ingredients permitted to be used in the making of beer to water, hops, barley, and yeast. Its influence can also be seen in our early microbrewers.

New craft beers from both of these traditions have found receptive markets in Ontario. In the early days of the craft beer revival in the province, there was a claim by some that the beer

TOP TEN BREWERIES

market in Ontario was separated by Yonge Street. To the east, it was said, customers preferred ales, because of their British traditions and heritage. To the west, drinkers supposedly preferred lagers, due to their Germanic roots. Whatever truth there might have been to this claim has, as the market has diversified over the last thirty years, become diminishingly accurate to the point of irrelevance. However, the central premise that lies at the heart of this insight does help to illustrate why Ontario provided such a robust market for beer in the twentieth century and why so many beer lovers in the province were quick to take up brewing in the 1980s: the majority of the population had come from beer-drinking nations.

There has been tremendous growth in the business of brewing beer in Ontario since the 1980s. It is helpful to think

ONTARIO'S CRAFT BEER HISTORY

of this modern brewing history in Ontario in terms of three distinct periods: the founding of the first wave of small brewers (approximately 1984 to 1995); a second period following failure and shakeout, when conservatism reigned (approximately 1996 to 2007); and the current period, characterized largely by enthusiasm, expansion, and change to the market.

THE FIRST WAVE (1984–1995)

Ontario's first craft brewery, Brick, was founded in Waterloo in 1984, literally in the shadow of Labatt's converted Kuntz facility. Upper Canada opened in Toronto the same year, brewing a mixed selection of ales and lagers. Overall the selection of styles on offer in the province was very basic, with the varieties being direct lifts from English and German tradition. Frequently, brewers would cite their travels in Europe as their inspiration for a particular recipe. Latching on to any tradition, be it the "real ale" movement or the *Reinheitsgebot* regulations, provided ready-made talking points and a defined marketing context for small-brewery products. These specialty products helped to differentiate small brewers from their much larger, and more established, counterparts. The 1980s may well prove to have been the only period in Ontario history when people anticipated the annual release of a bock beer.

Small brewers were helped in their battle to capture the imagination of the market by a labour dispute at the Beer

Store, which closed down for the month of February in 1985. At the time the LCBO had not fully diversified into beer sales, offering only inexpensive American imports like Pabst Blue Ribbon and Lonestar. With the province's only real outlet for beer sales closed and the LCBO struggling to keep up with orders, small local breweries became important in the short term. Customers were lining up in order to purchase their beer, and sales were so strong that the small breweries were pleading in newspaper interviews for the return of empties so that they could package more beer.

One of the hallmarks of this period was the ambitious attitude toward the market. For decades, the beer industry model in Ontario involved an attempt to sell beer to the whole province through the Beer Store. It was a model dictated by the largest players in the market, and many start-up breweries attempted to emulate it. The small breweries founded in this period were huge by today's standards. By the end of its first decade of operation, Brick was producing 40,000 hL of beer annually and was publicly traded. Sleeman, partially funded by Stroh's in Michigan, began producing beer in 1988 at 200,000 hL annually. In point of fact, of the thirteen microbreweries listed in 1993's *Ontario Beer Guide*, the very smallest produced just under 10,000 hL of beer, and the majority were vastly larger.

Toward the end of this period, the industry was plagued by two issues. The first was quality. The drive to create large volumes of beer for sale led to issues with consistency on the part of brewers who were, after all, relatively inexperienced, having started only a decade previously. Adding to the problem of inconsistent quality was the proliferation of extract brewing systems in brewpubs across the province. By 1993, Ontario had thirty-one brewpubs, many of which operated with these systems. Extract brewing was touted as something anyone could do, as replacing all-grain brewing with malt extract removed much of the effort from the process. A small number of these brewpubs simplified things even further by simply using imported wort, removing even the necessity of adding extract to hot water and making them responsible only for fermenting it on premises. Without sufficient training, information, and respect for cleanliness, however, the quality of the beer being served suffered enormously. It is not a surprise that the majority of those that survived employed all-grain brewing methods.

TOP FIVE AMERICAN IPAS

1.	BRONAN	p. 278
2.	KARMA CITRA	p. 266
3.	INSTIGATOR	p. 290
4.	ROMAN CANDLE	p. 104
5.	LAZY BONES	p. 429

The second issue was the emergence of the discount beer segment at approximately the same time. In late 1992, President's Choice launched its own brand, which managed to capture fully 2 percent of the market by spring of the following year. Loblaws, which had commissioned the beer, struggled to keep up with demand. Imitators were spawned, and the large brewers entered the discount-beer market. Ontarians, perhaps sensibly in the wake of a recession, decided that, rather than paying a premium for inconsistent beer produced by small brewers, they would prefer to pay much less for a dependable product that was somewhat inferior in flavour. Even those who enjoyed a more flavourful beer increasingly avoided the not-always-dependable small breweries and brewpubs. Instead, they began taking advantage of the numerous brew-on-premises outlets that opened at the time. These allowed anyone to walk in off the street and make small batches of beer of a relatively high quality at a massive discount.

As a result of these issues, sales in the craft beer market declined significantly. Brewpubs folded left and right. Small breweries closed or were consolidated into the holdings of larger companies. The effects of the shakeout of the mid-1990s can be seen to this day. Some of Ontario's early craft brands are owned by odd companies. Brick has ended up with Conners and Northern Algonquin. Sleeman still produces Upper Canada Lager and Dark Ale (which are shells of their former selves).

THE SECOND WAVE (1996–2007)

If the second period in our recent history has a theme, it is that of caution. As one might expect following such a period of tribulation, the late 1990s saw craft breweries reining in experimentation. Instead, the surviving breweries focused on quality and consistency. It had become apparent that the key to long-term success in the beer market in Ontario was not the size of the brewery, but rather the ability to grow predictably while maintaining the quality of the product.

The good news was that the first generation of small brewers in Ontario had produced a significant number of personnel capable of running breweries that conformed to this model. Of the relatively small number of start-ups that emerged following the shakeout, the majority had employees who had formerly worked in successful breweries. Steam Whistle is the most famous example, with founding partners who had worked at Upper Canada. The "3FG" code on its bottles stands for Three Fired Guys. Mill Street was founded with personnel from Amsterdam. Magnotta entered the beer industry, having already developed expertise in wine production. Other new ventures were frequently staffed by veterans of existing breweries who had outgrown their positions or found themselves without an employer. The pattern repeated throughout the industry, creating a sense of continuity in the slow but steady recovery.

During this period, the quality of the beer on offer increased dramatically. However, the variety of beer styles being brewed remained approximately the same and, at various points, may even be said to have decreased. Ontario developed a reputation internationally for beers that were of high quality even if they were not particularly interesting. By way of contrast, in the United States, which had always been a more adventurous market and somewhat less bound up with tradition than Ontario, brewers created mould-breaking, highly experimental beers.

In the defence of Ontario's craft brewers, it can be said that, chastened more than a little by the troubles of the mid-1990s, they were justifiably timid. The decision to offer a new brand was not taken lightly. However, experimentation was minimal. After all, the beer was selling, and many brewers saw little benefit in developing new

TOP FIVE DOUBLE IPAS		
1.	LASER SHOW	p. 321
2.	ROBOHOP	p. 266
3.	TWIN PINES	p. 450
4.	SUCKER PUNCH	p. 518
5.	HOP CONE SYNDROME	p. 429

recipes. A residual effect of this, which persists to this day, is the sentiment among beer geeks that Ontario lags behind the United States in terms of interesting beer.

THE THIRD WAVE (2007–2016)

The term *craft beer* entered into popular usage midway through the first decade of the twenty-first century. The change in language helped to differentiate a category in which small brewers could participate. The Ontario Small

Brewers Association, originally founded in 2003, changed its name in 2005 to the Ontario Craft Brewers in order to take advantage of this development.

Gradually, over the course of the decade, the number of kinds of beer being offered began to expand. The hop-forward ales that had been popular in the United States began to have additional influence on recipe design north of the border. The earliest commercially available examples were still malt-heavy. The now retired Devil's Pale Ale from Great Lakes was considered extreme at its launch in 2006, containing a whopping 66.6 International Bittering Units' (IBUs) worth of hopping.

Slowly confidence returned to the market and new breweries began to crop up. The build-up was slow, however. In the first half of the decade there were entire years that went by without a brewery launch. From 2006 to 2010, the average was approximately four a year. An increase in the status of craft beer was helped along by the addition of bars and pubs focused specifically on the category. Events like Bar Volo's Cask Days and an increasing number of other festivals provided showcases for experimentation and challenged brewers to come up with something new to delight the public.

The focus of the business began to change. Rather than

intending to sell beer to the entire province, brewers focused on specific localities, in part because of the expense of dealing with the foreign-owned Beer Store chain. As a result, distribution through the LCBO has increased, and the focus in packaging has shifted from the traditional six-pack of bottles to a system that prefers single cans of beer. For the most part, very small craft breweries prefer to do business out of their front doors. Compared to the early brewers of the 1980s, the ambition of Ontario's new craft brewers is somewhat smaller. The size of these companies may not be as large, but the imagination on display is infinitely greater.

TOP FIVE STOUTS		
1.	SHIPS IN THE NIGHT	p. 486
2.	COBBLESTONE	p. 359
3.	BLACK SHEEP	p. 373
4.	BLACK KATT	p. 197
5.	FORTITUDE	p. 518

The caution that followed the shakeout of the 1990s has served us well. Many of the young brewers opening their own facilities gained experience under long-time industry veterans and have had the idea that quality matters drilled into them as a mantra. The cumulative wisdom is having a real effect.

The addition of the Niagara College Brewmaster and Brewery Operations Management program helps to ensure that brewery start-ups will survive and has engendered a greater sense of community in an already collegial industry. The addition of a Durham College program affiliated with Chicago's Siebel Institute should only bolster this effect.

Between 2012 and 2017, Ontario will have added two hundred breweries to the roster of brewing operations in the province, including individual brewpub locations, contract brewers, and bricks-and-mortar breweries. That surpasses the high point of the nineteenth century. During the five-month period in which the first edition of this book was written, Ontario launched more breweries than it did during the 1990s in total.

At the moment, there are very few styles of beer in the world that are not brewed in Ontario. In addition to the brewing industry, there are currently a burgeoning hop industry, a handful of maltsters, and suppliers of yeast starting up. The brewing renaissance is in full swing, and the province has taken notice. Recent changes to the retail system will ensure that this development continues.

BUYING BEER IN ONTARIO

As a result of a combination of factors, the Ontario beer market has changed drastically in a very short time. The addition of two hundred breweries over the last five years created a situation in which reform to the existing beer-retailing system was necessary in order to provide the province's breweries with a road to the market. The political will to make these changes was helped somewhat by the geographic allocation of breweries. There is now a small brewer in just about every riding in the province, which makes their survival an important issue for local government representatives.

In this section we will attempt to outline the players in the market. This comes with a caveat. Change to the retail portion of the Ontario beer market is going to come relatively slowly over the next decade. This is likely by design. Critics of the recent changes that have taken place assume that the laggard nature of change is designed to help the large brewers. More probably, the changes to the market are designed to be gradual and predictable in order to create dependable tax revenues for the Ontario government. Sometimes, in life, rather than exciting conspiracies, we get boring policy.

THE BEER STORE

In principle, the Beer Store is a good idea. Founded in 1927, it was a post-Prohibition answer to beer retailing. The twelve-year experiment with prohibiting alcohol left a market in which there was no system for retailing beer. The Province of Ontario created the Liquor Control Board of Ontario (LCBO) in order to retail wine and liquor, but it was stymied somewhat by the ever-present realities faced by brewers throughout history: Beer takes up a lot of space. Beer is heavy and the roads are poor. In order to sell beer, it is necessary to warehouse it and deliver it. Consider the cost of starting the LCBO from scratch, and then tack on additional warehousing.

Brewer's Warehousing, as the Beer Store was called when it was first created, was an attempt to outsource the warehousing and delivery of beer. Originally it delivered to mom-and-pop stores, which actually handled the retailing. The warehousing system was partially owned by each of the brewers in the province, a format that made it a co-operative.

Some brewers were larger than others, but that is a persistent market reality. Eventually, Brewers Warehousing became Brewers Retail and the warehouses developed their own network of stores. The cost savings for brewers as a result of the vertical integration of the business was part of the appeal.

With the benefit of hindsight, it is easy to see that the consolidation of Ontario's breweries was an inevitability following Prohibition. Many of them had been turned into vinegar factories or soft-drink bottling plants and were not really financially solvent. Prohibition had driven nearly all of Ontario's brewers out of business, but the creation of Brewers

TOP FIVE SAISONS		
1.	FLEMISH CAP	p. 244
2.	FARMAGEDDON	p. 104
3.	PEPPERCORN RYE	p. 234
4.	CHLOE	p. 486
5.	BRETT FARMHOUSE	p. 162

Warehousing in 1927 was not the ideal answer for many of the new breweries that opened following the relaxation of the province's liquor laws; in fact, it compounded the pressure. While the beer retailing co-op provided savings to the brewers who jointly owned it, the size of the operation and the fact that participating brewers were expected to provide enough beer to stock stores across the province meant that many brewers could not afford to be part of it. As a result, larger, better-financed breweries, such as E.P. Taylor's Canadian Breweries, were able to lessen competition by buying up the smaller, failing brewing operations.

While companies like Canadian Breweries certainly got the ball rolling, realistically, consolidation was happening in markets all over the world. This practice continued over the next few decades until, by the 1980s, there were only a handful of giant brewers left in Canada. In Ontario, this extreme consolidation of the brewery business resulted in the Beer Store having just two majority owners by 1989: Molson and Labatt.

By 2014, additional mergers and acquisitions in the international market meant that Molson had become Molson Coors and was, therefore, partially American owned. Labatt had been purchased by InBev in 1995 and subsequently became part of the Belgian-based Anheuser-Busch InBev. A small percentage is owned by Japan's Sapporo, which was able to make inroads to the market by purchasing Sleeman. As a consequence of corporate consolidations, the distribution and retailing of beer in Ontario, originally intended to be a co-operative for the province's brewers, was completely owned by three entities based outside the country. It was estimated by various analysts that the owners realized between $400 and $700 million worth of cost reductions annually as a result of this arrangement.

The 150 breweries that existed in Ontario at the end of 2014 had no ownership stake or decision-making ability in the system with which they were meant to do business. Criticisms included exorbitant listing fees and unequal representation on shelves and in display, both of which were entirely justified. Additionally, the Beer Store represents a mid-twentieth-century model of retail designed for a small number of year-round brands to be sold in large packaging formats. The craft beer model, which includes numerous seasonal releases throughout the course of the year, was completely ignored.

The Beer Store's failure to acknowledge the realities of the market have led to some mandated changes. Small brewers will be entitled to purchase nominal ownership. The board structure has been revamped to include independent members and representatives for non-majority owners. The creation of the position of Beer

TOP FIVE LAGERED ALES/KÖLSCHS		
1.	CREAM ALE (MUSKOKA)	p. 365
2.	COUNTRY CREAM ALE	p. 432
3.	BROWN VAN K.S.A.	p. 159
4.	NO NONSENSE	p. 254
5.	1857 KÖLSCH	p. 60

Ombudsman will hopefully shed light on any abuses customers witness or any perceived injustices small brewers may wish to voice. A reduction in the fee structure and a mandate requiring 20 percent of products be from small brewers may make the stores more accessible, but the question remains as to whether small brewers will want to do business with an entity that did not consider their needs until forced to by the government. It is likely that at some point in the near future craft brewers will participate, if only to take advantage of the guaranteed shelf space.

In light of other developments, the Beer Store's overall business will likely continue to wane. The LCBO diversified into beer two generations ago, and polling commissioned by the authors suggests that 50 percent of customers under the age of forty-five are unlikely to shop for beer at the Beer Store. Its unwillingness to cater to an emerging market rendered the Beer Store irrelevant to Ontario's brewers as a retailer for years and did serious damage to its reputation with beer drinkers. It remains to be seen exactly what will happen, especially as the packaging format in the province has shifted to cans, decreasing the importance of the Beer Store's associated recycling facilities.

THE LCBO

As mentioned, the LCBO was not designed to handle beer. Its mandate was to sell the province wine and liquor. There was a time when it did so begrudgingly, forcing people to carry liquor-permit books with them until 1962. In the modern era, it supplies glossy magazines that highlight the qualities of various types of alcohol and provide food–pairing possibilities. This suggests that change is possible as long as the government gets a cut of the profits.

The LCBO has done quite a good job with the beer segment, especially when you consider that it was not designed for that purpose. Its position as the largest purchaser of beverage alcohol in the world means that it has frequently achieved economies of scale in dealing with foreign producers. That means Ontarians have access to world-class Belgian and German beers at incredibly reasonable prices. In fact, the LCBO is the only retail organization in Ontario that actively imports beer from other countries. While the choices made in terms of which beers to import is certainly a bone of contention, the LCBO hits on winners about 50 percent of the time.

The real difficulty with the LCBO is the fact that it is limited in terms of retail space because it predominantly sells wine and liquor. Traditional beer-packaging formats are large and cumbersome. An agreement from the year 2000

TOP FIVE LAGERS		
1.	MOUNTAIN LAGER	p. 462
2.	HELLER HIGHWATER	p. 302
3.	LITTLE NORWAY	p. 450
4.	GASLIGHT HELLES	p. 363
5.	HONEST LAGER	p. 530

arranged that the LCBO would limit itself to six-packs as the maximum volume in the majority of its stores (agency stores excluded), allowing the Beer Store exclusivity on twelve- and twenty-four-bottle formats. While this caused public outcry upon revelation, it's not an insensible policy. The Beer Store was designed to handle those volumes. The LCBO was not.

The LCBO has done quite well for Ontario's small brewers, which have made up one of the fastest-growing segments in the store for a number of years. In fact, the explosion of Ontario's craft scene could not have happened without the LCBO as a partner. There are, however, a few intrinsic problems. For one thing, brewers are not guaranteed shelf space at the LCBO and frequently profess a desire for a more transparent product-selection process. For another, limitations in shelf space mean that the preferred formats for craft beer are cans and single bottles. A side effect of this limitation is that people do experiment with different products more willingly; a real positive if you're a very small brewer, but a mixed blessing if you're in the mid-tier. In 2010, brewers didn't have to work terribly hard to sell a six-pack. Now moving a single can is often a fight for established brands.

The LCBO has recently launched the Craft Beer Zone, a specialty area in a small number of stores that will focus on showcasing Ontario's brewers and give them the attention that the exploding industry deserves. That being said, the LCBO is ill-equipped to deal with the approximately 250 breweries that currently exist, let alone the hundred that are in planning.

GROCERY STORES

The announcement in April 2015 that grocery stores would be permitted to sell beer in Ontario was met with skepticism. It had been so long since there was any change to the structure of beer retailing in the province that a certain amount of wariness was understandable. According to the new framework, over the course of the next decade 450 grocery stores will be granted licences to sell beer, creating approximately the same number of retailers as currently exist in the Beer Store chain. While the initial bidding process has allowed for sixty grocery stores to obtain licences at time of writing, 150 stores will have the ability to sell beer by May 1, 2017, and sixty more shortly thereafter. A reasonable effort has been made to ensure the distribution of licences is equitable and that they do not fall solely to larger chains of stores.

There are justifiable concerns about the manner in which beer is sold in grocery stores. An upper limit of 7.1% alcohol on products to be sold in these stores seems somewhat arbitrary, but it should not represent a barrier to the vast majority of brands. Stores will apparently not be allowed to sell their own brand of products. A soft cap on volumes of beer being sold through each location means grocery stores will pay a 1-percent penalty beyond a certain amount of beer sold, with that penalty going to the brewer owners of the Beer Store. The authors suspect that this amount will in no way be large enough to compensate the Beer Store for its loss of business. The convenience of being able to purchase beer and food in a single trip should prove to be extremely attractive to beer drinkers.

A mandated 20-percent quota for small-brewer inventory and the massive increase in shelf space that grocery stores represent means that this development is likely to disproportionately benefit craft brewers in Ontario. If one views grocery store sales in the United States or other provinces as an example, it's likely that, while large international breweries will be represented, they will not be able to dominate. Grocery stores are prohibited from accepting money or inducements for shelf space. In point of fact, most grocers have indicated that they plan to exceed the craft beer quota significantly. It is something of a loss leader. The more frequently people come back to purchase a variety of brands, the more likely they are to also purchase food. This development represents a huge amount of potential growth for Ontario's brewing industry and should be exciting to watch over the next few years.

WITHOUT LEAVING YOUR COUCH

A recent development in retail in Ontario is the ability to have beer delivered to your home via an online ordering service. While it has always been possible to have beer delivered through a local service, customers were largely dependent on the existing selection at the local LCBO or Beer Store. At one time you might have needed to put on pants. No longer.

The LCBO service is a good one, featuring the majority of the products that are available through their stores and a number that are not. At one time, if you lived outside of a major city, your chances of ever getting your hands on sought-after products was very slim indeed. Thanks to the LCBO's online ordering system, Ontarians now have the ability to order just about anything the chain carries. Naturally, there are some conditions. The minimum order is fifty dollars plus shipping and taxes, and it will take up to a week to arrive. Considering the potential upside for people living in rural Ontario, it's hard to consider these to be significant problems.

Private subscription services like Brew Box and Savvy Hip Hops offer consumers beer delivered to their homes on a monthly basis at varying rates, depending on the length of the subscription and the breweries involved. In the case of some packages, the prices may seem a little high, but when you consider that it removes the cost of travel and that some offerings are extremely rare, you may find it worth your while to become a subscriber.

TOP FIVE KETTLE SOURS/ BERLINERS		
1.	TOTALLY	p. 269
2.	YALLA YALLA CITRA	p. 268
3.	JELLY KING	p. 104
4.	CITRA GROVE	p. 109
5.	SPADINA MONKEY RASPBERRY	p. 290

Finally, breweries are beginning to take the option of shipping by mail seriously. Standouts like Seaforth's Half Hours on Earth and Hamilton's Collective Arts provide consumers anywhere in the province with the ability to try their beer. And you should. Even factoring in shipping, the brewery's margin on online sales remains fairly high when compared to traditional retail channels.

BARS AND RESTAURANTS

One of the best places to enjoy craft beer is at a bar that specializes in serving it. To that end, we have created an appendix with a list of some of the better destinations in Ontario for your delectation. In this edition, we have expanded the appendix to over one hundred listings. Because craft breweries tend to sell and deliver directly to bars and pubs, that's where you're likely to find their most interesting products. Seasonals and one-off beers are in high demand across the province for rotating taps, and offerings can change daily. Many better pubs post daily changes on Twitter or Instagram.

Some of the better bars will have dozens of choices. A word of caution: beyond a certain point, you may notice diminishing returns on taplist size. A bar with over a hundred craft beers on tap is almost certainly not turning over kegs at the speed of a bar with a dozen. Although this is not a certainty, you may want to keep in mind that variety has drawbacks as well as advantages.

Bars that do not carry some manner of craft beer are becoming increasingly rare in urban parts of Ontario. That said, breweries purchasing or otherwise acquiring taps at bars for recompense remains a real problem in the province. Doubtless you will have walked into a bar in which all of the taps are from a single large brewing company. Perhaps you have witnessed the annual blossoming of the promotional patio umbrellas. These are sure signs something is untoward.

Theoretically, these practices are illegal. In practice, the law remains very difficult to enforce, and it has existed in perpetuity since the advent of industrialized brewing. The Alcohol and Gaming Commission of Ontario does not currently have a realistic path toward the enforcement of this policy and handles complaints as they come in. As a consumer, you have significantly more power. We urge you to vote with your dollar. Choose to drink in a bar with more flavourful beer that's made in Ontario by a small producer. Not only will you be helping the province's economy, but the food will probably be better and the people will almost certainly be more interesting.

BREWERIES

If you enjoy beer and you'd like to support Ontario's craft breweries, the place that makes the most sense to buy beer is at the brewery. Whether it's a brewpub that sells growlers out of their retail store or a full-size brewery with bottles, cans, and a selection of novelty glassware and bottle openers, the reality is this: The beer is going to be better coming out of the brewery. It will be fresher and tastier. When we taste beer for this book, we prefer to go directly to the brewery because it is often the best showcase for what the brewery is capable of.

TOP FIVE IMPERIAL STOUTS/ PORTERS		
1.	OLD KENTUCKY BASTARD	p. 386
2.	BARREL-AGED DOUBLE TEMPEST	p. 68
3.	DONKEY VENOM	p. 105
4.	HEARTS COLLIDE	p. 430
5.	LONG, DARK VOYAGE TO URANUS	p. 451

While buying through a retail channel may be more convenient, depending on where you live, there may be issues with freshness when you're buying a product from a store that stocks several hundred different items. In the case of craft beer, which is almost always unpasteurized and frequently unfiltered, the product is probably shelf stable for up to four months. That said, the difference between a fresh can and a four-month-old can is probably noticeable in a side-by-side tasting, even to the uninitiated.

Many small breweries have tasting bars that will allow you to try a small amount of a beer before you purchase it, just in case you want to be sure that you'll like it. In some parts of Ontario you could put together a pretty good afternoon wandering from brewery to brewery and doing just that. (In Toronto there is a single block with three breweries, which saves walking time.) The majority of these breweries will have knowledgeable employees behind the bar, willing to talk you through the finer points of their products. In some cases it may be the owner of the brewery working the bar. It's always good to know the person whose product you're buying.

Also, because the beer at the brewery is not subject to retail markups, brewers will make a better margin on beer that they sell out their front door. This, in turn, will allow them to invest in their businesses and improve the beer that you're buying from them. When you buy beer from the brewery's retail store, you're part of a delicious economic cycle. This will allow you to feel virtuous during your inevitable hangover.

INGREDIENTS

If there's ever been a marketing slogan that's rung true, it's Foodland Ontario's persistent jingle, "Good Things Grow in Ontario." Ontario has a lot going for it from an agricultural standpoint. For one thing, there's a lot of room for growing: Ontario is four times the size of the United Kingdom. With most of the heavily developed agricultural land between the forty-second and fiftieth parallels, we're ensured a cold winter and long days of sunlight in the summer. These growing conditions are proving to be excellent for grapes and apples, along with all of the other local fruit and vegetable produce we've come to enjoy.

The fact is that they are also excellent conditions for raising all of the crops that go into the making of beer. A symbiotic secondary agricultural industry is growing up around the edges of Ontario's craft brewing industry in service of brewers' increased need for ingredients.

As we detailed in the chapter on the province's craft beer history, the story of brewing in the twentieth century had largely to do with consolidation and standardization. At one time it was necessary even for large brewers to maintain plants across the country in which to produce their beer. For the sake of maintaining a large national brand's reputation for consistency, uniformity of ingredients was necessary, as was ease of handling. For this reason, local production of brewing ingredients became less desirable in the 1930s and 1940s as technological advances in ingredient processing and significant mechanization of agriculture made it possible to handle ingredient production on an enormous scale.

TOP FIVE PALE ALES

From purely an agricultural production standpoint, this has not been a bad thing. In Canada we're blessed with prairie provinces that produce some of the best malting barley in the world. What has been a triumph of agricultural production is, however, something of a blow for biodiversity and range of flavour, which are two of the tenets of craft beer. In an increasingly crowded market, brewers need to set themselves apart in order to thrive.

Consider a winery for a moment. From the outset, terroir has to be taken into account in order to guarantee a quality finished product. Once the grapes are in the ground, you are at the mercy of the elements. The wine may change between vintages, depending on moisture or temperature or other uncontrollable variables. The vintner's job is to make it show as best they can, and in doing so they are rewarded with a unique product.

In beer, it has not really been that way for a long time. A brewer begins by designing a recipe and ordering the ingredients that they believe will create the flavours they want in the finished product. In some ways this means there are infinite permutations of possible ingredients that may well result in myriad different beverages. This book details over a thousand such permutations. However, if brewers are all ordering their ingredients from the same suppliers, there can sometimes creep in an inevitable sameness, regardless of each brewer's intention. Everyone wants to play with the new hop variety or yeast strain, and a series of fairly similar one-off beers will crop up across the province within months of each other. The conceptual element is limited somewhat by availability and by influence from other beer scenes around the world.

With developments taking place in the agricultural sector, however, the ecology of the brewing scene in the province should become more diverse.

GRAINS

Beer is made up predominantly of water, but the next most significant ingredient by volume is grain. Depending on the cultural background of the region or the style of beer being made, the variety of grain can change, although the largest portion of the grist is usually barley. In the case of some very large brewers, you might be looking at significant volumes of corn grits or high-fructose corn syrup as adjuncts. Small brewers tend to use a wider variety of grain in order to create a variety of flavour profiles. While the majority of their recipe will be barley, they might include rye for a robust spiciness, wheat for added protein and a lighter body, or oats for a rounded, fuller body.

Essentially, brewers are looking for two things from grain: fermentable material and flavour — the sugars that the yeast will turn into alcohol and the unfermentable material that will remain as a flavour component.

With barley, the way that you ensure there are fermentable sugars in the liquid you're producing is through the malting process. Regardless of the technology involved in the process, maltsters are essentially attempting to trick the barley into thinking that it is time to sprout by wetting it and letting it sit. When the kernel germinates, the biochemical reaction is to turn stored starch into sugar. By stopping the barley's growth at the point where it is about to expend its stored energy, maltsters suspend the enzymatic action until a time in the future when a brewer mashes the barley. In some ways it is a cruel trick to play on a barley corn. It is all geared up to become a plant, but instead brewers are using that energy to feed yeast and produce alcohol for you to enjoy.

Flavour in barley has mostly to do with the specific kind of barley being grown and the way in which the maltster stops germination. Putting the wet barley into a kiln allows maltsters to stop that process. However, they are also able to control the temperature, duration, and final moisture content of the barley that's being kilned. These variables allow for control over the produced flavour, from light, nondescript barley sugar down to deeply chocolatey roast. While the majority of barley gets a standard treatment and becomes pale malt (which tends to make up the majority of an ale's malt bill), there is an entire range of treatments available that produce different flavours. If you have been to a number of breweries as a customer, you will likely have seen the iconic Weyermann malt frame: a red frame with yellow labels and a rainbow of different malt treatments. I believe every brewery gets one in the first few weeks of their existence.

Not to take anything away from Weyermann, but this item's nearly obligatory presence tends to highlight a certain limitation in ingredient sourcing.

At one point in the nineteenth century in Ontario, brewers mostly malted their own barley, which would have been sourced locally. In some cases, the brewers actually owned the farms on which the barley was grown. Although this became untenable much beyond 1860 due to the volumes involved, Ontario had a large number of industrial maltsters that exported all over North America. The period between 1860 and approximately 1890 was incredibly lucrative for barley farmers, especially in Prince Edward County. For the most part, the crop was the higher protein six-row barley, as two-row varieties had not yet been introduced.

As the industrialization of brewing continued past prohibition and the population of a growing nation pushed west, it made more sense to source barley from the prairie provinces. If you were a brewer making a beer that was very light in colour and in flavour, the important aspect of barley swung toward ensuring the amount of fermentable material was dependable. By the 1980s, when the brewing renaissance began in North America, there existed a dichotomy in supply. Basic two-row pale malt from the prairies provided the majority of the fermentable material in a recipe, while specialty malt that provided accents of flavour came from Europe or specialty producers.

Over the last year in Ontario, we've seen the beginnings of local malting for the first time in many decades. It would, however, be a mistake to consider that a throwback or a return to history. Producers of barley in Ontario are now largely using two-row varieties like AC Newdale and AC Metcalfe. Barn Owl Malt in Hastings County is using the traditional method of floor malting rather than a pneumatic malting system, but they are doing it in a modern, controlled environment that was custom built to purpose. Harvest Hop and Malt in Guelph is producing not only base malt, but also specialty rye malt with an uncompromisingly spicy character. The combination of two-row malt with modern equipment and Ontario's terroir is something entirely new — this combination of circumstances and ingredients has never existed before, and we are on the cusp of something exciting.

The benefits of locally produced malt are many, although the acreage is yet small. The employment and revenue that they provide for the province's farmers could be significant. Ontario is not just its cities, and an underused agricultural sector could seriously benefit from this activity. Additionally, it is likely to expand the palette of flavours from which the province's brewers can choose, possibly resulting in a range unique in the world. While we are still likely to depend on the prairie provinces for the majority of barley, and while European specialty malt is irreplaceable for some purposes, Ontario may well develop a character all our own.

HOPS

While it's relatively easy to point to an era in the past when barley was a significant factor in Ontario's development, with hops there is less recorded information.

Hops are a rhizome that grows to full maturity over the course of three to four years. They grow between thirty-five and fifty-five degrees latitude in both hemispheres but tend to thrive closest to the forty-eighth parallel. They grow out of the ground in shoots that become bines, which are most commonly trained up eight- or ten-foot trellises of wire situated in parallel lines, although non-conventional growers may use different techniques to produce results. When they are just beginning their growth for the year, they resemble nothing so much as asparagus stalks, but they flower and develop cones that hold a resin called lupulin. This resin is quite bitter and is responsible for the bitterness of beer and some of the less subtle aromatic compounds.

In terms of practical use, hops are added to the wort at different points in the boil in order to achieve different results. To create bitterness, they're added right at the beginning. The amount of bitterness is dependent on the amount of alpha acid in the hops or simply the quantity of hops used. Adding hops at the beginning of the boil tends not to result in a specific flavour. Adding hops toward the end of the boil creates flavour and aroma. Adding hops in the fermenter, a technique known as dry hopping, focuses aromas. It may be helpful to think of hops in beer as equivalent to spices in a stew. Adding them at the beginning provides background flavour, but for sharpness, you need to add them at the end.

While there are some wild varieties in North America, the vast majority of hop varieties that beer drinkers are familiar with are the descendants of European landrace varieties. When brewers came to Ontario in the nineteenth century, they brought hops with them from England or Germany or New York State. The difficulty is that very few of the varieties we are familiar with now existed at that point in time. Even if we knew which varieties had been transplanted to Ontario, those that were not wiped out by downy mildew in the early twentieth century have by now grown wild.

While the consolidation of breweries resulted in something resembling monoculture for malt, hops actually thrived during the twentieth century. As brewers and growers sought higher alpha acid hops in different countries in order to maximize production, the end result was multiplicity as iterations were bred. In fact, some of the earliest purpose-bred hops in England featured a wild Manitoban variety. At this point in history, hops are bred for the refinement of certain aromatic qualities as much as they are grown for specific levels of bitterness. For this reason, we tend to use the names of varietals as shorthand for the tasting notes in this book. Amarillo, for instance, tends to impart clementine and a small nuanced pine character. Equinox (now Ekuanot because of a naming dispute) smells of the flesh of green bell peppers. Saaz is classically peppercorn, lemon, and sharp floral sting.

At this point, factors of breeding and terroir have become important in creating hop designations. Perhaps unsurprisingly, the aromatic compounds in hops tend generally to mimic the flora of the biome or terroir in which they're grown. Classic Czech and German hops tend to emulate the spices and flowers of middle Europe, while English varieties tend to be more brightly floral and fruity, imparting some twiggy hedgerow. Pacific Northwest hops tended for a long time to produce pine and citrus. New Zealand varieties can lean toward herbal minerality and sharp tropical fruit, while Australia produces sweeter pineapple and passionfruit. There are, naturally, exceptions to these generalities, but they are useful in terms of thought process.

In Ontario, we now have dozens of hop growers attempting to develop their own hop yards by transplanting varieties that are popular in brewing in Europe and the Pacific Northwest in order to create a product that Ontario brewers will want to brew with. One of the difficulties we face is the size of Ontario. It is worth pointing out that the hop gardens of Kent in England and the hop yards of Zatec in Czechia are actually about as far apart as Thunder Bay and Toronto, and only slightly greater than the distance between Windsor and Cornwall, for that matter. Ontario is large enough to have different growing regions. As hop growers experiment with loamy soil in Norfolk County, or the rocky Canadian Shield in eastern Ontario, or the Pelee, Niagara, or Prince Edward County microclimates, we are going to see some interesting developments and possibly terroir–dependent varietals over the next decade. One thing the authors have noticed while tasting through wet hop beers for this edition is that hops typically known for their citric qualities tend to express them more herbally. Lemon becomes lemon balm and lime becomes lime leaf. That may not be a bug, but rather a feature. It is up to the brewers to find a way to use that to their advantage, and it is up to the growers to tweak the crop.

Some hop growers are already pointing the way by working with the wild varietals that either are North American landraces or were abandoned at the turn of the twentieth century. Clear Valley Hops in Nottawa has a variety called Wild Turkey that develops peach, mango, and slight citrus aromas. The Tavistock Hop Company has a reclaimed nineteenth–century variety, possibly a Canada Red Vine variant, with notes of strawberry, melon, and sharply bitter endive. Pleasant Valley in Prince Edward County has a variety they

ROBIN'S PICKS

1.	SLEEPING GIANT NORTHERN LOGGER	p. 467
2.	NICKEL BROOK UNCOMMON ELEMENT	p. 387
3.	NEW ONTARIO BREWING FRISKY PETE'S ENGLISH PALE ALE	p. 376
4.	GRANITE GREAT NORTH MILD	p. 263
5.	BRASSERIE ÉTIENNE BRÛLÉ CITRALE	p. 144

INGREDIENTS

are calling Wild Loyalist that displays earthy, floral, and spice character not dissimilar to Saaz.

If decades have driven these flavours into wild hops in this terroir, imagine what could be bred with the hardy stock that will have survived over the coming decades. With the acreage and growing season available, it's possible that Ontario could develop its own sought-after varieties.

YEAST

Typically, guides like this will tell you that there are two basic kinds of yeast: ale yeast and lager yeast. Any home brewer will tell you it's not that easy.

It's true that yeast is generally categorized by those two species — *Saccharomyces cerevisiae* for ale yeast and *Saccharomyces pastorianus* for lager yeast — but different strains have individuated over the course of brewing history. While ale yeast tends to be top fermenting and to perform best at room temperature or higher, there are a hell of a lot of different strains that contribute different aromatic compounds. While lager yeast tends to be bottom fermenting and to perform best at cellar temperature or below, there are a number of variants that give different breweries their house character. There are also wild yeasts like Brettanomyces Bruxellensis that are responsible for dry, horsey character in an ever-expanding range of styles.

If you're a brewer designing a recipe, you might use your house lager or ale strain for everything. If you're, for instance, the Granite, in Toronto, you use an ale yeast called Ringwood for just about everything you make. It is a southern English strain that ferments fairly quickly and was popularized in North America by a brewer named Alan Pugsley. It sets your beer apart from everyone else's, but it does mean that you can make only so many styles of beer.

If you're a brewer and you set out to design a beer in a specific style, you're going to want to order a specific strain of yeast to make sure that beer has the character you want. Any given beer style might conceivably be made with any number of different yeasts. If you wanted to make an IPA, you might go with a clean-fermenting California ale yeast to get out of the way of the aroma hops, or you might go with the now-popular Conan yeast out of Vermont in order to get that peachy, vanilla character popular in Vermont IPAs. There are dozens of reasonable choices, all of which will provide subtly different esters and phenols. Some would be more unorthodox than others but would do the job without noticeable problems.

The difficulty many brewers face is that it is hard to maintain a large number of yeast strains on site at their optimum condition. Yeast propagation is necessary to ensure that each batch of beer has enough viable cells to ferment properly and without off flavours. Over the course of several generations, the character of the yeast may change through mutation or develop unwanted properties. For this reason, many brewers simply order yeast for one-off batches from suppliers in the United States or Europe. This creates logistical difficulties with international shipping and customs.

Founded in 2013, Escarpment Laboratories has become Ontario's answer to those American yeast suppliers. Located in Guelph, Escarpment has a number of popular yeast strains on the go for home brewers and professionals alike, taking shipping delays off the table for brewers looking for fresh pitches of yeast. The real draw here, though, is that owners Angus Ross, Richard Preiss, and Nate Ferguson are able to provide specialty strains because of their experience in molecular biology and brewing.

Some strains, such as their Old World Saison blend, actually combine two separate classic saison strains, while the New World version combines Saccharomyces with brett. This customization is enhanced by their ability to plate new strains from the wild. Wild Thing was harvested from within an apple orchard and is native to Ontario. Sawdust City's Limberlost used a strain of ale yeast harvested from the Limberlost Forest and Wildlife Reserve. As Escarpment undergoes expansion in the coming years, it's likely that the selection of strains on offer will increase and become more diverse and iconoclastic.

WHAT DOES THIS MEAN TO YOU, THE DRINKER?

This year, it was possible to walk into a bar and order a beer with malt, hops, yeast, and water all sourced from within the province of Ontario. In the case of Mackinnon Brothers Brewery in Bath, it was possible to produce an estate beer for the first time, a practice that has probably not been seen on a widespread basis in the province since the 1850s. If their Harvest Ale is any indication, we're in for some real treats.

With each year that passes, it's likely that we will have more Ontario ingredients in beer made within the province. Production will become more focused and more sophisticated over time, and Ontario will set itself apart from other regions based partly on its terroir, a factor that, as little as five years ago, was not remotely in play. Not only is every day that passes the best day for beer that the province has ever had, but every day also sees us becoming more ourselves and less like other brewing regions.

ABE ERB BREWERY & RESTAURANT

 @abe_erb

🌐 abeerb.com

📍 15 King Street S, Waterloo

📞 (519) 886-4518

🕐 Mon–Thu 11a.m.–12a.m., Fri 11a.m.–2a.m., Sat 10a.m.–2a.m., Sun 10a.m.–11p.m. No tours necessary, as equipment is prominently displayed.

🛒 Daily 11a.m.–11p.m.

📍 151 Charles Street W, Kitchener

📞 (519) 954-0151

🕐 Mon–Thu 11a.m.–12a.m., Fri 11a.m.–2a.m., Sat 10a.m.–2a.m., Sun 10a.m.–11p.m.

Named after Waterloo's first settler, Mennonite Abraham Erb, these brewpubs, which opened in 2014 and 2016, not only manage to produce a variety of styles, but look good doing so. The owner, Rob Theodosiou, has gone for an interior design he calls "boutique industrial" that effectively uses the large, worn spaces.

The airy, high-ceilinged room of the Waterloo location has a windowed garage door as a front wall and chandeliers made out of repurposed barrels from the now defunct Seagram's distillery. The brewery cellar is unique in that its fermenters are housed on a catwalk above the dining area, supported by steel beams driven eight feet into the concrete floor. Within this rough space are elegant touches, such as repurposed window sashes fitted with stained glass, custom leather couches, and even specially commissioned wallpaper.

The Kitchener location acts as a production facility and a popular lunchtime establishment for nearby tech-sector giants, such as Google. The 20 BBL brewhouse overlooks communal dining tables in a high-ceilinged complex that once served as a tannery. Double-sized fermenters outside the dining-room windows serve as a reminder that this is a working brewery, while oversized incandescent bulbs keep it whimsical. The aroma of mashing barley serves as an appetizer.

The food menus focus on local produce and traditional pub fare, making good use of the in-house smokers for barbecue dishes while providing a number of healthy options and some innovative fusion twists.

———

1857 KÖLSCH is a refreshing version of the hybrid style, light and crisp due to its pilsner-malt base and Hallertau finish, which imparts a snappy, woody bitterness above light banana and pear yeast esters (4). **ALTERIOR MOTIVE** is also a German hybrid beer but eschews the traditional earthiness, instead deriving light chocolate and biscuit from the specialty malts, with a hint of tart raspberry jammy-ness in the middle, not unlike a Viva Puff (3.5). **BUGGY WHIP IPA** has peach and mango aromas leading to a balanced pine bitterness on the finish (4). **COFFEE PALE ALE**, brewed with a single origin roast from Abe Erb's sister company Settlement Co. coffee roaster, is bright with green vegetal coffee notes that fade to dry roast and blend seamlessly into grassy hops (4).

BRITISH MILD has a light pear ester that develops into a full-bodied middle swaddled in leather, true to more aggressive southern English versions (3). **MEN OF NIGHT STOUT** produces a deceiving dry roast and dark chocolate aroma that develops into a surprisingly sweet body and equally surprising dry finish (3.5). **GATEWAY SMOKED PORTER** begins with a pronounced, slightly porky smoked-malt character that disappears into chocolate, tobacco, and leather in the mid-palate (4). **SPECIAL BITTER** has a pleasing stewed apple and sugared barley character with a grassy English hop bite on the finish (4).

ACE HILL BEER

 10 Alcorn Avenue, Suite 304, Toronto

 @AceHillBeer

 acehillbeer.com

The people behind Ace Hill Beer are five friends with diverse backgrounds in marketing and restauranting. Originally brewing out of his garage, brewmaster Blake Anderson developed a recipe for their sole beer based on his home brew, Jaromir Lager Czech Pilsner, which won gold in the lager category and silver for best in show at the 2014 Canadian Amateur Brewers Association Awards. Now contracting out of Big Rig Brewery in Ottawa, the five have made good use of the contacts from their previous careers to create an eye-catching brand seen throughout the province, from stores to high-end restaurants in Toronto.

———

ACE HILL PILSNER has come a long way since its Jaromir days, made thinner and lightly hopped by design to appear more approachable. Tastes are very subtle notes of grass and toffee, with a slight phenolic note (1.5).

ALL OR NOTHING BREWHOUSE

📍 1156 Speers Road, Oakville

📞 (905) 337-0133

🐦 @allornothingbh

🌐 allornothing.beer

🕐 Daily 10a.m.–5p.m.

Since the summer of 2014, All or Nothing has been a staple of the Toronto beer scene, appearing on tap at a number of the better bars around the city. The original name of the brewery ties nicely into the sentiment shared by many small brewers in Ontario about their place in a market dominated by large international conglomerates. In November 2015, the brewery was forced to change their name from Underdogs as part of a trademark dispute; the beer remains identical.

In the early days of 2016, All or Nothing purchased Oakville's Trafalgar Ales and Meads, which was affiliated with Black Creek Historic Brewery and Trafalgar Artisanal Distillery. A significant amount of expense and effort has been expended in order to update the facility, and as of December, additional fermentation and brite tanks and a new glycol system have been installed, allowing a transition from their

ONTARIO CRAFT BREWERIES

63

current contract arrangement with Cool Brewing in Etobicoke. Plans exist for a range of wheat beers, which may come to fruition in 2017.

———

ALL OR NOTHING HOPFENWEISSE is a hop-forward take on German wheat beer. The smooth, wheaty body produces a doughy aroma highlighted by banana, tropical fruits, and freshly juiced oranges (3.5).

AMBER BREWERY

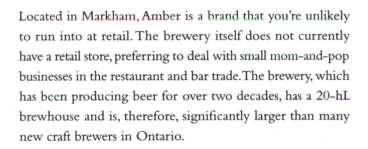

 130 Riviera Drive, Markham

 (905) 305-8383

 amberbrewery.com

 Sales by phone and email for kegs, including free delivery within the GTA.

Located in Markham, Amber is a brand that you're unlikely to run into at retail. The brewery itself does not currently have a retail store, preferring to deal with small mom-and-pop businesses in the restaurant and bar trade. The brewery, which has been producing beer for over two decades, has a 20-hL brewhouse and is, therefore, significantly larger than many new craft brewers in Ontario.

———

The focus at Amber is on value, with their two brands, **TORONTO AMBER LAGER** (NR) and **CHICAGO DARK** (NR), being positioned as competitively priced compared to similar choices in the Toronto market.

AMSTERDAM BREWING COMPANY

AMSTERDAM BREWERY

📍 45 Esandar Drive, Toronto

📞 (416) 504-6882

🐦 @amsterdambeer

🌐 amsterdambeer.com

🕐 Tours Sat 1p.m.–5p.m.

🛒 Mon–Sat 11a.m.–10p.m., Sun 11a.m.–6p.m.

AMSTERDAM BREWHOUSE

📍 245 Queens Quay W, Toronto

📞 (416) 504-1020

🐦 @AmsterdamBH

🌐 amsterdambrewhouse.com

🕐 Tours Mon–Tues 4p.m., Wed–Sun 12p.m.–6p.m.

🛒 Mon–Wed 3p.m.–10p.m., Thu–Sun 11a.m.–10p.m.

Toronto's oldest craft brewery has had its share of change over the years. Beginning as a brewpub under Roel Bramer at 133 John Street in 1986, its second location, the Rotterdam, was added on King Street West in 1988. In 2003, they acquired Kawartha Lakes Brewery and their current brew-master, Iain McOustra. From 2005 to 2012 the brewery occupied a space at the bottom of Bathurst. The current incarnation includes a large-scale production facility in Leaside and a massive brewpub on Queens Quay West with a commanding view of Toronto Bay. The 2016 expansion of the Leaside production facility included the purchase of a state-of-the-art Krones brewhouse, which became necessary in order to keep up with consumer demand.

Amsterdam's core product lineup has changed significantly since the beginning of the decade; only three of their nine year-round offerings existed before 2010. In fact, their most popular beer is now Boneshaker, rather than their Blonde. Under McOustra, the brewing team has proved to be as versatile as any in the province in creating beers for their seasonal and Adventure Brew ranges, with farmhouse ales and barrel-aging programs being specialities. Amsterdam now walks the line between providing extremely affordable beer for the masses and specialty products for enthusiasts, while slowly converting the former to the latter. They continue to improve.

———

3SPEED is an all-malt light lager, one of relatively few in Ontario made without adjunct and one of the cleanest takes on the style available, with a lightly sweet grain character and a small amount of hop bitterness (4). **BLONDE** is a brewery staple representing the older mentality at Amsterdam. A competently made adjunct pale lager, it's a step up from macro beers that has been revamped in 2016 (3). **LEMON GINGER GRISETTE** does precisely what it says on the tin, with fresh lemon zest and lightly pickled ginger making it a refreshing summer quaffer (3.5). **MAVERICK AND GOSE** is a Chardonnay barrel–aged gose with a hint of salinity and peach on the nose. Originally a collaboration with Toronto's Great Lakes, it looks to become a seasonal staple in 2017 (4). **CRUISER** is a contemporary pale ale with bright lemon and grapefruit from Citra, Simcoe, and Centennial hops that uses grapefruit juice to adjust the PH in the mash (3.5). **BONESHAKER** is more an oversized red ale than an IPA and fits a huge amount of pine and zest into its wide body, which has become drier and nuttier in recent years (4). **STARKE PILSNER** is a recent addition to the mix that merges a massive Hallertau lime bite and spicy whole leaf hop presence with a crisp finish (4). **BARREL–AGED DOUBLE TEMPEST** will hold its own against any of North America's super-heavyweight imperial stouts and ought to be shared (5).

ANDERSON CRAFT ALES

ANDERSON
· CRAFT ALES ·

📍 1030 Elias Street, London

🐦 @andersoncales

🌐 andersoncraftales.ca

🕐 Wed–Sat 11a.m.–9p.m., Sun 12p.m.–5p.m.

Opened in the summer of 2016, Anderson Craft Ales is overseen by Gavin Anderson, who has a doctorate in microbiology and previous brewing experience at New Brunswick's Brasseurs du Petit-Sault. With his father, Jim, contributing to the construction of the facility, sister Aynsley designing the hip and minimal branding, and many other members of the Anderson clan, from cousins and siblings to in-laws, contributing to the upkeep of the space, it's safe to say that its status as a "family-run brewery" isn't just for publicity.

The brewhouse holds a 15-BBL system, and the amount of space — two floors in a large industrial building, plus a large parking lot — practically demands that it be available for community events. Of further excitement to beer geeks is that Anderson has forgone the use of tallboys in favour of the classic 355 mL can.

ONTARIO CRAFT BREWERIES

Anderson has two mainstays. **IPA** has notes of pine intermingling with grapefruit, melon, and orange rind, complemented well by a gentle malt backbone before going into a bitter finish (3.5). **AMBER** has chocolate and toffee aroma that makes its way into the taste and includes a firm roasted finish (4).

ARCH BREWING COMPANY

📍 4-110 Pony Drive, Newmarket
📞 (888) 391-7670
🐦 @ArchBrewingCo
🌐 archbrewing.ca
🕐 Mon–Thu 12p.m.–8p.m., Fri 10a.m.–8p.m., Sat–Sun 12p.m.–6p.m.

For Suzie and Billy King, the road to Arch has been a long one. It took eight years for them to realize their dream of opening a brewery, testing the waters with a contract-brewed product before jumping into the market with both feet. Retaining Paul Dickey to design their initial recipe, Arch produced a single beer out of Wellington Brewery in Guelph, which introduced their brand to the market. The transition to a physical brewery in Newmarket has proved to be an interesting one, vastly expanding their lineup and introducing styles of beer that were not suggested by their initial offering. The 10-BBL brewhouse allows for a lot of variability and is comfortably viewed from a gallery that overlooks both the brewery and retail shop. Brewer Mark Dodwell's creations are available from the retail store in cans or in the brewery tap, which features light snacks and a charcuterie board.

Their initial product, **DINNER JACKET O'RED IPA**, has changed considerably since moving production to Newmarket from Wellington. A bright lemon hop character cuts through a caramel body exempting some of the previous Ringwood complexity (3.5). **CHESTERFIELD KSA** is in the kölsch style, light grainy honey and apple on the nose with healthy solidity in body (3). **OLD HOMESTEAD** is an altbier with a gently bready body beneath its soapy, floral, noble hop aroma (3). **DUNKEL LEO** is raisin and banana with a touch of chocolate in the body before a small alcoholic warmth (3.5). **WHISKEY BROWN** is an English brown stout aged on oak chips and soaked in Collingwood whisky; raisin, dried cherries, and honey in the body are supported by the roundness the oak imparts (3.5).

ASHTON BREWING COMPANY

113 Old Mill Road, Ashton

(613) 257-4423

@AshtonBrew

ashtonbrewpub.ca

Daily 11:30a.m.–11:00p.m.

Originally built as a grist mill on the bank of the Jock River, the Old Mill at Ashton is a brewpub with a deeply historic feel. Some of the original wooden foundation still shows signs of a fire. The brewery is owned by the Hodgins family, who began pouring their beers for the public in 2011. The Hodgins patriarch, Art, has had a long career as a publican, having owned many establishments in the area since 1975. This, his first brewpub, required additional expertise. To set up the brewing side of the Old Mill, the family enlisted the help of Lorne Hart, founder and owner of the famous Hart Brewery, which opened in 1991 and closed its doors in 2005 to the upset of many.

Currently the Ashton Brewing Company (using the ABC brand throughout their lineup) makes accessible, flavourful beers with regular seasonal offerings. While ABC beers are

ONTARIO CRAFT BREWERIES

poured across the Ottawa region, they can also be found in the Bank Street tied houses of Patty's Pub and Quinn's Ale House, as well as the Old Mill itself.

If you find yourself at the Old Mill, keep a look out for George, the resident ghost.

———

SESSION ALE is a mild and easy beer that has many of the malt characteristics of a blonde ale (3). **CREAM ALE** has a pilsner-like aroma thanks to the Saaz hops (3). **AMBER** has robust roasted-coffee notes blending with creamy caramel flavours (3.5). **HARVEST BROWN** features an unmistakable nutty character, with cocoa flavours moving toward the finish (2.5). **HOPSTRAVAGANZA** is an English-influenced IPA with a medium body, citrus undertones, and a lingering bitter aftertaste (2.5). **VANILLA STOUT** is served on nitro and features intense coffee notes with a smooth mouthfeel (2.5).

BAD APPLE BREWING COMPANY

📍 73463 Bluewater Highway, Zurich

📞 (519) 236-7908

🌐 badapplebrewingco.ca

🕐 Sat–Sun 10a.m.–5p.m.

Very few Ontario breweries start with the purchase of an apple orchard, but Bad Apple has made it a hallmark of their approach to brewing, focusing in part on the combination of beer and cider for home consumption. Founded in 2016 by husband-and-wife team Jason and Sarah Ingram, they have chosen packaging options for their beer and cider to benefit local sales, with 750 ml swing-top bottles and growlers available from the brewery.

Although the brewery does create straightforward beer styles in both hefeweizen and pale ale styles, its flagship **BORN IN A BARN** is styled as a cyser (NR), as are several other blended offerings.

BAMBOO BEER LIMITED

 @KawayanMovement

 bamboobeer.ca

Launched in 2013 in Hamilton by Vincent Cruz Villanis, **BAMBOO BEER** is predicated on the interesting idea that some of the fermentable material for beer could come from bamboo leaves rather than barley or other grains. The beer, contract brewed at Cool, is one of only a few varieties in the world using bamboo as a fermentable material (others exist in mainland China), is something of a proof of concept for the versatility of bamboo, and is one of a very few beers from Ontario that are exported to southeast Asia. The company is currently involved in a partnership with the Philippine Bamboo Foundation and has a following within Filipino communities in Canada (NR).

BANCROFT BREWING COMPANY

📍 2 Hastings Street N, Bancroft

📞 (613) 334-8154

🌐 bancroftbrewing.ca

🕐 Sun–Wed 11a.m.–10p.m., Thu–Sat 11a.m.–1p.m.

In 2014 the Bancroft Brewing Company, under the ownership of the Krupa family, took over the Southern Algonquin Pub and Eatery on 4 Bridge Street West and installed a brewpub. One of the first breweries to take advantage of the Hastings County Economic Development Office's handbook on starting up a brewery, Bancroft Brewing supplies beer to their eatery. After starting with a small system, the demand was so high that the brewery underwent significant growth, now sporting a 7-hL brewing facility along with a retail store. Their brewpub is still the best place to enjoy Bancroft's beers.

———

To date, Bancroft's lineup includes four beers. **BLONDE LADY** is a light blonde ale that fills the role of being the brewery's accessible beer for those who may be new to craft (NR). **IRON MAN IPA** fits squarely into the Ontario pale ale category with a selection of West Coast hops meeting sweet malt and roasted character (NR). **BLACK QUARTZ ALE** is a dark ale named after a gem specific to the region. Containing six malts, it has notes of coffee and caramel (NR). **LOGGERS ALE** is a straight-ahead English brown ale (NR).

BANDED GOOSE BREWING COMPANY

📍 31 Division Street S, Kingsville

📞 (519) 733-6900

🐦 @jacksgastropub

🌐 bandedgoosebrewing.com

🕐 Mon 11:30a.m.–8p.m., Tue–Sat 11:30a.m.–9p.m., Sun 11:30a.m.–8p.m.

Started in early 2014, Banded Goose is a nanobrewery-sized expansion to Jack's Gastropub and Inn 31 in Kingsville, themed to take advantage of the migratory patterns of birds over Lake Erie. The brewing set-up at Banded Goose is diminutive even by nanobrewing standards, coming in initially at just under fifty litres per batch. The goal for Banded Goose is not to brew enough to sell off site, but rather to brew beers that complement the pub's menu, using seasonal ingredients where possible. They are often able to take advantage of local hop yards in Leamington. At present they are usually able to manage two draft taps of their own beer at once to go alongside eight other taps of Ontario offerings. The menu features produce from

ONTARIO CRAFT BREWERIES

local farms and artisans, and provides pairing suggestions of both wine and beer. _____

Because of the extremely small size of the brewhouse, Banded Goose affords itself a certain amount of flexibility in terms of brewing. Different beers might be made at any time, but these are some past examples. **NOTTY BLONDE** is a citrus-forward blonde ale that uses zest and Saaz hops to add punch (NR). **POT O' GOLD AMBER ALE** is a slightly sweet amber that uses Cascade hops and locally grown Centennial for dry hopping (NR). **FALSE ALARM IPA** is a single-hop Centennial beer that develops grapefruit bitterness (NR).

BANDIT BREWERY

📍 2125 Dundas Street W, Toronto

📞 (647) 348-1002

🐦 @Banditbrewery

🌐 banditbrewery.ca

🕐 Mon–Thu 5p.m.–12a.m., Fri 5p.m.–1a.m., Sat 2p.m.–1a.m.,
Sun 2p.m.–12a.m.

🛒 Daily 11a.m.–11p.m.

A converted auto shop located, to the amusement of many Toronto beer geeks, next door to a Beer Store, Bandit Brewery is the work of business partners Stephane Dubois and Shehzad Hamza, who drew inspiration from German beer gardens to create a spacious brewpub adorned with the iconic Toronto mascot of a raccoon and featuring one of the best patios in the city. Head brewer Ben Morris, a graduate of Niagara College's brewmaster program, has spent a good deal of time refining his recipes since the grand opening in the spring of 2016. Beers that range from simple and accessible styles to more adventurous offerings are frequently on tap and available in their bottle shop.

FARMED & DANGEROUS is a farmhouse ale made with Escarpment Labs yeast that features slightly sweet Belgian swirl and a dry, peppery character throughout (3.5). **BANDIT'S AMERICAN PALE ALE** goes heavy on the citrus and pine notes, with roasted malt flavours balancing things out somewhat (3). **CONE RANGER IPA** has flavours of pine, grapefruit, and orange blossom honey complementing the malty base nicely (3). **TSARINA BOMB**, a double IPA, is rife with orange and honey notes, with a gentle jab of bitterness three-quarters of the way into the palate (3.5). **WIZARD OF GOSE** has dry coriander notes that are clearly the star of the show, followed along with a slightly salted and tart rhubarb note (4). **SMOKE ON THE PORTER** is rather heavy on the smoke, leather, tobacco, and cocoa notes in its light body (2.5).

BAR HOP BREWCO

📍 137 Peter Street, Toronto

📞 (647) 348-1137

🐦 @barhopbar

🌐 barhoptoronto.com

🕐 Mon–Fri 12p.m.–2a.m., Sat–Sun 1p.m.–2a.m.

Toronto beer lovers will be familiar with Bar Hop. The original location on King Street West rapidly became one of the most popular craft beer destinations in the province when it opened in 2012. With thirty-six beers on tap, Jim MacDonald and Rob Pingitore's first venture gained notoriety for its careful balance of high-quality established offerings and exciting new brewery experiments. The popularity of the spot frequently leads to lineups and crowding at the bar.

The second location on Peter Street expanded the ownership, bringing on Tashi Sundup as a partner. It has the welcome advantage of additional size: three floors, including a rooftop patio with a view of Queen West. Mark Cutrara's presence as head chef has resulted in a menu of updated pub classics and some truly eye-catching fare (Pig's Head Nachos, anyone?). Rumours swirled during construction that a small

ONTARIO CRAFT BREWERIES

brewpub was in the cards, but it was not until the latter half of 2016 that Bar Hop Brewco was able to produce anything on site. Brewer Matt Bod's beers are not intended to take over the lineup but to complement the carefully curated tap selection, filling in gaps where they exist.

———

Their inaugural beer, **TREMOLO**, is a complex blended saison featuring spelt in the grain bill and *lambicus* and *lactobacillus* in 20 percent of the barrel-aged portion. The aroma comes through as pear, orange, and toasted coconut above a full, light, sour body that leads to a short, dry finish (4). Designed as a summer quaffer, **MIRACLE CURE** is a saison featuring pear and clove esters with a gentle spiciness from Styrian Golding that folds into a bone-dry finish (4).

BARLEY DAYS BREWERY

📍 13730 Loyalist Parkway, Picton

📞 (613) 476-7468

🐦 @BarleyDaysBrews

🌐 barleydaysbrewery.com

🕐 Summer: Sun–Thu 10:30a.m.–6p.m., Fri–Sat 10:30a.m.–7p.m.
   Winter: Fri 12p.m.–5p.m., Sat–Sun 11a.m.–5p.m.

First opening as Glenora Springs Brewery in 2000, Barley Days changed their name in 2007 to commemorate the period in Prince Edward County's history as a producer of malted barley. Barley Days has long been regarded as the brewing ambassador of their home region, and is featured prominently in Prince Edward County promotional material. They also set up shop at the Barley Days Pub, alongside Waupoos Winery and 401 Cider Brewery, in the tourist landmark the Big Apple on Highway 401. Brewmaster Brett French heads the team, producing a number of beers that are distinctive yet accessible.

———

Most of Barley Days' beer names feature a common theme, referencing the rich history of Prince Edward County. Their selection includes **LOYALIST LAGER**, which has a fairly light body and a quick hint of spiced toffee before heading toward a cereal finish (3); **WIND & SAIL DARK ALE**, with its very prominent roasted-caramel flavours and light to medium mouthfeel with chocolate and a light leather note (3); **SACRED MULE SPARKLING ALE**, a Czech pilsner perplexingly brewed with sparkling-wine yeast that showcases how yeast can change the profile of a beer, contributing an acidic and bitter flavour not unlike black mustard seed in the finish (1); **SCRIMSHAW OYSTER STOUT**, made with real oysters in the boil, is heavy with chocolate and has a slight salty brine note mid-palate, going toward a dry finish (3); **COUNTY IPA**, made with Barn Owl malt, is quite thin in mouthfeel with an assertive bitterness hitting a bit too close to the finish (2); **COUNTY LIGHT**, the brewery's light beer, has very light and swift citrus notes and a touch of nutmeg before the quick cereal finish (2.5); **SNAKE BITE APPLE ALE**, made with locally pressed apple juice, is a good balance between malt and apple, with an expected touch of acidic character and an apple skin bitterness (3); and **HARVEST GOLD PALE ALE**, a nicely bitter beer with dry floral notes and a mild, bitter finish (2.5).

BARNCAT ARTISAN ALES

📍 1600 Industrial Road, Unit B5, Cambridge

📞 @Barncatales

🌐 barncatales.com

🕐 Fri 5p.m.–8p.m., Sat 12p.m.–4p.m.

Centrally located as Cambridge's second brewery, Barncat is the work of award-winning home brewers Matt Macdonald and Jeremy Skorochid, who made the jump to professional by taking out a five-year lease on a 2,400-square-foot industrial space and opening to the public on April 1, 2016. Named after the series of beers Skorochid became known for in homebrew circles, Barncat is content for now to brew a number of special-release beers, made available in their retail shop every weekend.

At the time of writing Barncat has no mainstays, with a lineup that is constantly changing. The ratings below act as a representation of the quality to expect.

———

EMINENCE IPA is as thick and brightly coloured as a glass of orange juice that sets the expectation for the taste, which is a medley of orange, grapefruit, and pineapple asserting dominance (4). **CAT FACTORY INDUSTRIAL RUSTIC ALE** is aggressively carbonated, with flavours of large melon notes and a hint of lemon with a dry, bretty mouthfeel (4). **CAT REACTIVATOR** is a coffee barley wine that has the aroma of a freshly brewed mocha, coming through in the taste with an added creamy body (4.5).

BARNSTORMER BREWING COMPANY

📍 384 Yonge Street #3, Barrie

📞 (707) 481-1701

🐦 @BarnstormerBeer

🌐 barnstormerbrewing.com

🕐 Mon–Thu 11a.m.–11p.m., Fri–Sat 11a.m.–1a.m.,
Sun 11a.m.–11p.m.

🛒 Daily 11a.m.–11p.m.

Opened late in 2013 in a shopping plaza on the south side of Kempenfelt Bay, Barnstormer Brewing is Barrie's first brewpub. The brewpub has taken on an aeronautical motif that extends across the entire enterprise, from the nose cone pin-up mascot on through to the names of the food items on the menu. The spent-grain pizzas are among the best brewpub pizzas in the province, and the Flying Spicy Pig is not to be missed. The bar area features walls covered with diagrams of aircraft and, despite cozy wooden fixtures, retains the feel of a small aircraft hangar.

The year 2016 saw a significant expansion of the brewery facilities, which included a shift to a 10-BBL brewhouse and much larger fermentation vessels. The floorplan increased, expanding through walls into other portions of the shopping plaza in which Barnstormer is located. Under Niagara College–educated brewer Jeff Woodworth, the beers have become more stable. Barnstormer has been planning ahead for their increased volume by attending beer festivals across Ontario in order to build a following, and they now find themselves with several listings at the LCBO and the Beer Store. Plans currently exist to begin distilling in addition to brewing at the beginning of 2017.

––––

FLIGHT 400 is a lightly fruity blonde ale with Bosc pear and garden herbs over a straight-ahead cereal body (3). **WINDSHEAR WATERMELON SUMMER ALE** is a light-bodied American wheat made with watermelon juice that comes across more as rind than pulp due to the wheaty tang and light bitterness (2.5). **CIRRUS SESSION PALE ALE** is a light pale ale with bright lemon, orange, and tropical fruit character from the hopping schedule (4). **BILLY BISHOP BROWN** fits somewhere between a brown ale and a mild because of its relatively low alcohol and light body, but it features toasted grain, chocolate, toffee, and a relatively gentle finish (3). **FLIGHT DELAY IPA** is a West Coast IPA that neatly balances northwest pine and grapefruit with mango and guava in the aroma (3.5). **ACCELERATED STALL** is included here as an example of the seasonals being produced. While the Widebody series features single-hop double IPAs, this one combines hops from three continents to create a big lemony bitterness drafting a smooth body in its slipstream (3.5).

BATCH

📍 75 Victoria Street, Toronto

📞 (416) 238-1484

🐦 @BatchToronto

🌐 batchtoronto.com

🕐 Sun–Wed 11a.m.–1a.m., Thu–Sat 11a.m.–2a.m.

🛒 Daily 11a.m.–11p.m.

The space at 75 Victoria Street in Toronto has quite a history of being involved in the city's beer scene. It was the first home of Michael Hancock's Denison's Brewing Company, and after that Duggan's Brewery, which lasted a few years before closing. In 2012 the building gained new life as a brewpub owned by Creemore Springs and British Columbia's Granville Island called Beer Academy, which featured beers made by Stephen Rich (Cowbell Brewing) and became the debut space of Creemore's Mad & Noisy Brewing series, which still exists today. However, at the end of 2014, after only two short years, Creemore shut the space down for renovations. In early 2016 the space reopened as the Creemore-owned Batch, a hip, rustic brewpub serving modern takes on pub food favourites, a wide selection of cocktails and local craft beers, Creemore's flagships, and in-house beers made by former Northwinds brewer Andrew Bartle. Since starting his time at Batch, Bartle has enjoyed making flavourful and accessible styles that appeal to the constant traffic of people the area enjoys.

———

CREAM ALE has healthy grain character, smooth mouthfeel, and a slight fruity note toward the slightly smoky finish (3). **PALE ALE** is blood orange sweetness with honey stepping in mid-palate, leading toward a soothing, dry finish (4). **IPA** has notes of lychee, mango, melon, and ruby red grapefruit hitting hard in this rather bright-tasting beer, with a malt backbone that rather firmly keeps the flavours in check (3.5). **WITBIER** is all orange peel, coriander, and Belgian candi dancing around in a creamy blanket (3.5). The **PORTER** is the personal favourite of patron and staff alike, and for good reason. Light to medium body with cocoa and espresso notes taking the wheel, before a licorice sweetness hits into the finish (4).

BAYSIDE BREWING CO.

♀ 970 Ross Lane, Erieau

☎ (519) 676-8888

🐦 @BaysideBrewery

🌐 baysidebrewing.com

🕐 Daily 11:30a.m.–9p.m.

Located on the Erieau peninsula at the south end of Rondeau Bay, Bayside Brewing Co. has been a very popular addition to the Erie coast. Opened in 2013 with equipment repurposed from the noted Windsor brewpub Charly's and with the same brewer, Bayside is something of a summer destination because of their large patio and proximity to the beach. The menu largely consists of standard pub fare, although the selection of pizzas from their wood-fired oven is a clear highlight.

The beers on offer are in fairly basic, accessible styles, possibly due to the extract brewhouse currently in use. **LIGHTHOUSE LAGER** is a light lager with a banana chip ester and a dry finish (1), while its big brother **LONG POND LAGER** produces juicy fruit and melon character with its more substantial body

(1.5). The most successful offering is their **HONEY CREAM ALE**. Made with honey from a local Chatham–Kent apiary, it has a floral nose and a balanced sweetness (2.5).

BEAU'S ALL NATURAL BREWING COMPANY

 10 Terry Fox Drive, Vankleek Hill

 (866) 585-2337

 @beausallnatural

 beaus.ca

 Daily 10a.m.–6p.m.

You would be hard-pressed to find anyone in Ontario who hasn't heard, in some way or another, of Vankleek Hill's Beau's. In their ten years of existence they have earned awards and critical acclaim for everything from their eye-catching packaging, environmental sustainability efforts, and employee-owned status to their continual releases of new beers, unique and well-publicized collaborations, and almost cult-like fan base.

Beau's was started by father and son Tim and Steve Beauchesne, who left their respective jobs (Tim was the owner of a long-running textile company and Steve ran Go! Go! Go! Records and kept a government job) in order to pursue their dream of running a brewery. Since officially opening in 2007, they have already seen tremendous success in sales and have managed to do what few breweries have been able to do: stretch their distribution borders outside of Ontario and into New York and Quebec. Additionally, Beau's has managed to become the face of Ontario craft beer and environmental sustainability, emphasizing the importance of supporting local businesses, remaining active in their community through charity work, and doing their best to encourage green practices in other businesses.

———

Beau's flagship beer, **LUG-TREAD LAGERED ALE**, is a very approachable beer for newcomers to the brewery, with mild grain notes in a slightly sweet finish (3). **THE TOM GREEN BEER!**, a milk stout brewed in collaboration with famed Canadian comedian and cow "milker" Tom Green, is smooth and chocolatey, with strong flavours of roasted coffee and sweet lactose (3). **WAG THE WOLF** is a wheat beer with New Zealand hops added, creating a cocktail of banana, clove, papaya, and mango (3.5). Part of Beau's Farm Table series is the **MÄRZEN**. Formally known as Night Märzen, the autumn seasonal beer contains lovely bread pudding notes, with toffee, raisin, plum, and brown sugar in a bready body (4). **ST. LUKE'S VERSE** is one of Beau's famous gruits, made with lavender, rosemary, and thyme. The beer itself is a rather epic battle of dominance between lavender and rosemary, with hints of ginger following behind and leaving for a touch of thyme in the finish (2.5). **80 SHILLING** is a Scottish-style ale with warm toffee and roasted coffee beans, finishing off with a quick, coppery finish (3.5). **KISSMEYER: NORDIC PALE ALE** is a beer made in collaboration with Danish brewer Anders Kissmeyer, and part of the Beau's B-Side Brewing Label. The beer has a distinct herbal and citrus character, with a crisp finish and grassy aftertaste (4).

BEER LAB LONDON

📍 420 Talbot Street N, London

f Beer-Lab-London-212759812268247

A collaboration between London's extremely popular venue for craft beer, Milos' Craft Beer Emporium, and talented brewers the Denim Brothers (Adil Ahmed and Nick Baird) has resulted in a small bespoke line of beers. Having previously brewed under contract at London's Forked River, Ahmed and Baird have opened their own facility right next door to Milos'. Previously, the focus has been on extremely experimental small-batch beers, frequently brewed on a diminutive pilot system that can hardly meet the high demand of the brewer's enthusiastic patrons.

With such a small operation that concentrates on variety, it is difficult to suggest what will change between the writing and publication of this guide. The following ratings are included as examples of where the brewery is likely to go in the future.

———

BRETT LAM BERLINER is a Brettanomyces-finished Berliner weisse, light in alcohol with a refreshing, bone-dry finish. The aroma is peach, apricot, and light barnyard funk (4.5). **GALAXY SAISON** has a nose of papaya, mango, and passion fruit and delicate peppery Belgian yeast over a light wheat cracker (4). **MIMOSA GOSE** is bright orange peel and fresh-squeezed juice with an understated salinity throughout the core of the palate and a scrubbing carbonation (4). **BREAKFAST STOUT** is full of chocolate syrup depth, but may be a little overwhelmed by roast on the finish (3.5).

BELL CITY BREWING COMPANY

📍 51 Woodyatt Drive #9, Brantford

📞 (519) 900-6204

🐦 @bellcitybeer

🌐 bellcitybrewing.com

🕐 Wed–Thu 12p.m.–6p.m., Fri–Sat 12p.m.–8p.m., Sun 12p.m.–4p.m.

Located in Brantford and inspired by the works of that city's most famous resident, Alexander Graham Bell, Bell City has taken on the theme of famous inventors for their lineup of beers. Beginning as a contract player with a single brand in May 2013, Bell City opened their bricks-and-mortar location in February 2015. The result has been a sharp increase in the number of brands supported and the addition of a retail store and taproom that has made the brewery more a part of the Brantford community. A small but considered food menu focuses on Cornish pasties, until now a sadly overlooked beer snack in Ontario.

Bell City shifted their contract production in 2016 from Railway City to Toronto's Brunswick Bierworks, and demand

ONTARIO CRAFT BREWERIES

for their beer across the LCBO system means they will likely contract for the foreseeable future while producing the majority of their core and seasonal beers onsite at their Brantford facility.

———

EUREKA CREAM ALE is, stylistically speaking, more like an amber ale than the cream ale it professes to be, but it is accented by lemony citrus and meadow grasses, underpinned by a deep toasted toffee malt character (3.5). **LENOIR BELGIAN ALE** (named for the inventor of the combustion engine) lies somewhere between a Belgian golden ale and a tripel, with a clove nose and candied pear body (2.5). **ELIJAH'S REAL MCCOY** is a kölsch–style hybrid, lightly orchard fruited with a more robust grain character than traditional versions (3.5). **EDISON'S PEEPSHOW IPA** is a heavily bittered West Coast IPA with orange and lemon on the aroma and pine on the finish (4). **GALAXY HOPPER IPA** uses Galaxy in combination with other hops to bring tropical fruit and melon character to a lightly hopped session IPA (3), while **THE LOST BUST OF NEW BERLIN** is a properly bready marzen with an earthy, spicy Tettnang hop character (4).

BELLWOODS BREWERY

📞 (416) 535-4586

🐦 @bellwoodsbeer

🌐 bellwoodsbrewery.com

📍 124 Ossington Avenue, Toronto

🕐 Mon–Wed 5p.m.–12a.m., Thu 5p.m.–1a.m., Fri 4p.m.–1a.m., Sat 2p.m.–1a.m., Sun 2p.m.–12a.m.

🛒 Daily 11a.m.–11p.m.

📍 20 Hafis Road, North York

🕐 Wed–Sat 12p.m.–9p.m., Sun 12p.m.–6p.m.

Opened in April 2012 in a converted garage near Dundas and Ossington, Bellwoods has rapidly developed an international reputation as one of Canada's best breweries. The small space that the brewery began in proved insufficient to keep up with local demand, and by their second year Bellwoods had expanded next door, adding additional fermentation capacity and a permanent bottle shop. Demand for their beer rightly remains high, periodically causing the bottle shop to sell out completely, while special releases now result in polite queues.

ONTARIO CRAFT BREWERIES

Owners Mike Clark and Luke Pestl spent the majority of 2016 working on the renovation of a secondary facility in North York, which will significantly expand production. The Hafis facility features a 30-BBL brewhouse, a number of large fermenters, and several 60-hL wooden foeders in addition to a large barrel warehouse. Although the facility has a great deal of potential for expansion, it is likely to produce only 3,000 hL to 4,000 hL in the immediate future as Bellwoods tests market options that were previously inaccessible to them, since all of their volume had been selling out their front door.

――――

FARMAGEDDON is a farmhouse ale that begins with citric lemon aromas running to reedy grass as it warms. The body develops mandarin orange and horse blanket character prior to a dry finish with a light oak character (4.5). **FARMAGGEDON WITH MONTMORENCY CHERRIES** is a special edition using Niagara cherries to good effect. The whole of the fruit is represented, through skin, flesh, and stone, retaining the wood and dry brettiness of the standard Farmageddon (5). **JUTSU PALE ALE** manages to combine grapefruit, lemon, and nectarine with the hazy creaminess of an oaty body before a resinous finish (3.5). **ROMAN CANDLE** is a textbook example of an American West Coast IPA, with grapefruit, orange, and lemon leading to a finish like a blanket of pine needles (4.5). **JELLY KING** is a mixed fermentation dry-hopped sour that takes on guava and stone fruit character in a surprisingly full body, with a lemon-like acidity that is assertive but not detrimental (4.5). **GRANDMA'S BOY 2016**, brewed with Niagara shiro plums, is a delicate interplay between stone and orchard fruit in a vibrant, spicy body that dries out as a result of the Brettanomyces (4.5). **3 MINUTES TO MIDNIGHT** is an enormous imperial stout with notes of cherry, prune, maple, brandy, and deep roast that may cause fallout the morning after (4). **DONKEY VENOM**, for all its barrel character and wild fermentation, remains shockingly clean. The tart, lightly sour character plays into dark fruit, chocolate, roast, and a wisp of smoke, creating a nuanced offering, especially given the high alcohol content (5).

BELMONT LAKE BREWERY

Belmont Lake
BREWERY

📍 53 Fire Route 17, Havelock

📞 (705) 803-3001

🌐 belmontlakebrewery.com

🕐 Fri 3p.m.–6p.m., Sat–Sun 12p.m.–6p.m.

Located in the small community of Havelock in Peterborough County, Belmont Lake Brewery was opened in June 2016 by husband and wife Norrie and Julie Bearcroft, two English expats from Brighton who arrived in Canada with their dog Jack, intent on building a brewery in the beloved community they frequently holidayed in. And build it they did. Put together with local lumber and situated on the shores of its namesake, Belmont Lake features a 4-hL brewing system and access by both road and boat.

———

CROWE RIVER IPA has a deep malt backbone that supports flavours of orange and grapefruit, ending with a slightly sweet, biscuity finish (2). **CORDOVA GOLD BEST BITTER** has a light to medium body with biscuit, berry, and a subtle hint of pineapple working well together before its overwhelmingly bitter finish (2). **BLACK BEAR STOUT** is a pleasant dance of semi-sweet chocolate and light roast coffee followed by a nice wood-like, dry finish (3).

BENCH BREWING COMPANY

📍 3991 King Street, Beamsville

📞 (905) 562-3179

🐦 @benchbrewing

🌐 benchbrewing.com

Founded in 2016, Bench Brewing is one of the single most ambitious projects ever undertaken in Ontario. Housed in the disused Maple Grove Public School in Beamsville, Bench intends to harness the terroir of Ontario wine country in order to make unique beers. Owner Matt Giffen is no stranger to the region; his Giffen Vineyards provided their entire crop to Norman Hardie in Prince Edward County. The appreciation of the region's potential is a significant part of the overarching goal.

In addition to a 50-hL brewhouse and a 5-hL pilot, Bench is equipped with a three-acre hop yard planted with four varieties. Brewing team Mark Horsley (Nickel Brook) and Joe Wells (Hangar 24) plan to bring sour beers to Ontario in quantity. In addition to a coolship for the open inoculation of wort, Bench has acquired fourteen foeders, allowing for over 1,300 hL of fermentation space for sour beers. This fact, in combination with the ready availability of wine barrels from industry partners, suggests that, when the project is brought to fruition, Ontarians will be in for a real treat.

———

In the meantime, Bench has been producing their initial offerings out of Collective Arts in Hamilton. **BALL'S FALLS SESSION IPA** packs more body than the majority of beers in the style, with a peachy nose from its Vermont ale yeast and melon and citrus from dry hopping (4). **CITRA GROVE DRY HOPPED SOUR** is one of a series of single-hop sour beers, showcasing the variety of flavours that dry hopping can represent anchored by a tart, refreshing body (4.5). **TWENTY MILE FARMHOUSE ALE** produces banana aromas and a dry body from its yeast strains and a complex tropical fruit and berry flavour (4). **CLEAN SLATE BRETT SAISON** is the first venture into properly sour territory, with a sharp barnyard and pineapple nose that practically desiccates the tongue (3.5).

BEYOND THE PALE BREWING COMPANY

📍 5 Hamilton Avenue N, Ottawa

📞 (613) 695-2991

🐦 @BTPBrewing

🌐 beyondthepale.ca

🕐 Tues–Sat 12p.m.–8p.m., Sun 12p.m.–5p.m.

One of the early success stories from Ottawa's recent explosion of breweries is Beyond the Pale. Their initial goal was simple: brew more adventurous beer than what existed in Ottawa at the time — beer the brewers wanted to drink. Beginning in 2012, in a Hintonburg location barely 1,000 square feet in size, the brewery expanded rapidly with the loan of some fermenters from Beau's All Natural in Vankleek Hill.

On opening day, owners Shane and Al Clark and Rob McIsaac sold through the entire volume of beer they had produced, initially having estimated it would last three weeks. The fanaticism for locally brewed beer in Ottawa means that they have been able to open a much larger facility at City Centre, with a 15-BBL brewhouse five times the size of their original equipment. With recent changes to Ontario law, it is likely that the second location will have a retail store of its own, which may become necessary as the original location becomes more dedicated to brewing funkier styles with wild yeast and barrels. Additionally, 2015 saw the expansion of Beyond the Pale into LCBOs across Ottawa.

———

PINK FUZZ is an American wheat ale that is deceivingly light in body, given its 6% alcohol. Each batch includes the zest of twelve boxes of grapefruit, creating a bright, vibrant citrus character (4). **RYE GUY** is a West Coast IPA that uses rye as an accent grain, lending a spicy character and also a mellow mouthfeel that balances the orange and pine from Cascade hops (4). **IMPERIAL SUPER GUY** is Rye Guy's big brother, taking the same flavour profile toward the extreme at 9% (3.5). **THE DARKNESS** is an American-style stout with a heavy coffee and chocolate character and a hint of salted caramel in the body (4).

AROMATHERAPY is a double dry-hopped Vermont-style IPA with a giant peach aroma and a juicy citrus and stone fruit body that doesn't come across as overly bitter (4.5). **SAISON TROPICALE** is a saison/IPA hybrid leaning into pineapple and melon, with a spicy character bolstered by rye in the grist and a Belgian yeast strain (3.5). **JUICY DREAM** is a creamy, turbid East Coast IPA with significant wheat and oat in the grist to bolster the body and papaya, mango, and guava from late hopping (4). **FOXHOLE** is billed as a red winter IPA, with deep caramel and toasted malt notes holding back a pine-branch swat to the senses (4).

BICYCLE CRAFT BREWERY

OTTAWA | ONTARIO

📍 850 Industrial Avenue, Unit 12, Ottawa

📞 (613) 408-3326

🐦 @BicycleBrewery

🌐 bicyclecraftbrewery.ca

🕐 Thu–Fri 12p.m.–7p.m., Sat 11a.m.–7p.m., Sun 12p.m.–4p.m.

Located on Industrial Avenue in Ottawa, Bicycle Craft Brewery is operated by husband-and-wife team Laura and Fariborz Behzadi. Their love for the outdoors inspired the name and general theme of the brewery, which they started in 2014. Great care has been taken to decrease their carbon footprint and be cost-efficient, and they are a regular host to community events.

———

Bicycle's flagship beer is the **VELOCIPEDE IPA**, featuring a lot of melon and ruby red grapefruit with a moderately piney finish (3.5). Other beers include the **CRIMSON CASCADE** American amber, with a thin mouthfeel and distinct flavours of toasted caramel, chocolate, and orange zest that bloom out toward the middle of the palate (2.5), **TRILLIUM IPA**, originally a summer seasonal, which has floral notes, with a hint of lime in the aroma, that make their way into the taste (2), and the **SIR JOHN A PALE ALE**, which has a mild toffee sweetness throughout leading to a fairly dry finish (3).

BIG RIG BREWERY

BIG RIG BREWERY & TAPROOM

📍 103 Schneider Road, Kanata

📞 (613) 591-6262

🐦 @BigRigBrewery

🌐 bigrigbeer.com

🕐 Tues–Thurs 11:30a.m.–6p.m., Fri 11:30a.m.–8p.m.,
Sat 12p.m.–4p.m.

BIG RIG KITCHEN & BREWERY

📍 2750A Iris Street, Ottawa

📞 (613) 688-3336

🐦 @BigRigBrewery

🌐 bigrigbrew.com

🕐 Mon–Wed 11a.m.–11p.m., Thu–Fri 11a.m.–1a.m.,
Sat 8a.m.–1a.m., Sun 8a.m.–11p.m.

BIG RIG KITCHEN & BREWERY

📍 1980 Ogilvie Road, Gloucester

📞 (613) 552-3336

🐦 @BigRigBrew

🌐 bigrigbrew.com

🕐 Mon 11a.m.–10p.m., Tue–Wed 11a.m.–11p.m., Thu–Fri
11a.m.–12p.m., Sat 8a.m.–12a.m., Sun 8a.m.–11p.m.

Award-winning Big Rig is perhaps one of the fastest-growing breweries in the city of Ottawa. Opened in 2013 by brewmaster Lon Ladell, Clocktower Brewpub co-founder Pierre Cleroux, restaurateurs Jimmy Zourntos and Angelis Koutsos, and famed Ottawa Senators defenceman Chris "Big Rig" Phillips, Big Rig has seen tremendous growth over the years. The brewery now boasts two brewpub locations (authors' note: try the pizza) and a full-on brewery and taproom in Kanata, which has become one of the top contract-brewing facilities in the province, along with Cool Beer Brewing.

———

Big Rig's signature flagship beer is the **GOLD**, which has sweet biscuit notes with a delicate hop presence (3.5). The **CANADIAN AMBER** has a grassy characteristic with notes of honey followed by a dry, almost abrupt, finish (3). The **SHAKEDOWN APA** is a wonderful combination of tropical fruits and citrus, providing a slightly sweet tang in the finish (3.5). **ALPHA BOMB** is a dry-hopped IPA with plenty of alpha acids from the Chinook, Columbus, and Mosaic hops used, creating a beer with distinct notes of mango and pine (3.5). **MIDNIGHT KISSED MY COW** is a double-chocolate milk stout with creamy notes of chocolate with warming roasted and alcohol notes (4). **RELEASE THE HOUNDS BLACK IPA** contains traces of chocolate, roasted coffee, and leather with pine bitterness (4). The **BIG BOOT HEFE** is a remarkable example of the style, featuring the usual banana and clove with a hint of vanilla (4). **BOCK ME GENTLY** is a traditionally dry beer that contains lightly toasted grain and caramel notes with dried fruit and cinnamon (4).

BIG ROCK
BREWERY

@bigrockbrewery

bigrockbeer.com

📍 42 Liberty St, Toronto

📞 (416) 304-9465

🕐 Mon–Wed 11a.m.–1a.m., Thu–Fri 11a.m.–2a.m., Sat 10a.m.–2a.m., Sun 10a.m.–1a.m.

📍 1589 The Queensway, Etobicoke

📞 (647) 351-7837

🕐 Mon–Tue 11a.m.–5p.m., Wed–Fri 11a.m.–7p.m., Sat 11a.m.–5p.m.

Founded in 1985 in Calgary, Alberta, by Ed McNally, Big Rock has long maintained a presence in Ontario. While the Alberta craft brewing scene lags behind Ontario's, Big Rock's early dominance in that market allowed for a huge amount of growth throughout the eighties and nineties, resulting in a company that is likely the second-largest independent brewer in Canada behind Moosehead. Expansion beyond Alberta had proven difficult to maintain because of logistics and competitive markets. While the end of the last decade saw them chasing big beer trends like lime flavouring and low carbohydrates, the change in direction under former CEO Robert Sartor has been profound. In Alberta, brewer Paul Gautreau has released a number of seasonal offerings. This experimental tendency has been reinforced by a national strategy: the addition of local breweries in Vancouver and Toronto.

In Toronto, brewer Connor Patrick is the hand responsible for steering both a plant in Etobicoke and the Liberty Commons brewpub in the trendy Liberty Village neighbourhood. This does mean that, instead of shipping everything for consumption in Ontario from Alberta, Big Rock's beer is now produced locally. The addition of an Oliver & Bonacini restaurant to a protected industrial building has resulted in some truly impressive development and a serious rehabilitation of the Big Rock brand. Where once there was only Grasshopper, there's now a well-judged selection of products that runs on a thirty-one-year development timeline.

———

GRASSHOPPER is somewhere between a kristallweizen and an American wheat ale, and is fairly subtle in character, with a gentle wheaty tone throughout (3). **WARTHOG** falls under the mild ale category, although without the traditional English yeast interest; a relatively sweet toasted grain and honey affair (3). **TRADITIONAL ALE** is a wholesome, standard brown ale from the early days of craft brewing, with light touches of toffee and chocolate in the body and a gentle fruity nose (4). **RHINE STONE COWBOY** is a light, floral kölsch-style beer with a touch of fruity pear and white grape at the head of the swallow (4). **PILSNER**'s hops come across as lightly perfumey barley with a bite of pepper throughout the top end of the clean body (3.5). **CITRADELIC IPA** is a single-hop affair that showcases lemony Citra against a fairly robust light brown malt body without losing the interest (3). **CASHMERE CROONER** is a single-hop lager that trades on the Cashmere hop's lemon, lime leaf, and white grape must above a soft barley body (3.5). **LIP SUMAC-ER FAUX GOSE** features sumac, lemon balm, and Hawaiian sea salt, which create salinity and acidity on the front half before a bump of barley sugar intrudes at the head of the swallow (3.5).

BIG WATER BREWING COMPANY

📍 123 McIntyre Street W, North Bay

📞 (705) 999-0001

🅕 Big-Water-Brewing-Co-1766580816942596

Located in a rather hidden spot in downtown North Bay and named after the English translation of the Ojibwe tribe's name for Lake Nipissing, Big Water Brewing is a very small operation put together by two friends who have collective backgrounds in home-brewing. While the brewery has proven elusive, keeping rather quiet in terms of social media presence, the beer initially released under a subscription service has proven to be a hit with its members. For now, progress on the brewery is ongoing, with construction of a dedicated taproom, event space, and lakeside-view restaurant on the top floor all planned for development.

———

Despite the small brewing operation, Big Water has a rather large selection of beers on offer, many of which use rye as an ingredient. The **RYE ESB** has a somewhat thin body, with slight pepper and toffee notes and a mild candy corn element at the end (2.5). **RPA** is a balanced mix of tropical and citrus notes in a light to medium body with a clean finish (3). The **PALE ALE** has an almost Belgian sweetness to it, with flaked oats adding a creamy note to the body (3.5). **BDG**, a Bière de Garde, has an earthy character with toffee notes and a slightly peppery finish (3). **SAISON** is very malt-heavy, with flavours of caramel and biscuit and a dry, peppery note at the end (3). Finally, **RYE IPA** is definitely on the English side, with a strong malt backbone and with papaya and tangerine notes from the Mosaic hops striking a surprisingly nice balance (4).

BITTE SCHÖN BRAUHAUS

 68 Huron Street, New Hamburg

 (519) 390-2000

 @Bitteschonbrau

 bitteschonbrauhaus.com

🕐 Tue–Sat 11a.m.–9p.m., Sun 12p.m.–5p.m.

Opened in the fall of 2016, Bitte Schön has been immensely popular with local drinkers, selling out of growlers incredibly rapidly over the course of its first two weeks. Housed in a nineteenth-century storefront in downtown New Hamburg, the brewery features relatively small dual direct-fire brewing systems that produce double batches for the onsite fermenters. Brewer Robin Molloy from Descendants in Kitchener is pulling double duty in order to produce beer for the small company, which makes it no surprise that the majority of their offerings are German styles of beer, given his training in that country. The interior design of the brewery is sparse and intentionally follows a minimalistic sensibility, making this Ontario's first Bauhaus brauhaus.

ONTARIO CRAFT BREWERIES

GOOD NEIGHBOUR registers light in colour for the German schwarzbier style, with a nutty malt character in the middle and a dry, roasty, slightly astringent finish to the body (3). **NEW HAMBURG HELLES** is bitter for a helles, with a small amount of citrus and sulfur in the nose leading to a medium grainy body (2.5). **HURON STREET HEFEWEIZEN** seamlessly blends clove and banana yeast character into a light, creamy, vibrant body with a tangy yeast character (4).

BLACK BELLOWS BREWING COMPANY

 @Black_Bellows

blackbellows.com

Black Bellows was founded by childhood friends Peter Braul and Scott Brown, whose decision to take up brewing professionally came on a canoe trip. The combination of Scott's entrepreneurial background and Peter's ten years of home-brewing experience seemed like a good basis for a new business. Based out of Collingwood and contracting out of Collingwood Brewery, Black Bellows joined the Ontario market in 2016 and has the intention of moving rapidly from brewing on a contract basis to operating a plant of their own.

———

BLACK BELLOWS WHITE is their first offering, a complex take on the Belgian witbier that includes more than just the standard orange peel and coriander. Bolstered by key lime and elderflower, the aroma is full of bright citrus, although the herbal and floral qualities muddle somewhat on the palate (3.5). **BLACK BELLOWS BROWN** falls stylistically

ONTARIO CRAFT BREWERIES

125

somewhere between dubbel, Belgian brown ale, and dunkel-weizen, with a clove and banana note from the yeast strain that recedes into a dark bready body (3).

BLACK CREEK HISTORIC BREWERY

📍 1000 Murray Ross Parkway, Toronto

📞 (416) 736-1733

🐦 @blackcreekbeer

🌐 blackcreekbrewery.ca

🕐 Times vary seasonally. Daily tours at 2p.m. and tastings at 12:30p.m. and 3p.m.

Located within the much-loved open-air heritage museum that is Black Creek Pioneer Village, the Historic Brewery is located in the town's Half Way House Inn and Restaurant. Making use of brewing methods commonly used in the 1800s, award-winning brewer Ed Koren has been creating historically themed beers for Black Creek since the brewery's inception in 2009. While the public can purchase their beers at liquor stores, thanks to large-scale contract brewing at Trafalgar Brewing, the real treat is to visit Pioneer Village, learn about the brewing landscape and methods of the 1800s, and sample the beers made with the brewery's historical equipment.

———

ONTARIO CRAFT BREWERIES

For the benefit of readers, ratings for Black Creek's beers will be of their offerings made at Trafalgar Brewing, as the more modern technology yields a more consistent end product. The **PORTER** is the brewery's first commercial offering and yields notes of espresso, roasted nuts, and cocoa in a light to medium body (3). **RIFLEMAN'S RATION** is a brown ale with flavours of toffee and brown sugar blending nicely with a roasted malt character (3.5). The **PUMPKIN ALE**, an annual favourite, is rife with pumpkin pie spices like cinnamon and nutmeg, with real pumpkin giving it some added character (3).

BLACK OAK BREWING COMPANY

📍 75 Horner Avenue, Unit 1, Toronto

📞 (416) 252-2739

🐦 @BlackOakBrewing

🌐 blackoakbeer.com

🕐 Tours available on Saturdays.

🛒 Mon–Fri 10a.m.–7p.m., Sat 10a.m.–4p.m.

Founded in Oakville in the last days of 1999, Black Oak was one of a handful of breweries to open in Ontario during the period following the brewing industry shakeout of the mid-1990s. Although the brewery's two core brands have always been available, an early experiment with a premium lager proved to be something of a setback and it was discontinued in 2004. Ken Woods, owner and president, has frequently acted as a spokesman for small breweries in Ontario.

Black Oak has been based out of Etobicoke since 2008, a move that did the brewery good. While the core range of seasonals has always been stable, the new facility has allowed for expansion and experimentation. Changes in staff over the last half decade have resulted in additional one-offs and seasonal

ONTARIO CRAFT BREWERIES

products, the vast majority of which have hit their mark and driven new customers to the brewery. The switch in packaging in 2015 to cans for core products has met with universal approval and is a positive sign for the brewery's prospects.

———

PALE ALE has a light, bready body and has leaned more toward North American citrus and pine hop character over the last few years (3.5). **NUT BROWN** is, as the name suggests, nutty and toasted in body with chocolate and toffee accents and a balanced bitterness (4). **10 BITTER YEARS** holds the distinction of having been the first regularly available double IPA in Ontario, dank with piney resin and brightened by clementine and tangerine citrus (4.5).

The cinnamon-accented **NUTCRACKER PORTER** is a perennial holiday favourite (4.5) while **OAKTOBERFEST** has a bread-crust body and a mild herbal, grassy character (4). **BEAT THE HEAT** is something of a masquerading witbier, but a pleasantly lemony summer quaffer nonetheless (3). **TRIPLE CHOCOLATE CHERRY STOUT** performs as advertised, with deep kirsch and black cherry notes (4), while **NOX AETERNA** is a full-bodied and lightly smoky take on the oatmeal stout made with locally roasted coffee (4).

BLACK SWAN BREWING

 144 Downie Street, Stratford

 (519) 814-7926

 @blackswanbeer

 blackswanbrewing.ca

 Mon 12p.m.–5p.m., Tue–Sat 11a.m.–7p.m., Sun 12p.m.–5p.m.

Both owners of Black Swan were teachers in Stratford before they decided to venture into brewing professionally. As younger men, Bruce Pepper and Ryan Stokes had become aware of good beer in Montreal and Detroit, respectively, and the duo have been home-brewing for a significant period of time. The brewery location was, until recently, a lingerie store, which may not have been its highest and best use in a town of 30,000. The shop now fits a 10-hL brewhouse into an ultra-low-budget, DIY setup that still manages to produce beers that seem to have captured the imagination of Stratford's beer scene. Black Swan has come a long way in a very short time, and their main brands have become so popular that they only infrequently have time to brew seasonal offerings.

———

131

ENGLISH PALE ALE is properly British with earthy allotment-garden flowers and hedgerow hops over biscuity, bready malts, but still fairly light in body (4). **PORTER** is lightly sooty in the aroma with a touch of freshly roasted espresso. Brown malt lends a touch of sweetness and a friable snap to the body (4). **IPA** is dominated by pineapple and juicy fruit, quince and clementine, and relatively light in body in the southern California manner (4.5). **RASPBERRY WILD CHILD** is a raspberry flavoured version of the brewery's Berliner weisse, which has become so popular that it is now available year-round (NR).

BLOCK THREE BREWING COMPANY

📍 1430 King Street N, Unit 2, St. Jacobs

📞 (519) 664-1001

🐦 @BlockThree

🌐 blockthreebrewing.com

🕐 Tours available during retail store hours. Call ahead for groups larger than ten.

🛒 Mon–Wed 11a.m.–6p.m., Thu 11a.m.–8p.m., Fri–Sat 11a.m.–9p.m., Sun 11a.m.–6p.m.

Block Three's story began in 2012, when four friends (a brewer and three accountants) decided to expand their monthly beer club in a drastic way. By April 2013 renovations on their chosen site had begun, and by September beer was flowing out the front door. Block Three has continued to upgrade and expand as they go along, adding fermenters, a thirty-two-piece barrel-aging program, and a wooden foeder. In 2016 they hired ex-Wellington brewer Kevin Freer to add some needed consistency to their core offerings and to help keep up with demand through the LCBO. Their tasteful tile-accented taproom is much roomier than you might guess from the building's exterior, and frequently hosts open mic nights and features board games for the entertainment of their fans, whom they refer to as "Blockheads." For the culturally inclined, the room features paintings from local artists and sculptures from local resident Tim Schmalz.

While Block Three tends to focus on rotating selections and experimentation, many of their most frequently available beers are in Belgian styles. This does not come close to representing the number of options available over the course of the year, which might fall anywhere stylistically.

——

KING STREET SAISON is a bright, citrusy saison with spicy yeast and herbal characteristics thanks to the addition of coriander and peppercorn (3). **BEAUTY AND THE BELGIAN** is a Belgian amber ale with a nutty, lightly roasty malt character and an aroma of plump raisins (3.5). **SINGLE TRACK MIND** is something of a patersbier or Belgian single in design, with scrubbing carbonation and a spicy Hallertau bite on the finish (3). **FICKLE MISTRESS** is a dry-hopped kettle sour using Citra, Columbus, and Mosaic for that tropical fruit edge (2.5). **FRANKENSTOUT** is so named because of the ever-changing malt bill. At time of writing it contains a deep coffee aroma with a whiff of creosote and heavy roast (3).

Perhaps the beer that will give the best example of the brewery's long-term direction is **DULLE GRIET**, a two-year-old barrel-aged red ale, fermented with Brettanomyces, that takes on aromas of grape must, spicy wood, and appropriate red fruit acidity in a pleasing dry body (4.5).

BLOOD BROTHERS BREWING

 165 Geary Avenue, Toronto

 @BloodBrothersTO

 bloodbrothersbrewing.com

🕐 Daily 12p.m.–9p.m.

Originally located in the basement of an industrial warehouse off Dupont and Dufferin in Toronto, Blood Brothers Brewing had given an almost literal meaning to the term "hidden gem," with only two signs indicating the location of their taproom. The brewery was first opened in 2015 by brothers Dustin and Brayden Jones, who started brewing using retrofitted dairy equipment. Since then the two have expanded well beyond their original location, finding a home in Indie Alehouse's barrel room, which provides them with enough space to triple their capacity and provide a comfortably small taproom and retail area, complete with snacks, a respectable number of taps, and a beautifully rustic atmosphere, with a beer altar behind the bar. The space is often frequented by local residents to the emerging neighbourhood and plays host to a weekly trivia night.

While the goal of Blood Brothers is to brew a number of unique beers throughout the year, some of the more long-standing ones include **SHUMEI IPA**, with tropical fruit notes backed by bursts of citrus and a slight hint of honey (3.5), the **INNER EYE PALE ALE**, with massive amounts of pineapple and a sweet, effectively sharp finish (4), and **FALL OF THEBES**, a brett farmhouse ale made with grape must from nearby Macedo Winery, with heavy wine notes more prominent than the slight tart character at the end that grows as the beer warms (3). A much-loved seasonal offering, **GUILTY REMNANT**, is a white stout with a significant flavour of vanilla cookie dough and cold brew coffee with a milk chocolate swirl (4). Variations of this beer have also been made with peanut butter, raspberry, and salted caramel.

THE BLUE ELEPHANT CRAFT BREW HOUSE

📍 96 Norfolk Street S, Simcoe

📞 (519) 428-2886

🐦 @BlueElephantInc

🌐 blueelephant.ca

🕐 Mon–Sat 11:30a.m.–12a.m., Sun 2p.m.–8p.m.

Heather Pond-Manorome has been the proprietor of the Blue Elephant, a beloved Simcoe institution, since 1992. Since the restaurant's shift in 2012 from focusing on Thai cuisine to becoming a brewpub, it has been a popular location for beer drinkers of all stripes in the region, continuing to carry a small number of macro brands alongside its own. The century mansion in which it is located seats over 350 and is visually a curious combination of influences: an eclectic manor house decorated in beer memorabilia and Thai ephemera. The Blue Elephant's menu is similarly diverse, and there is a gentle waft of chilies from the kitchen, which features local Norfolk County produce wherever possible. This local ethos may be what accounts for their success in using fresh hops; their relationship with Carolinian Hop Yard resulted in brewer James Grant's victory in the 2014 Great Ontario-Hopped Craft Beer Competition.

The Blue Elephant's enthusiasm for creating a following for better beer (not just their own, but in general) is impressive. They offer customers the opportunity to participate in a monthly brew camp using interesting ingredients, and they designed their own Ale Trail to help promote other breweries in Ontario's southwest region.

––––

NORTH SHORE LAGER is a straight-ahead American-style lager with a fairly clean barley grain body (3). **GENTLEMEN'S PILSNER** was originally brewed for the Simcoe stopover of Gentlemen of the Road. It is a light, doughy North American pilsner with a slightly sour finish (2.5). **RED DEVIL** is an earthy amber ale with a caramel and toast-grain body, served on site with a lime segment (2.5). **SWEET LEAF** is a brown ale with an earthy, vegetal hop presence and a deep malt body leaning toward Tootsie Roll and molasses (3).

S.S. MINNOW is subtly accented with coconut and ginger, while barley and coconut water seem to blend in the body (2.5). **STRAWBERRY LAGER**, a summer flagship, has a vibrant frozen strawberry daiquiri quality to it and is popular on the patio (2.5). **NORFOLK HARVEST** uses locally grown hops to add tobacco, pepper, and spicy herbal character to a Grape-Nuts malt body (3). **KRIPKE'S WHAGER** is a wheat lager named for *The Big Bang Theory* that develops biscuity malt character and a certain depth of bazinga in the body (3.5).

BOBCAYGEON BREWING COMPANY

📞 (705) 243-7077

🐦 @bobcaygeonbeer

🌐 bobcaygeonbrewing.ca

Founded in 2015 in Bobcaygeon and contract brewed in Ottawa, the Bobcaygeon Brewing Company is enjoying some early success on tap around the province of Ontario, focusing predominantly on the area between Toronto and Ottawa.

––––

The selection of products that Bobcaygeon offers has tripled in the last year. **COMMON LOON** American pale ale leans gently toward malt in its balance with a light, sweet cereal character balanced by a dandelion aroma and a hint of orange peel bitterness (3). **DOCKSIDE** is a red ale in the style of the English midlands with a leather and fallen leaf aroma with the faintest whiff of smoke in the lightly grainy mid–palate (3). **PORTER AFTER NINE** is closer to English than American, with a hint of salinity and black olive minerality on the aroma before reaching roast coffee and a touch of sweetness on the way to a deep, dark finish (3.5).

BOSHKUNG BREWING COMPANY

📍 9201 Highway 118, Minden Hills
📞 (705) 489-4554
🐦 @BoshkungBrewing
🌐 boshkungbrewing.com
🕐 Tue–Thu 11.a.m.–6p.m., Fri 11a.m.–9p.m., Sat 11a.m.–8p.m., Sun 11a.m.–6p.m.

Catering to both locals and the cottage crowd, Boshkung has seen so much success since opening in 2014 that construction is currently underway for a second location slated to open this summer, situated in the heart of downtown Minden in a former Beer Store on 20 Water Street. The award-winning brewery is an ideal destination for visitors to the Haliburton region. In addition to a tasting room and retail store, Boshkung has licensed seating at picnic tables on Mirror Lake and take-out pizza for customers looking for a bite to eat. Couple that with neighbouring restaurant Rhubarb, which is under the same roof and ownership, and this brewery is a must-visit.

Founding brewmaster Johnny Briggs is an early graduate of the Niagara College brewing program and has nicely judged the balance between flavour and accessibility in the core lineup of beers.

———

NORTH COUNTRY KELLERBIER is deeply bready for a kellerbier, verging into the sweetness of a Vienna lager. The leafy, lightly spicy noble-hop character imparts a light herbal bitterness with lime in the aroma (3). **35 & 118 CREAM ALE** is a quite fruity number, with pear, peach, and McIntosh apple, fading into a distinct cereal note and a light herbal finish (3.5). **BLACK ROCK DARK ALE** has a sweet malt character, smooth and creamy but full of dried berries and milk chocolate on the palate (3). **KUNGAROO IPA** is a nice representation of an American pale ale, with grapefruit, lime, and orange blending with caramel, malt bitterness, and earthy spices (3). **CAMPFIRE RYE** is a fall seasonal beer with an aroma reminiscent of its namesake, thanks to the oak-smoked wheat malt. The spicy bite of rye blends well with notes of caramel, with a smooth and creamy mouthfeel (3.5).

BRASSERIE ÉTIENNE BRÛLÉ

📍 893 Notre Dame Street, Embrun

📞 (613) 370-3000

🐦 @BrasserieEb

🌐 etiennebrule.ca

🕐 Tue–Sat 11a.m.–11p.m., Sun 11a.m.–8p.m.

Located in Embrun and named for the famed French explorer, Brasserie Étienne Brûlé is a brewpub that opened in the spring of 2016 by friends Mathieu Jérôme, Pierre-André Roy, and Richard Ménard. Housed in a building that was previously a firehouse, the brewery's immense space works well for its purpose, where locally sourced shareable platters are served alongside the house beers, sold on tap and in the iconic stubby bottles in their retail space by the bar. On the brewing side, Étienne has brought on Dan Beaudoin, formally of Boshkung Brewing and Bar Volo's famed House Ales, putting his experience and skill to very good use.

———

LE BOHÉMIEN DE NOTRE-DAME is a wonderful traditional take on a pilsner, with light and grassy hop character and a delicate caramel sweetness (4.5). **VAGABOND** blonde ale has spiced earthy berries up front, which make way for a warming caramel character that fades into the finish (4). **5W30** stout plays heavy on the coffee, but not the acidic quality of it, rather taking on a smooth, creamy body (3.5). The IPA, **CITRALE**, operates under the logic that hoppy doesn't necessarily mean bitter. The result is an altogether juicy beer with grapefruit and melon well showcased (4.5).

Sleeping Giant Brewing Co. in Thunder Bay does more than just promote their own brand — they promote the local area's beer scene as well.

With locations in Calgary, Montreal, and Thunder Bay, Canada Malting Co. is the largest malt producer in the country, providing over 450,000 metric tons per year to brewers, distillers, and the food industry.

Manitoulin Island currently has two craft breweries, Manitoulin Brewing Co. in Little Current and Split Rail Brewing Co. in Gore Bay.

Manitoulin Brewing Co.'s flagship beer, Swing Bridge Blonde, near its iconic namesake.

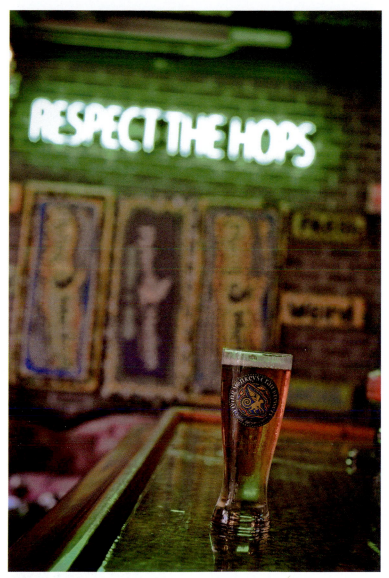

Since rebranding from their original name in 2009, Barrie's Flying Monkeys Craft Brewery has been proudly and unapologetically weird.

Woodstock's first craft brewery, Upper Thames Brewing Co., has received immense community support right from the start.

Niagara Oast House Brewer's second-floor event space features a breathtaking view, overlooking row upon row of grape vines and a hop trellis.

Brasserie Étienne Brûlé's Dan Beaudoin gained brewing experience at Boshkung and most notably at House Ales, the in-house brewing facility at the legendary Bar Volo. He has clearly put the lessons he's learned at both places to good use.

New Ontario Brewing Co. and their well-made beers have proven to be a welcome addition for the people of North Bay since opening in 2015.

Originally, Haliburton Highlands Brewing opened their Abbey Gardens brewery with a traditional Mongolian yurt for a retail space. Their new location, a 4,500-square-foot building, is definitely a lot more stable.

BREW WINDSOR

📍 635 University Avenue E, Windsor
📞 (226) 246-0720
🌐 brewwindsor.com
🕐 Tue–Thu 12p.m.–9p.m.,
   Fri–Sat 12p.m.–11p.m., Sun 5p.m.–9p.m.

Started in 2014 by hospitality-industry veterans Joseph and Jordan Goure, Brew is one of a handful of recently opened breweries in Windsor. The brewhouse itself is a rarity: one of a very few recently commissioned extract systems in Ontario. It is partitioned off from the taproom by a glass wall, which fits seamlessly into the retro-industrial look of the building. Many of the food items on the taproom's tightly focused menu integrate beer into the recipe, including spent-grain pizza crust and pretzels with beer-brined sauerkraut. In summer a rooftop beer garden provides a comfortable patio for customers. In colder weather, beer to go is available in the brewery's custom blue glass swing-top bottles. Brew excels as a Halloween destination, really getting into the spirit of things with an adult-oriented haunted house.

Improvements for 2016 include upgrades in Brew's fermentation vessels, which have been changed from plastic to

ONTARIO CRAFT BREWERIES

145

steel and have contributed a noticeable improvement to their products on tap.

———

Brew is thoroughly focused on the crowd just arriving at craft beer. As such, their main offerings are what you might consider gateway beers. **PROPER LAGER** is a light-bodied take on a pale lager, with a hit of rising bread dough (2). **THE WALKING RED**, a spiced red ale, approximates a gingerbread cookie nicely, a good fit for autumn (3.5). **BLACK 'N' BREW** chocolate stout is slightly thin, but redeemed by dry cocoa on the finish (2.5). **CANADIAN MAPLE BREW** is unmistakably a maple beer and the closest you can get to sucking sap from the spigot (3).

BRICK BREWING COMPANY

📍 400 Bingemans Centre Drive, Kitchener

📞 (519) 742-2732

🐦 @waterloobrewing

🌐 brickbeer.com

🕐 Mon–Sat 10a.m.–7p.m., Sun 10a.m.–6 p.m.

Brick Brewing was Ontario's first craft brewery, founded by Jim Brickman in 1984 in the shadow of a much larger Labatt plant. While the focus of Brick's portfolio has shifted over the years (not very long ago they led the discount segment with their buck-a-beer brand Laker Lager and its variants), the company has invariably enjoyed a great deal of success. Their sadly discontinued Anniversary Bock has attained legendary status within Ontario's short craft-brewing history. With changes to the structure of beer pricing in the province and the emergence of the craft sector since 2007, Brick's focus has become their Waterloo brands. Don't assume the shift has diminished their size; they still brew nearly 350,000 hL a year. The new facility in Kitchener-Waterloo contains state-of-the-art equipment, beginning operations just as the brewery entered their fourth decade. For a brief period in 2015, Brick actually

ONTARIO CRAFT BREWERIES

147

possessed the most efficient brewhouse in the world: a Krones model that achieved 98 percent efficiency.

———

The shift in attention to craft brands has created some significant improvement in recent years. **CLASSIC PILSNER** has a gentle bready body and a grassy hop aroma with lime accents from the Hallertau hops (4). **WATERLOO DARK** has gained roast and is currently fuller bodied than it has been in a decade (3.5). The **IPA** is a muted British expression of the style (2.5), while the **AMBER** is a practically unclassifiable oaked rye bock weighing in at 6.8% and suitable for autumn sipping (3). The biggest success the brewery has enjoyed in the craft segment has come from its line of radlers, which have sold incredibly well over the last two summers. The **GRAPEFRUIT RADLER** manages to balance soda-like sweetness with effervescent carbonation and a healthy squeeze of tart, acidic juice (4). New for 2016 is the **DOUBLE-DOUBLE DOPPELBOCK**, which achieves exactly what it's meant to, aping the classic Tim Hortons two cream and two sugar experience but without a rim to roll (3.5).

BRIMSTONE BREWING COMPANY

📍 209 Ridge Road N, Ridgeway

📞 (289) 876-8657

🐦 @BrimstoneBrew

🌐 brimstonebrewing.ca

🕐 Wed–Thu 4p.m.–10p.m., Fri 4p.m.–11p.m., Sat 12p.m.–11p.m., Sun 12p.m.–5p.m. Contact in advance for tours.

🛒 Mon–Tues 12p.m.–4p.m., Wed–Thu 12p.m.–10p.m., Fri–Sat 12p.m.–11p.m., Sun 12p.m.–5p.m.

The goal of any small brewery is to fit into the community that it serves. Brimstone has been aided in achieving that end by operating out of the basement of Ridgeway's Sanctuary Centre for the Arts, which routinely hosts everything from yoga classes and gallery shows to live music. In its first two years, the brewery expanded from a modest nanobrew set-up to a much larger system, and it maintains a taproom catered by Crave Local Fresh Catering, which occupies the same building. In summer, a patio extends the taproom to the outside of the converted church. The addition of brewer Zack Gagnon in 2015 has focused

Brimstone's offerings and allowed for some expansion of their seasonal program, with very positive results.

———

Given the name of the brewery and the fact that it occupies a converted church basement, it is no surprise that the beer names have taken on a darkly liturgical theme. **ENLIGHTENMENT** blonde ale is sweet, with a robust barley aroma and a pepper and grass hop bitterness, an approachable offering for initiates to the order (3.5). **MIDNIGHT MASS** oatmeal stout takes the step of using chicory in the fermenter in place of the more traditional coffee in order to deepen roast character and add bitterness, developing a cherry and wood presence in the middle of the aroma (4). **LAUTER TUN SAINTS** is a hybrid pale ale that uses oats, wheat, and rye in the grist. The grassy, mineral dankness of Nelson Sauvin segues seamlessly into the rye spice for a truly cohesive experience (4). **SINISTER MINISTER** is an extremely assertive India pale ale, with pine and citrus bitterness vastly overmatching caramel malt sweetness (3).

BROADHEAD BREWING COMPANY

📍 81 Auriga Drive, Unit 13, Nepean

📞 (613) 695-9444

🐦 @BroadheadBeer

🌐 broadheadbeer.com

🕐 Tue–Thu 10a.m.–6p.m., Fri 10a.m.–7p.m., Sat 10a.m.–5p.m.

Located in Nepean, just outside the borders of Ottawa, Broadhead's brewing facility and taproom will make any DIY enthusiast go green with envy. The walls, flooring, bar, grain-mill chute, and much of the equipment was hand built by home-brewing friends Shane Matte, Jason Smale, Jamie White, and head brewer Josh Larocque. Even the computer system that controls the brewery was developed from scratch (and includes a *Star Trek: The Next Generation* interface that makes the nerd inside of us smile approvingly). Brewing out of their own facility, as well as at Big Rig, Broadhead distributes as far north as Temiskaming and can be found in most bars in the Ottawa region.

———

Broadhead has six year-round beers. **BACKBONE STANDARD** is a golden ale with a crisp, medium body and a slight bitterness rounded out with a sweet finish (3). **LONG SHOT WHITE** is a fairly sweet and spicy wheat beer with a lot of coriander and orange character (2). **GRINDSTONE AMBER** has a fairly light body, with a bit of graham cracker sweetness and a touch of grassy bitterness in a rather clean finish (2). **UNDERDOG PALE** has a lot of sweet caramel notes with a grounded, earthy undertone and a balanced mouthfeel (3). **WILDCARD ALE** is a pale ale with a frequently changed hop addition in each batch. The one that has Centennial hops has a very light body with a bitter tangerine character (1.5). **DARK HORSE STOUT** features a lot of rich espresso and brown sugar, with a creaminess brought on by the addition of oatmeal (3).

BROCK STREET BREWING COMPANY

📍 1501 Hopkins Street, Unit 3, Whitby

📞 (905) 668-5347

🐦 @BrockStBeer

🌐 brockstreetbrewing.com

🕐 Mon–Wed 9a.m.–8p.m., Thu–Sat 9a.m.–9p.m., Sun 11a.m.–6p.m.

Named for the historical downtown street that was the stopping point for travelling dignitaries, politicians, and even royalty, Brock Street Brewing was opened in the spring of 2015 by partners Mark Woitzik, Chris Vanclief, Victor Leone, and Scott Pepin and proved to be just what Whitby needed. In the first six months an outpouring of support saw sales rise 20 to 30 percent each month. Brock Street is currently in the process of putting together their second location, a brewpub on the corner of Brock and Dunlop at 244 Brock Street South that is expected to open in the summer of 2017. There is so much excitement for the space that wedding parties have already been booked there over a year in advance.

ONTARIO CRAFT BREWERIES

BLONDE is a simple North American take on the style, with an aroma of sweet citrus and apricot with a lightly bitter crest in the mid–palate (2). **AMBER** has light toffee notes with a hint of berries and a lightly earthy hop presence in the tail (2.5). **PORTER** is essentially a cup of mocha, with a long, dry, roasty finish (3.5). **BROCKTOBERFEST LAGER** plays white grape off deeper stone fruits and toffee, with earthy hops leading toward the finish (3.5). **IRISH RED ALE** has a delightful light peppery character with sharp and spicy notes in a lightly smoky finish (3). **DOUBLE VISION IPA** has large notes of caramel backing up an assertive earthy bitterness (2.5). **PREMIUM PILSNER** is definitely in the German style, with crisp biscuit notes and rather sweet accents, leading toward a mildly bitter finish (3).

BROKEN STICK BREWING COMPANY

📍 5450 Canotek Road, Unit 78, Ottawa

📞 (613) 366-3599

🐦 @BrokenStickBrew

🌐 brokenstickbrewing.com

🕐 Thu–Fri 12 p.m.–7 p.m., Sat 11 a.m.–6 p.m., Sun 11 a.m.–4 p.m.

While Broken Stick did not open until 2014, the plans for the brewery had been in development since 2007, when much of the necessary equipment was sourced from Quebec. Located in an industrial park in the Orleans section of Ottawa, Broken Stick has already seen production triple. Special attention has been given to the retail section of the small brewery, which has a custom refrigeration unit nearly as wide as the store, featuring a wide selection of growlers for take-home consumption. Custom equipment is part of Broken Stick's modus operandi, since one of the owners, Eric, operates an industrial controls business, ensuring that the brewery will see incremental improvement in processes for the foreseeable future.

ONTARIO CRAFT BREWERIES

TIPSY PALE ALE has changed in the last year, lightening the malt character and developing a more pronounced English hop character with a hint of bark and shrub in the finish (3).

SPRING FLING is straight down the middle of the American amber ale style, with a gently sweet malt body and pronounced roast and toffee making up the beer's middle (3).

DOWNTOWN LEROY BROWN PORTER is full of chocolate and hazelnut, and is smooth on the way to a dry finish (3).

PART OF A "HEFE" BREAKFAST leans toward the darker end of the hefeweizen spectrum, with minimal clove on the aroma and a healthy banana bread character (3).

BROTHERS BREWING COMPANY

 15 Wyndham Street N, Guelph

 @BrothersBrewery

 brothersbrewingcompany.ca

While many brewers come to the trade later in life, by their senior year of high school Asa and Colton Proveau had a plan in place to open a brewery. Goal-directed learning led them to brewing and business school, respectively, and allowed them to convert a music studio on the family farm in Pelham into a nanobrewing facility. Just a few years later they are poised to open Brothers Ale House in downtown Guelph, with the help of Niagara College graduate Michael Bevan. The renovation of the Petrie building to facilitate the new brewpub has taken somewhat longer than expected, but interest has remained high, in part because of the gradual revelation of the brewpub's lineup on social media. A crowdfunding campaign has helped with funding, and the brewpub should be open and producing beer by early 2017.

———

TROPIC THUNDER, a glimpse into the potential of the Ale House location, is an American pale ale with Mosaic, Amarillo, and Citra developing a relatively mellow fruit salad character: pineapple, mango, peach, and tangerine (3.5).

BROWN VAN BREWING

 (613) 316-5245

 @brownvanbrewing

🌐 brownvanbrewing.com

Many contract brewers come to the industry with little in the way of expertise on subject matter. The same cannot be said of Brown Van's owners Paul and Erica Braunovan. Paul is a specialist in intellectual property and trademark law and has frequently worked with breweries, even participating as a subject matter expert at the Ontario Craft Brewers Conference. While their single offering, a kölsch-style beer, is one of many in the province of Ontario, it is set apart by the brewing expertise of Don Harms, who mans the kettle for them at Kichesippi. The speed with which they have permeated the Ottawa market, becoming nearly ubiquitous in just seven months, speaks to the quality of the product.

———

KÖLSCH STYLE ALE has a healthy, round barley character topped by a slight apple skin and wildflower character on the aroma, finishing in a clean, grassy bitterness (4).

BRUNSWICK BIERWORKS

 25 Curity Avenue, Toronto

 (647) 444-2337

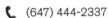 brunswickbierworks.com

In a market with a thriving contract brewing industry, Brunswick Bierworks is something of an anomaly. For the most part, brewers contract their space out to other people to make up a shortfall in their own capacity. In the case of Brunswick, there is no own-brand product, as the facility is given over entirely to the local production of other companies' beer, and in considerable volume. The main brewing system is 50 hL in volume, with a pilot system at 20 hL (bigger than the majority of breweries in Ontario have for production). Brunswick produces locally, as in the case of Bell City, or internationally, as it does for Sweden's Omnipollo.

Founded by Mike Laba and Chris Goddard, owners of the Craft Brand Company, Brunswick is a novel solution to some of Ontario's more stringent importation difficulties and has the potential to be a facilitator of change in the market in both the long and short term. By summer 2017, it is likely that they will have an operational tasting room and bottle shop.

BURDOCK BREWERY

Burdock

📍 1184 Bloor Street W, Toronto
📞 (416) 546-4033
🐦 @BurdockTO
🌐 burdockto.com
🕐 Daily 5p.m.–2a.m.
🛒 Daily 11a.m.–11p.m.

Since its opening in the summer of 2015, Burdock, located near Dufferin and Bloor, has earned itself a solid reputation in Toronto's beer scene from hardened critics and picky drinkers alike — a very strong debut after two years of planning. While many factors have gone into making Burdock so popular so fast (convenient location, excellent atmosphere, and seasonal, locally focused food), much of the critical praise of the beer goes down to the brewing skill of the team as well as the innovative recipes, several of which were originally developed by Burdock's original brewer Siobhan McPherson. Now under the supervision of co-owner Matt Park, Burdock continues to produce a number of year-round and seasonal offerings for sale either at the bar or through its bottle shop.

While there are several beers that Burdock will keep year-round, the recipes will be tweaked seasonally. As of writing, the **WEST COAST PILSNER** is a hoppy take on the pilsner style, with intense lime notes in the aroma and taste, with a dry, bitter finish (3.5). **BLOOR LAGER** is light and grassy, with delicate floral notes in the aroma (3.5). **VERMONT BLOND** has a lovely peach character and notes of grapefruit, thanks to a combination of the Vermont Ale yeast and Citra hops (4). **AMERICAN PALE ALE** is actually a series of beers made with different hops. The variation mentioned here contained Citra and Galaxy hops, and was an aggressive punch of mango, pineapple, and papaya hitting hard up front followed by a very quick finish (3.5). The **SESSION SAISON** is rather sweet, with delicate white pepper notes and a dry, somewhat spicy finish (4). **BRETT FARMHOUSE SAISON** is beautifully dry, with notes of spiced tropical fruits (4.5).

BUSH PILOT BREWING

 (905) 399-5885

 @BushPilotBeers

🌐 bushpilotbrewing.com

Among contract breweries in Ontario, Bush Pilot has a significant advantage in context and in collaborating brewers. Founded by Vlado and Liliana Pavicic from Roland & Russell Importers, Bush Pilot has relationships with some of the best brewers in Scandinavia and takes advantage of them with their high-quality, high-concept brews. As of 2016, Bush Pilot is attempting to establish a site for a production facility in Hastings County and temporarily contract brews out of Burlington's Nickel Brook. With limited presence in Ontario grocery stores, much of their business is made up of exports to Alberta, Saskatchewan, and Manitoba.

———

Each beer pays tribute to the story of a plane or pilot that braved the Canadian wild. **STORMY MONDAY**, brewed in collaboration with Danish brewer Anders Kissmeyer, Niagara College, and Nickel Brook, is a barley wine aged in Calvados

163

barrels. With a plethora of fruits and spices involved in the brewing process, it's a complex fireside sipper reminiscent of mulled cider and meant to be lingered over (4). **NORSEMAN**, a collaboration involving Nøgne Ø and Nickel Brook, is an eisbock aged in Armagnac barrels. The massive 14.5% eisbock has a sticky sweetness from aroma to finish and is ideal as a sipper on a cold winter evening (4). **PENGO PALLY** is a vibrant saison including herbs one might find in the tundra. The complex aroma of grass, lemon, and peppery botanicals and the wheaty body make for a refreshing food-friendly beer (4.5).

CALABOGIE BREWING COMPANY

📍 12612 Lanark Road, Calabogie

📞 (613) 752-2739

🐦 @calabogiebrewco

🌐 calabogiebrewingco.ca

🕐 Mon–Thu 1p.m.–5p.m., Fri 11a.m.–6p.m., Sat–Sun 11a.m.–5p.m.

Started in 2015, Calabogie is a project from three friends (Mike Wagner, Ken McCafferty, and Greg Gilson) who were serious enough about their brewing venture to bring in a ringer. Head brewer Jamie Maxwell has had stints at Harpoon in Vermont and Union Station in Rhode Island. Brewing commenced during the late spring of 2015. The facility itself is carefully laid out and features a tasting station situated in the middle of the brewery's cellar, juxtaposing industrial steel and concrete with an elegant bar and tiled backsplash. Across the road is the Redneck Bistro, owned by the same partnership that runs Calabogie, which features their beer and the beer of other local breweries. The brewery's approach to funding includes a founders club, which gives members first dibs on special releases throughout the year and a number of other benefits.

While the brewery produces a number of styles of beer over the course of the year, these were available at the time of writing. **FRONT PORCH** is a light and accessible floral and soap hopped German kölsch-style ale with a honeyed grain character and lightly slick texture (2.5). **WHISTLING PADDY** is an American-style pale wheat ale with a juicy fruit and apricot nose and a body lightened by its wheat content (3). **FIVE ISLAND** is a peach gose with an orchard-ripe peach aroma and bright salinity, a sort of summer quencher (3.5). **SUMMER SOLSTICE PALE ALE** contains a big West Coast hop character and an aggressive bitterness (2.5). **BOGIE WEST COAST AMERICAN IPA** is a standard 1990s Pacific Northwest IPA with huge pine aroma (3.5). **BROWN COW MILK STOUT** is sweet mocha and Hershey's syrup with a small amount of lactose for a balancing sweetness (3.5).

CALEDON HILLS BREWING COMPANY

 caledonhillsbrewing.ca

Founded in 2016, Caledon Hills is actually something of a rarity in the Ontario landscape: a family-owned brewery with a second-generation Ontario brewer. Stefan Riedelsheimer has been brewing in varying capacities in Ontario for a quarter of a century and is passing the experience down to his three sons. Sebastian Riedelsheimer is the company's brewer, but the entire family is involved. Taking their branding from a pair of pileated woodpeckers that live nearby, Caledon Hills has opted for a direct-to-licensee approach to the market, focusing largely on pub sales. Beer is available at the brewery, but it is best to contact them ahead of time to arrange a purchase.

———

PREMIUM LAGER is a relatively lightly coloured Vienna lager with honey-sweet toasted, nutty malt notes and light noble hop interest in a very smooth body (3.5).

CAMERON'S BREWING COMPANY

📍 1165 Invicta Drive, Oakville

📞 (905) 849-8282

🐦 @CameronsBrewing

🌐 cameronsbrewing.com

🕐 Mon–Fri 9a.m.–5p.m., Sat 12p.m.–5p.m.

Founded by former chemical engineer Cameron Howe, this brewery truly is an example of a hobby flourishing into a sustainable business. In the early days, Cameron's was most well-known for selling their initial beer — an award-winning cream ale — in packs of nine. Called the "Cameron's Cube" and personally signed by Howe himself, the packaging format was enough to plant the name of the brewery into the minds of the public. In 2003 the brewery moved out of their small location in Etobicoke and relocated to a larger facility in Oakville.

In 2010 Bill Coleman, an experienced marketing pro who, notably, was involved in Molson's "I Am Canadian" ad campaign, purchased a stake in Cameron's and became president and co-owner. Under his leadership, the brewery began hosting cask nights and brought forth more adventurous beers by brewmaster Jason Britton to accompany their original core lineup. This is further evidenced by the brewery's recent rebranding effort, which has shifted away from the traditional look into something more modern to reflect their outlook.

———

The brewery's first offering, the **COSMIC CREAM ALE**, pours a lovely golden colour and contains notes of caramel, biscuity grain, and a touch of honey with a light, bitter finish (3.5). The **AMBEAR RED ALE** contains lightly toasted caramel and an earthy character that lingers after the quick finish (3.5). **CAPTAIN'S LOG LAGER** has a wonderfully warming biscuit note with a light, sweet hay character nearing the end (3.5). **NEW WOOD BRETT SAISON** is a serious departure from the brewery's core lineup, with notes of mango, pineapple, and starfruit hitting nicely, with the brett adding a dry support base (4). **ONE-EYED GROUSE ESA** has distinct toffee and dark fruit character, with an earthy backbone (3). **12 MILE IPL** contains tropical notes of melon with a citrus twist at the end (3.5). **EARLYBIRD BREAKFAST BARLEYWINE** has rich crunchy toffee, with a light coating of chocolate and coffee in a smooth, creamy mouthfeel (4). Finally, the much-loved **DEVIATOR DOPPELBOCK** is aged in oak barrels and has beautiful toffee with dark fruits in a rich, bready body (4.5).

CARTWRIGHT SPRINGS BREWERY

📍 239 Deer Run Road, Pakenham

📞 (613) 295-3377

🐦 @CSBbeer

🌐 csbeer.ca

🕐 Tours are available on Saturday and Sunday at 1p.m.

🛒 Fri–Sun 11a.m.–5p.m. Call for service on Monday, Wednesday, and Thursday.

Opened in the late spring of 2015, Cartwright Springs is a partnership between brewer Andre Rieux, and co-owners Eduardo Guerra and Hien Hoang. Named for the freshwater spring from which the brewery sources its water, Cartwright Springs has also been able to harness another resource: the Internet. One of a very few breweries in the province with a Kickstarter success story, they were able to fund the addition of a taproom to their Quonset-housed brewery in July 2015.

The brewery has opted to sell their beer in custom blue-glass, returnable, swing-top bottles that give their product a distinctive look and tie into the ecologically responsible theme that runs through their facility, from spring water to advanced effluent treatment.

———

So far, Cartwright Springs' most popular beers have been their **KÖLSCH**, which they profess is light and grassy in terms of hop character (NR); their **SMASH**, a single-malt, single-hop session ale with a pleasant citrusy aroma (NR); and their **MAPLE PORTER**, an 8.5% strong beer brewed entirely with maple sap in place of water, creating a walnutty sledgeham- mer of a beer (NR).

CASSEL BREWERY

📍 715 Principale, Casselman

📞 (613) 369-4394

🐦 @CasselBrewery

🌐 casselbrewery.ca

🕐 Wed–Fri 1p.m.–6p.m., Sat–Sun 10a.m.–5p.m.

Opened just in time for the first edition of the National Capital Craft Beer Festival in 2012, Cassel is the result of Mario Bourgeois's long-term interest in home-brewing. Beginning in 2000 with extract kits, he graduated to all-grain brewing and eventually to opening a shop of his own. While Cassel was initially something of a DIY affair, the 3-BBL brewhouse is slated to be replaced with a brand new 15-BBL system and a number of additional fermenters. The brewery has expanded to take on a second building, and the number of offerings has steadily increased over the last three years. A new website and an increased presence in LCBO locations across the province suggest that Cassel will continue to be an important player in Ottawa's beer scene for the foreseeable future.

———

WHITE FOG is the brewery's take on Belgian witbier, complete with orange peel and coriander. In addition to that light citrus and spice, there's a hint of field berry on the aroma ahead of the full wheaty texture of the body (3). **GOLDEN RAIL** is a honey brown ale that takes on a deeply nutty malt presence in the aroma, and is fruity with a touch of clove on the palate (2.5). **LIL' RED STEAMER** is full of robust toffee malt, almost nutty brittle, with fruit and light milk chocolate (3). **STATION CRAFT LAGER** would be a pilsner if not for the use of Mosaic and New Zealand hops that give it a bright, vibrant minerality with sharp herbal leaf and bright lemongrass notes (3.5). **CABOOSE IPA** is slightly berryish, leading into tangerine and bitter scrub pine over a nutty caramel body (3). **SLEEPER CAR** is a double chocolate porter with bittersweet chocolate, Swedish Berries, and hazelnut, a good choice as a seasonal fireside sipper (3.5)

CECIL'S BREWHOUSE & KITCHEN

📍 300 Wyld Street, North Bay

📞 (705) 472-7510

🐦 @cecilsbrewhouse

🌐 cecils.ca

🕐 Mon–Tue 11a.m.–12a.m., Wed–Sat 11a.m.–1a.m.,
Sun 10a.m.–12a.m.

Cecil's Brewhouse & Kitchen is one of the few places in North America that makes use of New Zealand brewer Brian Watson's "SmartBrew" automated brewing technology. Essentially, custom, pre-fermented beer (known as wort) is brewed and delivered to a location, leaving the employees with little to do except load the wort into onsite fermentation tanks, add yeast and hops, press Start, and wait until the beer is ready. The food on offer at Cecil's is traditional pub fare, though their famous double-dusted chicken wings are an obvious highlight.

———

The mainstays of Cecil's are **NIPISSING LIGHT**, with hints of lime and a dry, somewhat sweet finish (2.5); **NIPISSING**

LAGER, with a distinct grapefruit note and a swirl of malt at the end (2); **KING COUNTRY DOUBLE IPA**, which has notes of citrus that become somewhat overpowered by the sweet malt notes following (1.5); **BLACK KNIGHT CREAM STOUT**, which is sweet and creamy with massive amounts of milk chocolate (3); **WYLD BLUEBERRY WHEAT ALE**, which definitely has a lot of blueberries present, followed by a pleasing dry note in the end (2.5); **TEMAGAMI AMBER ALE**, a fairly respectable representation of the style, with nice low–roasted caramel and brown–bread flavours to it (3); and **SHAMUS IPA**, an English-style IPA with a fairly light body, distinct tones of lemon and orange zest, and a warming, caramel-like body (3).

THE CEEPS

 671 Richmond Street, London

 (519) 432-1425

 @TheCeeps

 ceeps.com

 Daily 11a.m.–2a.m.

If you were a student who found yourself in London at some point in the last twenty-seven years, then chances are you have fond memories (or fond blurs) of nights at the Ceeps. Housed in an 1890s historical building and originally known as the Canadian Pacific Railway tavern, the Ceeps is the go-to destination for University of Western Ontario students looking for a good night out. Ambience is what you might expect from a long-time campus haunt, with events and food or drink specials constantly in rotation throughout the week and a spacious patio at Barney's, the connected venue. Most of the selection reflects the tastes of the student clientele, and as such doesn't cater to folks looking for a selection of craft beer.

That said, the Ceeps holds a very interesting place in history as one of the oldest brewpubs in Ontario — their brewing system was installed back in the early 1990s. Additionally, the original brewmaster of Ceeps was Ontario brewing legend Charles MacLean (MacLean's Ales Inc.). The current and long-time brewmaster, Ben Thompson, is a very skilled brewer who knows the patrons of Ceeps well enough to aim his all-grain beers in the direction of low alcohol and light flavour.

———

While Thompson brews a number of seasonal beers throughout the summer and winter holiday months, there is only one beer available during the school year. The **CEEPS TOASTED ALE** is definitely a step above the big beer alternatives sold at the bar, with a light, coppery mouthfeel and a very abrupt finish mid-palate followed by a lingering grain aftertaste (3).

C'EST WHAT?

TORONTO'S LOCAL

📍 67 Front Street E, Toronto

📞 (416) 867-9499

🐦 @cestwhattoronto

🌐 cestwhat.com

🕐 Mon 11:30a.m.–1a.m., Tue–Sat 11:30a.m.–2a.m.,
Sun 11:30a.m.–1a.m.

Since opening in 1988, C'est What has been a force in the Toronto scene, not only as a purveyor of the province's small brewers, but also, at different points, as a live music venue and an early adopter of Ontario wines. The basement pub features one of the most consistently impressive lineups of cask-conditioned beers in the province. The exposed lime-stone walls, cozy fireplace area, pool tables, and eclectic menu of beer-friendly fare make C'est What a perennial favourite in Toronto. Owner George Milbrandt has been important in providing the public with exposure to better beer as the host of the annual Festival of Craft Breweries. Perhaps more important at the moment is the bar's commitment to trying out new offerings from small brewers all over Ontario with the presence of an On Tap and Upcoming list on their beer menus.

The beers served under the C'est What brand are no longer brewed on premise. They are manufactured on a contract basis in most cases by Bruce Halstead from County Durham Brewing in Pickering, Ontario. This is a good fit, especially given the focus on cask-conditioned ales. **JOAN'S DARK SECRET** is the notable exception; this dark mild with a touch of peat smoke is brewed by Toronto's Granite Brewery (3).

***

AL'S CASK is a straightforward English-style bitter with spicy, herbal bitterness poking through over lightly toasted grains (4). **CARAWAY RYE** achieves what it sets out to, bringing rye spiciness to the fore over hints of leather, tobacco, and saddle soap (2.5). **MOTHER PUCKERS** is a refreshing North American wheat brewed with ginger that leans toward the candied end of the ginger spectrum, with a touch of lemon-drop brightness (3). **HOMEGROWN HEMP ALE** really shows off its character in the mouthfeel with smooth vegetal bitterness on the finish (2.5). **STEVE'S DREADED CHOCOLATE ORANGE ALE** manages nicely to retain the milk chocolate character of the whack-and-unwrap variety (3.5), while the **COFFEE PORTER** has a massive espresso aroma with a lightly sour finish that nicely sates the caffeine jones (3.5).

CHEETAH INTERNATIONAL BREWERS INC.

📍 #12-75 Milliken Boulevard, Toronto
📞 (416) 292-3434

Based in the Toronto suburb of Scarborough, Cheetah International Brewers began operations in 2004 with a focus on creating beers that would complement a broad range of food, with a specific focus on spicy Indian cuisine. Their beer is contract brewed at Great Lakes Brewery and Cool Brewing, with distribution stretching throughout North America and Europe. While you would be hard pressed to find their beer in retail stores or bars, many Indian restaurants usually have one or both of their beers in the drinks menu.

———

Their two primary beers include the **CHEETAH LAGER**, which has a light mouthfeel and a low caramel sweetness (2), and **CHEETAH DARK LAGER**, which is distinctly toffee sweet, with a quick and dry finish (2.5).

CHESHIRE VALLEY BREWING

Cheshire Valley
B R E W I N G   C O .

 @CheshireValley

 cheshirevalleybrewing.com

Housed at Black Oak Brewing in Etobicoke, Cheshire Valley is the project of long-time brewer and respected beer judge Paul Dickey. Over the years, he has brewed for Black Oak and Pepperwood Bistro in Burlington, and has developed recipes and provided guidance for several start-up breweries in Ontario. While Cheshire Valley's footprint is more modest than that of some of the breweries Dickey has influenced, the beers have generated substantial respect. It's not surprising that he has kept some of his best ideas for his own brand.

A highly experimental brewer, many of the one-offs available from Cheshire Valley are single-hop pale ales designed to showcase the potential of new hop varieties. Different iterations may show up throughout the year and are unlikely to repeat. More frequently available are **MILDLY AMUSING**, a highly sessionable, dark English mild ale with nutty toasted grain, chocolate, and coffee that is even better on cask (4), and the American-style **ROBUST PORTER**, featuring coffee, chocolate, and roasted malt with a vinous fruitiness and a full, smooth body (4.5).

CLIFFORD BREWING COMPANY

🐦 @CliffordBrewing

🌐 cliffordbrewing.com

Clifford Brewing Company is the solo project of Brad Clifford, an award-winning home brewer, co-founder of the Ontario Beer Company, and brewmaster of the now defunct brewing side of Toronto's arcade/bar Get Well. Officially launched in 2015, Clifford currently contracts his beers out of Etobicoke's Cool Beer Brewing, though plans for his own physical space in Hamilton are in the works for spring.

———

Clifford has two mainstays. **PINBALL WIZARD** is an American pale ale brought over from Clifford's Get Well days, featuring notes of pineapple, melon, grapefruit, and pine, with a light biscuit and caramel backing (3.5). The award-winning **CLIFFORD PORTER** is a very creamy beer with flavours of coffee, cocoa, leather, and dark fruits in a soothing finish (4.5).

ONTARIO CRAFT BREWERIES

CLOCKTOWER BREW PUBS

 @The_Clocktower

 clocktower.ca

CLOCKTOWER GLEBE (BREW HOUSE)

- 575 Bank Street, Ottawa
- (613) 233-7849
- Mon–Fri 11:30a.m.–12a.m., Sat 10:30a.m.–12a.m., Sun 10:30a.m.–11:45p.m.

CLOCKTOWER ELGIN STREET

- 200 Elgin Street, Ottawa
- (613) 724-4561
- Mon–Fri 11a.m.–12a.m., Sat–Sun 10a.m.-12a.m.

CLOCKTOWER NEW EDINBURGH

- 422 MacKay Street, Ottawa
- (613) 742-3169
- Mon–Fri 11:30a.m.–12a.m., Sat 10:30a.m.–12a.m., Sun 10:30a.m.–11:45p.m.

CLOCKTOWER BYWARD MARKET

- 89 Clarence Street, Ottawa

📞 (613) 241-8783

🕐 Mon–Fri 11:30a.m.–12a.m., Sat 10:30a.m.–12a.m.,
Sun 10:30a.m.–11:45p.m.

CLOCKTOWER WESTBORO

📍 418 Richmond Road, Ottawa

📞 (613) 680-5983

🕐 Mon–Fri 11:30a.m.–12a.m., Sat 10:30a.m.–12a.m.,
Sun 10:30a.m.–11:45p.m.

Clocktower is a chain of brewpubs located in Ottawa. Their first location, on Bank Street, opened in 1996 and is considered the city's oldest brewpub. Award-winning brewmaster Patrick Fiori joined Clocktower in 2007 with a master's in brewing and distilling from Scotland's Heriot-Watt University, and over the course of his first two years he began tweaking the recipes for the house beers until they were up to his standard.

Today Clocktower has five locations throughout Ottawa, and Fiori continues to develop his focus on special one-off beers and collaborations, a notable example being HefeWheaton, a hefeweizen brewed with famed *Star Trek: The Next Generation* star and uber-geek Wil Wheaton for Ottawa Comiccon.

———

The **KÖLSCH** has a very light body with flavours of graham cracker and honey, with a slight hint of fruit (1.5). The **RASPBERRY WHEAT** has a light to medium body, with dominant raspberry notes blending nicely with the dry characteristics of the wheat (3). **WISHART'S ESB** has a very strong and somewhat chalky malt character with a very dry finish (2). The **RED** is a North American amber ale and tastes distinctly of spiced caramel with notes of citrus and pine (2.5). **OYSTER STOUT** is rather light in body, with heavy notes of chocolate and a slight salty brine note in the finish (2.5). Finally, the **BYTOWN BROWN** is reminiscent of roasted coffee and nutty caramel in an altogether smooth mouthfeel (3).

COLLECTIVE ARTS BREWING

📍 207 Burlington Street E, Hamilton

📞 (289) 426-2374

🐦 @CollectiveBrew

🌐 collectiveartsbrewing.com

🕐 Tours available hourly every Saturday from 12p.m. to 5p.m.

🛒 Daily 11a.m.–9p.m.

The journey from contracting to owning a brewery can be fraught with difficulty. Collective Arts, however, has been an exception, seamlessly making the transition to their current home in Hamilton, in the building that once housed properties like Peller, Amstel, and Lakeport. The brewery's somewhat extreme decommissioning on the part of the previous Labatt ownership made renovation especially difficult, but may prove helpful in the long term, as new flooring and piping was required. Now, the building, sharing space with Nickel Brook Brewing, is fully renovated, with an outdoor beer garden and retail shop.

Much of the brewery's image is tied up in association with artists in various media, which has resulted in several series of vibrant labels that give the bottles a distinct look and the brewery indie-rock cred. Partnering with Toronto's Indie 88.1

ONTARIO CRAFT BREWERIES

for their Black Box Sessions has certainly delivered Collective Arts an audience. It would have been easy for skeptics to dismiss the colourful wrapper had the contents of the bottle not measured up. Fortunately, in the hands of brewer Ryan Morrow, the product has been uniformly impressive. Add to that a series of quality one-offs and even going so far as to enter the world of cider production, Collective Arts has become ubiquitous on shelves in a comparatively short number of years; an impressive accomplishment when one considers the number of breweries founded during that time.

———

The hallmark of Collective Arts' lineup has been the aroma generated by late hopping additions. **STATE OF MIND** is a light session IPA with orange, grapefruit, and pineapple, and a touch of papaya with very little bitterness (3.5). **SAINT OF CIRCUMSTANCE** incorporates citrus zest along with hops, becoming lemony with a floral presence (3.5). **RHYME & REASON** is billed as an extra-pale ale and features a nice aroma of pineapple and grapefruit. Its bitterness is primarily herb and pine (4). **RANSACK THE UNIVERSE** features Galaxy and Mosaic hops and should almost be considered as a perfect beer for brunch, as it is essentially tropical fruit salad in a glass (4). **STRANGER THAN FICTION** is the first departure from the lineup of hoppy pale ales; a full-bodied porter with a smooth, round mouthfeel and deep flavours of espresso and cocoa (4).

COLLINGWOOD BREWERY

📍 10 Sandford Fleming Drive, Collingwood

📞 (705) 444-2337

🐦 @CollingwoodBeer

🌐 thecollingwoodbrewery.com

🕐 Tue–Wed 12p.m.–5p.m., Thu 12p.m.–7p.m., Fri 12p.m.–8p.m.,
Sat 11a.m.–7p.m.

The Collingwood Brewery has rapidly become a staple since it opened for business in 2014, not only in their hometown of Collingwood but also in the competitive Toronto market. Rather than following trends, Collingwood has focused on making approachable beer for the local market — a good decision when you consider the amount of tourism that the Blue Mountain region generates over the course of a year, and the amount of beer that skiers and snowmobilers will carry away from a taproom.

Brewer Chris Freeman, a graduate of Niagara College, has created a lineup of accessible beers that would appeal to most people trying craft beer for the first time, in addition to a range of specialty items for the die-hard beer enthusiast. In 2015 the brewery's capacity climbed above 2,500 hL for the first time, partially due to sales in the LCBO and local licensees. The brewery continues to expand their production incrementally and the 35-hL brewhouse is seeing a considerable amount of use as the number of fermenters grows. Plans to expand the building should come to fruition in 2017 as storage and cellar space is increased.

————

DOWNHILL PALE ALE is a hybrid English/American pale ale with biscuity malts and a slight orange pekoe character in the aroma from Amarillo hops that descends into peppery bitterness on the finish (4). **KINGPOST ESB** is an American take on the style, eschewing funky yeast notes for a more medium-bodied robust toffee malt and red licorice nib character (3.5). **ROCKWELL PILSNER** is a lightly bready take on the style that lives up to its Czech billing with floral, herbal hops and a somewhat restrained bitter sting (3.5). **SAISON** mingles tropical fruit with clove and iron on the aroma, with a slightly off dry body (3).

KELLERBIER, originally part of the 1854 series but subsequently repeated, is an unfiltered, deeply bready version of the keller or zwickelbier with considerable floral, pepper, and lemon-balm character from noble hops (4). **VINTAGE ALE**, rather than emulating the genre of English vintage ales made popular by Fuller's, is an expression of each year's terroir through local honey. A harvest ale made with local hops, the character is largely of wildflower and gentle sweetness, lighter than other examples in the province (3.5).

COMMON GOOD
BEER COMPANY

📍 475 Ellesmere Road, Toronto

📞 (416) 639-6579

🌐 commongoodbeer.com

🕐 Mon–Wed 11a.m.–5p.m., Thu–Sat 11a.m.–7p.m.

Opened in the fall of 2016, Common Good Beer Co. is the work of Jamie Mistry, former brewmaster at Amsterdam Brewing Co. The brewery originally went under the name Craft Brewers Coalition during development, but they were forced to change to Common Good due to copyright issues. The primary focus of the brewery is to be a haven for contract brewers, a plan that has already set them up to be a strong addition to the market. Lost Craft Brewing was said to be their largest account early on, switching over from Etobicoke's Cool Brewing the previous summer. Already within the first year, business has been booming, with further expansion on the horizon. In addition to its contract accounts, Common Good also makes their own brands, with an exciting small-batch series available at the brewery in cans and in growlers.

ONTARIO CRAFT BREWERIES

Common Good's first LCBO brand, **SOCIABLE PILSNER**, is slightly grassy with a light fruit sweetness and a mildly dry and grainy finish (3).

COOL BEER BREWING COMPANY

📍 164 Evans Avenue, Toronto

📞 (416) 255-7100

🐦 @coolbeerbrewery

🌐 coolbeer.com

🕐 Mon–Fri 10a.m.–7p.m., Sat 10a.m.–5p.m.

Founded in 1997 by Bobby Crecouzos, Cool Beer Brewing Co. saw immediate substantial growth after opening, moving from their original Brampton location to their current 28,000-square-foot Etobicoke facility in less than ten years. Since that time, they have seen much success both in their three award-winning core beers and, more notably, in their standing as one of the top contract breweries in Ontario. Brewmaster Adrian Popowycz is a former student of VLB in Berlin and has extensive experience in biotechnology, which he has put to good use at Cool and in his previous jobs at Great Lakes Brewery and Black Oak Brewing.

———

ONTARIO CRAFT BREWERIES

Cool's three core brands are **COOL LAGER**, which features a delicate dry cereal flavour in a very light body (2), **MILLENNIUM BUZZ**, a North American amber lager brewed with B.C. hemp and most notable for the dry notes found in the finish (2.5), and **STONEWALL LIGHT**, an excellent representation of the light beer style, achieving a nice balance with its delicate malt presence (3).

THE COUNTY CANTEEN

📍 279 Main Street W, Picton

📞 (613) 476-6663

🐦 @County_Canteen

🌐 thecountycanteen.com

🕐 Daily 11a.m.–12a.m.

Located right on Main Street in Picton, the County Canteen is easily one of the most impressive venues in Prince Edward County. Sporting a delectable food menu and a sizeable drinks selection that represents Ontario beer and wine well, the Canteen is run by Drew and Nat Wollenberg, who also operate the upcoming 555 Brewing Co., slated to open some time this year right down the road from the Canteen. While the majority of the Canteen's house beers will be contracted from 555, brewer Drew will also release small batches from the bar's own system every now and then.

——

An early example of the type of beers out of County Canteen is the **58 DEGREES OF WIT**, a wit that features coriander and orange peel with a hoppy presence near the end (NR).

COUNTY DURHAM BREWING COMPANY

📍 1885 Clements Road, Pickering

📞 (905) 686-3022

🕐 Please call ahead for tours.

Founded in 1996 by three partners with experience in home-brewing, County Durham became a one-man show over the course of the last two decades. Brewer Bruce Halstead produces ales that draw influence from both North America and England. While the year-round brands tend toward the American end of the spectrum, Durham's greatest strength are cask ales in traditional English styles and cellared properly. Much of the interest in the cask ales in Toronto can be explained by the consistency and quality of Durham's wares, which have been a constant presence on the city's beer engines for years. Perhaps the only difficulty in enjoying Durham's beer is getting to the pub before its devoted fans drain the firkin.

———

COUNTY DURHAM SIGNATURE ALE is an English pale ale with nutty amber malts and a fragrant floral, earthy bouquet

(3.5). **BLACK KATT STOUT** is best enjoyed on a nitro tap. It's a deeply roasty Irish dry stout with a slightly smoky whiff around autumn leaves and brandy beans (4). **HOP ADDICT** has had more low-end malt character in recent years, with spruce and citrus hopping underpinned by a touch of roast (3.5). **RED DRAGON** is included here as a single example of a range of cask-only ales. This amber ale is toasty and bready with a certain amount of toffee-apple sweetness and hops that run to bark and orange, with a slightly lingering finish after a full mouthfeel (4.5).

COUNTY ROAD BEER COMPANY

📍 1258 Closson Road, Hillier

📞 (613) 399-2903

🐦 @countyroadbeer

🌐 countyrdbeer.com

🕐 Daily 11a.m.–6p.m.

Nestled in the heart of wine country, County Road is the beer extension of the well-known Hinterland Wine Company. Known for their amazing sparkling wines, they share the same plot of land as the brewery, providing a nice balance for folks travelling to the county. Right next to Hinterland's retail space, the taproom provides visitors with a spacious resting point both indoors and at the beer garden outside, where wine and beer are served along with, from Fridays to Mondays, dishes from Chopped Canada winner chef Neil Dowson. Of note, the brewery is also one of the few currently offering mail-order service for its beers.

Using the land's own well water, brewer Chris Dinadis has started with crafting his own take on accessible beer styles, but plans are underway for a shift into sour beers and a barrel-aging program.

All of the brewery's beers are named after the — you guessed it — roads found within the county. **COUNTY ROAD 3 FARMHOUSE SAISON** was the first of the brewery's offerings to hit LCBO shelves and has an overall dry body with notes of cracked black pepper and a slight berry sweetness (3.5). **COUNTY ROAD 18 WITBIER** includes locally sourced sumac, which adds a welcome lemon tartness to the flavours of coriander and orange peel (3.5). **COUNTY ROAD 12 PALE ALE** has grapefruit, melon, and mango notes followed by a distinct grain bitterness (3.5).

COVERED BRIDGE BREWING COMPANY

📍 6–119 Iber Road, Ottawa

📞 (613) 915-2337

🐦 @CBBeer

🌐 coveredbridgebrewing.com

🕐 Thu 3p.m.–7p.m., Fri 12p.m.–7p.m., Sat 11a.m.–6p.m.

Since late 2013 biochemist and brewer John VanDyk has been selling his beers at the brewery's storefront in the small Ottawa suburb of Stittsville. Starting out as an avid home brewer, VanDyk's love for the limitless variation of flavours using limited ingredients led him to take the leap into commercial brewing. Since then, the award-winning Covered Bridge (named after an area on his home street) has made regular appearances at local beer festivals and has become an active member of the local community by taking part in various charity functions.

———

The **DIRTY BLONDE ALE** features a bready, toasted malt flavour with distinct, puckering lemon character (2). **THE MSB**

is a 9.1% ABV behemoth of a beer, with chocolate and nut profiles standing up with significant notes of pine (2.5). **ETERNALLY HOPTIMISTIC** is a dry-hopped American pale ale with large notes of citrus in a soothing, malty finish (2.5). **AMBER ROSE** is an American amber with a heavy-caramel malt backbone and an agressive, bitter finish (3). **LUMBERSEXUAL** is for those that love spruce and pine in their beers, featuring plenty of both (2). Finally, the very Canadian-themed **DOUBLE-DOUBLE** is a mocha stout that tastes just like that — coffee and chocolate with a slightly creamy mouthfeel (3).

COWBELL BREWING COMPANY

 (844) 523-4724

 @Cowbellbrew

 cowbellbrewing.com

The locals of the small Huron County village of Blyth are very familiar with this new brewery's owners, the Sparling family. Before it was sold in 2013, family-run Sparling's Propane was one of the largest retailers of propane and propane accessories in the country. With deep love for their home community, the family's discussion of economic development led to the natural conclusion: creating a destination brewery in Blyth. And by bringing three generations of business and development experience to the table, along with enlisting the brewing expertise of Stephen Rich, formally of Sweetgrass and the now-closed Beer Academy, the Sparlings stand a good chance of doing just that.

The brewery's initial offerings are currently available in LCBO stores and selected bars, with further flagships and a more adventurous seasonal Renegade series being rolled out over time. While currently contracting out of Brunswick

Bierworks, the large brewery will be opening soon on an 111-acre patch of land, along with a restaurant that can comfortably seat over two hundred people, a retail space, and a large outdoor event space that will be the future site of festivals and concerts. Interestingly, the brewery itself is set to be a "closed-loop" brewery, using water from the land's well and running wastewater through an onsite treatment facility. The brewery is also intent on offsetting their carbon footprint by taking part in a strong tree-planting initiative. As a way to further give back to the community, five cents of each can and pint of beer sold goes toward a selected charity.

———

Many of Cowbell's beers are steeped in Blyth's history, often referencing amusing anecdotes and colourful characters in the village's past. **ABSENT LANDLORD** is ostensibly a kölsch-style beer, but the bready sweet caramel flavours and floral hop character suggest it may be a bit too big for that style (3). **DOC PERDUE'S BOBCAT** bills itself as a West Coast red ale and contains a large hit of citrus and melon, with a creamy mouthfeel that leads into a bitter pine finish and sweet candy aftertaste (3).

CRAFT HEADS BREWING COMPANY

📍 89 University Avenue W, Windsor

📞 (226) 246-3925

🐦 @CraftHeadsBrew

🌐 craftheads.ca

🕐 Mon–Thu 10a.m.–1a.m., Fri 10a.m.–2a.m.,
Sat 11a.m.–2a.m., Sun 12p.m.–10p.m.

Located in Windsor's downtown core, Craft Heads is a small-batch brewery that focuses on experimentation and offers a variety of beer styles, as befits the owners' half decade of home-brewing experience. They will frequently have as many as thirty different variants on tap in their brewery-adjacent barroom. That's an astounding feat considering the diminutive size of the brewhouse — it's situated in a corner basement, and the half barrel system is currently used for sixteen brews a week in order to keep up with production. You can watch the brewer at work from the street prior to sampling his wares.

The feel of the somewhat sparsely decorated taproom leans heavily toward coffeehouse, in part because of the inclusion of a full barista set-up, including pour-over coffee. Wood-oven pizza is catered from the nearby Terra Cotta Gourmet Pizzeria. The brewery frequently hosts live comedy nights and live music, continuing a Windsor legacy from when it was the Aardvark Blues Cafe.

While time will allow for focus and refinement of the beer, the enthusiasm here is nearly palpable. The brewery is frequently in operation past midnight to keep up with demand.

———

While it's difficult to properly represent the sheer scope of the lineup, some staples have emerged as drinkers have made their preferences known. **MOTOWN HONEY BROWN** leads from a berryish nose into a thin, floral body with some residual sweetness from the honey used in brewing (2.5). **AARDVARK BLONDE** is honeyed malt accented by raspberry cane and lightly vegetal herbal hops (3). **NEXT ON STAGE AMBER** is toffee and light roast coffee malt with mellow orchard fruit on the aroma (3). **FEATHER HAT GUY P.A.** is a straight-ahead pale ale named after a local figure and his gauche chapeau. It has a pronounced clementine citrus character and a bright, vibrant carbonation (3.5).

BRETT "THE HIBISCUS" HART is a kettle-soured beer pushing gently into tart, floral territory with a drying body and refreshing finish (3). **TURBULENT CHOCOLATE PEANUT BUTTER PORTER** does exactly what you would expect. It is a Reese's cup in a glass from aroma through to swallow (4). **IMPERIAL COFFEE STOUT** incorporates the house-made cold brew coffee to good effect, balancing on the aroma with spicy hops that persist through a slightly thin body (3.5). **GALAXY IPA** emulates the turbidity and aggressive tropical hopping of the Vermont-style IPAs, practically a passionfruit smoothie (3).

CRAZY BEARD

☏ (647) 970-7994
🐦 @crazybeardale
🌐 crazybeardale.com

Launched in February 2015 by partners Cam McDonald, Bobby Besant, and Daniel Bartek, Crazy Beard is really an offshoot of a larger family of products operating under the title of Iconic Brewing Company, which diligent readers may recall from their appearance on *Dragons' Den*. The company specializes primarily in the ready-to-drink segment of the market and has had significant success marketing Dusty Boots Hard Root Beer, which has become popular among drinkers in their early twenties.

———

WILD APPLE ALE is basically a green apple Jolly Rancher in a glass, but without the cloying sweetness that you might expect from such a cider/beer hybrid product (3).

CREEMORE SPRINGS BREWERY

📍 139 Mill Street, Creemore

📞 (844) 887-3022

🐦 @creemoresprings

🌐 creemoresprings.com

🕐 Tours daily 12p.m.–4p.m. on the hour.

🛒 Mon–Sat 10a.m.–6p.m., Sun 11a.m.–5p.m.

Founded in 1987, Creemore Springs became one of the most important small breweries in Ontario by the turn of the century. Depending largely on the production of a single flagship lager, the brewery not only survived the economic crash of the 1990s, but continued to grow in size incrementally right up until their purchase in 2005 by Molson Coors.

Partially because of the new ownership, Creemore has become a ubiquitous brand in Ontario, with Molson Coors having wisely added resources and leaving an already successful product alone. The quality of Creemore's beer has remained stable or arguably improved since its purchase over a decade ago, which has seen an expansion of brewing capacity to just under 150,000 hL annually. The manner in which the expansion was completed in partnership with the municipality may prove a useful example for Ontario's small breweries as they continue to thrive.

Creemore's focus has always been on beers made according to traditional German brewing practices, and for that reason the Creemore lineup is dominated by lagers, many of which were introduced after the Molson Coors acquisition. The brewery's water is acquired from an artesian well two miles away.

———

PREMIUM LAGER has a small prickle of dry, herbal bitterness on the tongue, surrounded by fairly complex bread crust malt character and a full body (3.5). **LOT 9 PILSNER** replaced their Traditional Pilsner in early 2015. It is slightly lighter in alcohol and brighter in its profile, with wildflowers and peppery herbs settling in above crackery malt (3.5). **URBOCK** is a dunkel bock with a creamy mouthfeel and a dark brown bread character highlighted by molasses sweetness and baker's chocolate (4). **KELLERBIER** has a hefty dose of dry leaves, spicy pepper, and bready caramel finishing in a bitter snap (4.5).

ALTBIER, a collaboration with Dusseldorf's Zum Schlüssel, features an aroma of rain on dry earth and coniferous shrubs amid a lightly sweet mildly roasty body (4). New for 2016 is **KÖLSCH**, a restrained take on the other German hybrid style from farther up the Rhine. It is light, floral, and understatedly fruity with a crisp finish (4). **OKTOBERFEST** is a simple take on the Munich festival beer, with a Grape-Nut and cereal malt character and mild bitterness (3.5). **HOPS & BOLTS** is a sort of India pale lager sold under the Mad & Noisy label. It's a tangle of fruit and floral hop character above a light caramel body (3.5).

CROOKED MILE BREWING COMPANY

📍 453 Ottawa Street, Almonte

📞 (613) 256-7468

🐦 @crookedmilebeer

🌐 crookedmile.ca

🕐 Thu–Fri 12p.m.–6p.m., Sat 11a.m.–6p.m., Sun 12p.m.–4p.m.

Taking their name from a popular English nursery rhyme ("There was a crooked man and he walked a crooked mile / He found a crooked sixpence against a crooked stile"), Crooked Mile Brewing was founded by husband and wife Nick and Vicki Pruiksma with their business partner Dylan Bouleau, who opened the doors of their small but welcoming brewery, tasting room, and retail space in the fall of 2016. Head brewer Nick's primary focus is on British styles, and the trio aims for the space to be a social hub for the people in and around Almonte.

———

HIGHLAND HILLWALKER Scottish export has a heavy, roasted, dark coppery malt backbone with a sweet, lightly peppered finish (3). **CROW'S CASTLE BEST BITTER** strikes a nice balance between hops and caramel malt notes (NR). **STANDING STONE** is an English IPA that proves to be a comfort, with earthy hop character and deep malts going in for a slightly bitter finish (3.5). The regular seasonal offering, **DRUID'S DUSK**, is an Irish red with high biscuit and toffee notes, sweet berry flavours, and a slightly crisp finish (3.5).

DANFORTH BREWERY

🐦 @DanforthBrewery

🌐 danforthbrewery.com

The past few years have been good to the east end of Toronto. The area has seen several breweries opening their doors, attracting downtown beer geeks enough to take that perilous trip across the Don River for some pints and bottles that make the trip so very worthwhile. With more breweries on the way, the future looks bright for the area, and Danforth Brewery aims to be an active part of it. Founded by East Danforth resident Ed Carter, Danforth Brewery pays tribute to the iconic street, for what it was, what it is, and what it will be for the people of Toronto. The beer is currently under contract at Common Good, though plans to open a location are forthcoming.

———

Danforth Brewery's debut beer, **VIADUCT IPA**, is named after the Prince Edward Viaduct that crosses the Don River Valley. The beer is very heavy with grapefruit rind and pine, going in for an orange toffee finish (2.5).

DAWSON TRAIL CRAFT BREWERY

📍 905 Copper Crescent, Thunder Bay

📞 (807) 623-2337

🌐 dawsontrailcraftbrewery.com

🕐 Tue–Thu 3p.m.–8p.m., Fri 3p.m.–9p.m., Sat 12p.m.–7p.m., Sun 12p.m.–3p.m.

The duo behind Thunder Bay's second brewery, which opened in 2016, is filmmaker/animator George Renner and software engineer John Kivinen, long-time friends who took their passion for home-brewing to the next level. Originally the pair set out to become the smallest brewery in Ontario, and certainly their 3.5-BBL brewing system almost puts them in the running. The space itself is a small and fully renovated former cabinet store, with the aesthetic influenced by Refined Fool Brewing in Sarnia.

———

Despite their small size, Dawson Trail have a number of year-round beers on offer. **BORDER RUN CREAM ALE** has a very light mouthfeel and delicate biscuit notes, ending with a mildly bitter and dry finish (3). **RUNNING STONE**

IRISH RED ALE features caramel, stone fruit, and mild cocoa flavours, following up with an acerbic finish that turns sweet in the aftertaste (3). **OATER LIMITS OATMEAL STOUT** was intentionally made to be the lighter option to Sleeping Giant Brewing's Skull Rock Stout, and it certainly dances the line between light and medium bodied. Dark roast coffee and cocoa come together with a smooth cream note that gets cut off by a biting grain finish (2.5). **UP & AHTANUM** is an American IPA that feels more like a double IPA, with its 7.17% alcohol content. Melon and apricot notes hit hard and fast before making way for flavours of pineapple and grapefruit, with notes of stone fruit and geraniums scattered toward the finish (3).

DESCENDANTS BEER & BEVERAGE COMPANY

📍 319 Victoria Street N, Kitchener

📞 (226) 241-3700

🐦 @Descendantsbeer

🌐 descendantsbeer.com

🕐 Mon–Tue 12p.m.–8p.m., Wed–Sat 11a.m.–11p.m., Sun 12p.m.–5p.m.

One of a handful of breweries that began as contractors while attempting to locate a site for a bricks-and-mortar facility, Descendants has experienced more difficulty than most on the road to that goal. Fortunately, the brewery's Victoria Street location fits the 15-hL brewhouse admirably, with room to spare for additional fermenters in the future. Partners Robin Molloy and Lee Brooks continue to brew several of the Descendants brands at another facility on a contract basis for the LCBO, but the Bierhalle and bottle shop have given them the ability to create a number of other brands on site for local consumption. Molloy is a graduate of Germany's VLB, and that training is becoming more apparent as the lineup of available beer styles increases. With a limited menu of beer-friendly snacks and comfortable communal seating at long tables, the Bierhalle is a brightly coloured, festive space with ample parking in the rear.

———

At the moment Descendants has two brands available in the LCBO. **HARBINGER** is an American pale ale showing bready, caramel grain roughly around the edges of the body, with an aroma of light grapefruit and orange (3). **REYNARD THE FOX** is a golden ale subtly using rye as part of the grist, which peppers and bolsters a light, spicy hop character, resulting in a crisp finish (3.5). Their third year-round brand, **EL BUSCADOR**, is a Mexican-style cerveza in the vein of Tecate. It is light bodied with a slightly corny nose and a souring body that disappears in a short finish (2).

BOOTZAFRAU is a fairly standard Oktoberfest lager with a light, bready malt character and balanced hop bitterness (3.5). **RED HUGH II** is a heavily roasty red ale that leans toward the heavy end of the style on sweetness and fruit character (2.5). **SUGARMAN** is an American-style stout, heavy on dried fruit, grassy hops, and roast while remaining somewhat thin in the middle of the body (2.5).

DOG AND PONY BREWLAB

📍 315 Somerset Street W, Ottawa

🐦 @DogAndPonyBeer

📘 facebook.com/DogandPonyBeer

🕐 Mon–Tue 5:30p.m.–10p.m., Wed–Fri 11:30 a.m.–2p.m. and 5:30p.m.–2a.m., Sat 10a.m.–2p.m. and 5:30p.m.–2a.m., Sun 10a.m.–2p.m.

Brewing out of the kitchen (and front hall) of Union Local 613, a popular gastropub in Ottawa's Somerset Village, Dog and Pony Brewlab is one of the smallest breweries in the province of Ontario. The diminutive set-up manufactures approximately 150 litres of beer per batch while the bar is closed on Sunday afternoons. Partners Tristan Bragaglia-Murdock, Steve Fitzpatrick, and John Richardson, all previously employed in one capacity or another by Beyond the Pale, share duties creating recipes with interesting ingredients. With an eye toward upgrading to a second iteration of the company in the not-too-distant future, the trio are using Union Local 613's patrons as a captive audience upon which to hone their skills.

SAISON DUPONY is a saison brewed in the Wallonian style, with a nose of orchard fruit and gentle clove that leads into a round, full body before drying out on the back half of the palate (3.5). **SHENANIGANS** is styled as an imperial saison with haskap berries and hibiscus flowers; bright and juicy, it pours bright red, with a light sophisticated body that hides the alcohol (3.5).

DOMINION CITY BREWING COMPANY

DOMINION CITY
BREWING CO.

📍 5510 Canotek Road, Unit 15, Ottawa

📞 (613) 688-6207

🐦 @dominioncitybc

🌐 dominioncity.ca

🕐 Daily 11a.m.–6p.m.

Housed in a business park in the Orleans neighbourhood of Ottawa, in just over a year Dominion City has become one of the best representatives of Ottawa's brewing scene. While the owners Josh McJannett, Adam Monk, and Andrew Kent are home brewers from way back, the most impressive part of Dominion City's business is the commitment to community and representation of the area. Dominion is partnered with local farms and hop growers, coffee roasters, and food banks. The taproom at the brewery is panelled with boards from a recently dismantled local barn, and the bar itself is made of logs recovered from the bottom of the Ottawa River. The theme is completed by an annual celebration of Canadiana on July 1, Dominion Day.

As of the end of 2016, Dominion City has nearly doubled its production and is in the process of renovating two neighbouring units in preparation for additional expansion. While more fermenters and a larger brewhouse are certainly a priority, one of the main reasons for this growth is the potential for sour and barrel programs that will be among the first of their kind in eastern Ontario.

——

EARL GREY MARMALADE SAISON contains the zest of twenty-five cases of oranges in every batch, along with Earl Grey tea from Ottawa's Bridgehead Coffee. The pronounced orange sweetness melds with the bergamot in order to create a wildflower character that elongates the finish on the Belgian yeast (4). **EARNSCLIFFE ESB** has an aroma of toffee, raisin, and prune, with hazelnut and cocoa notes in its round toasted malt body (4). **TOWN & COUNTRY BLONDE ALE** is freshly grainy because of the use of Red Fife wheat and has a grassy hop presence in its lightly honeyed body (3). **TWO FLAGS IPA** is about the balance between sweet and bitter coming across as a blood orange lollipop of an IPA, made with Cascade hops from two Ontario growers (4).

 DEVIL'S BRIGADE is a take on a traditional Belgian golden ale, deceptively strong with a vigorous carbonation and an assertive citrus-and-pepper bitterness (3.5). **GALLOPING HESSIAN PUMPKIN BROWN ALE** is less about pumpkin spice than it is about toasted barley, coming across nearly as spiced Bundt cake (3.5). **SUNSPLIT IPA** is a completely opaque, turbid Vermont-style IPA, heavily dry hopped with Citra and Amarillo hops with a full body made up of oats (4). **HEARSAY ENTIRE PORTER** is a historical tribute to the origins of the style and an example of the future barrel program; a blend of three beers (mild, ESB, and porter) aged in a merlot barrel that contributes some red fruit and a light acetic tartness before the brown malt character comes through in earnest (4.5).

DOUBLE TROUBLE BREWING COMPANY

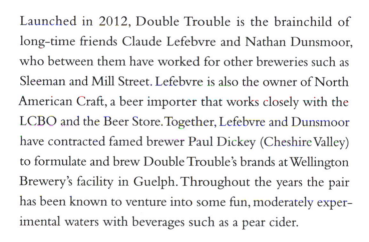

 (855) 467-5683

 @HopsandRobbers

 doubletroublebrewing.com

Launched in 2012, Double Trouble is the brainchild of long-time friends Claude Lefebvre and Nathan Dunsmoor, who between them have worked for other breweries such as Sleeman and Mill Street. Lefebvre is also the owner of North American Craft, a beer importer that works closely with the LCBO and the Beer Store. Together, Lefebvre and Dunsmoor have contracted famed brewer Paul Dickey (Cheshire Valley) to formulate and brew Double Trouble's brands at Wellington Brewery's facility in Guelph. Throughout the years the pair has been known to venture into some fun, moderately experimental waters with beverages such as a pear cider.

———

Their first offering was **HOPS & ROBBERS** sessionable IPA, which clearly has a strong English influence, with bready malts and brown sugar and a nice jab of pine (3). Further beers include **PRISON BREAK PILSNER**, a dry-hopped pilsner with herbal honey and lemon zest paving the way to a bitter finish (3); **REVENGE OF THE GINGER: KICKIN' GINGER RED IPA**, offers the fiery note of pure ginger in its aroma and taste, along with apricot and caramel (2.5); the winter seasonal, **FRENCH PRESS VANILLA STOUT**, contains — surprise, surprise — lots of espresso and vanilla in the aroma (3); and **FIRE IN THE RYE ROASTED RYE PALE ALE**, which features a very spiced and toasted-bread character along with grapefruit and pine, finishing with a distinct bitterness at the back of the throat (4).

Manantler Craft Brewing Co.'s speakeasy-inspired taproom features a number of pieces from local artists.

The folks at 5 Paddles Brewing Co. label bottles in the back room.

County Road Beer Co. in Prince Edward County has an impressive facility for a new brewery, with a barrel-aging program already in the works.

Rainhard Brewing Co.'s Hearts Collide Imperial Stout requires a patient pour.

Bellwoods Brewery's second location on Hafis Road in North York sports an impressive facility, including several wood foeders and a large barrel warehouse.

Located just north of Parry Sound, Norse Brewery is completely family-run and features some unique takes on simple styles.

When in Guelph, it's always worth stopping in at Royal City Brewing Co. for a flight.

Housed in a converted auto shop in Toronto's Roncesvalles Village, Bandit Brewery features a wide range of beers from accessible to adventurous.

Empty cans wait to be filled at Cool Beer Brewing Co. in Etobicoke.

Nepean's Broadhead Brewing Co. offers crafted beer made in a facility that is a DIY enthusiast's dream, with much of the equipment made by the owners themselves.

DRAUGHT DODGER BREWERY

📞 (416) 518-7363

🌐 draughtdodgerbrewery.com

Based out of Toronto, Draught Dodger is one of a handful of contract brewers to open in the city in 2015. Owned and operated by Matthew and Paola Di Iorio, the company has seen a certain amount of success on tap within the GTA, while also participating in the 2015 Great Ontario-Hopped Craft Beer Competition. Draught Dodger takes as its inspiration vignettes from the history of the city of Toronto. Brewzer, for instance, is directly inspired by legendary prize fighter George Chuvalo, who never fell, even against Muhammad Ali.

———

Currently brewing out of Stratford Brewery, Draught Dodger has a number of offerings that rotate through taps. Arguably their flagship, **YELLOW TRUCK** lands somewhere between a blonde ale and a steam beer, with a light, healthy grain character, pear ester in the nose, and a mild goldenrod hop presence (3.5). **LADY IN WHITE APA** is an exercise in cantaloupe, grapefruit, and tangerine bitterness where the hops outstrip the malt in balance (3.5). **BREWZER RED IPA** is brewed with Vic Secret hops and attempts to find a balance between guava and caramel in the body, remaining sweet through the finish (2.5).

DUGGAN'S BREWERY

📍 1346 Queen Street W, Toronto

📞 (416) 588-1086

🐦 @duggansbrewery

🌐 duggansbreweryparkdale.com

🕐 Tue–Thu 5p.m.–12a.m, Fri–Sat 12p.m.–1a.m., Sun 12p.m.–12p.m.

Michael Duggan has had a long brewing career in Ontario, serving time at Mill Street before launching a brewpub at 75 Victoria Street in the last days of 2009 after winning Bar Volo's inaugural Cask Days IPA Challenge. The closure of that initial location, after just under two years, left a small number of brands on the market, contracted out of Etobicoke's Cool Beer Brewing, and Duggan himself put work into developing recipes for new breweries.

In late 2014, Duggan opened a new facility in Parkdale at the corner of Queen and Brock after a brief period of pop-up openings. The brewpub is somewhat smaller than the old one, and works with a far more tightly focused menu featuring locally inspired dishes and an excellent rotation of live music. The good news is that the lineup of products has not changed

ONTARIO CRAFT BREWERIES

substantially. There is a lot of depth for the brewpub to draw on, and a game local audience on which to try out experimental batches.

———

NO. 9 is an IPA with nine different varieties of malt, reminiscent of toasted brown bread and raisin, with punchy Cascade pine and citrus (3.5). **NO. 5 SORACHI** lager is a pale lager that takes advantage of the Sorachi Ace hop to impart a bright dill and lemon character to the aroma (3.5). **NO. 13 HEFEWEIZEN** leans toward kristalweizen territory, with only light wheat haze and significant banana esters in the aroma (3). **NO. 46 PARKDALE BOMBER** is a throwback malt liquor, named as a tip of the hat to the neighbourhood's bad old days (3). **NO. 7 IRISH STOUT** is full bodied with a heavy roast and bittersweet cocoa in a creamy body, yet dry with a finish that doesn't become acrid (4). **100 MILE LAGER** is a beer from Michael Duggan's days with the Ontario Beer Company, and has a taste that is somewhat floral in the front, finishing on a soothing, honey-nut cereal note (3). **NO. 3 GERMAN PILSNER** is a nice representation of the style, with biscuity notes blending with flavours of hay and berries, drying out nicely in the finish (3). **NO. 25 APA** is on the copper side of appearance, with straight up herb and toffee notes in the aroma and flavours of pine and lemon peel, with a sweet note of dark fruits and bready malts taking it in for a comfortable, warming finish (3).

ELORA BREWING COMPANY

📍 107 Geddes Street, Elora
📞 (519) 805-2829
🐦 @EloraBrewingCo
🌐 elorabrewingcompany.ca
🕐 Mon–Thu 11a.m.–11p.m., Fri–Sat 12a.m.–1a.m.,
   Sun 11a.m.–9p.m.
🛒 Mon–Sat 11a.m.–11p.m., Sun 11a.m.–9p.m

A combination brewery, gastropub, and bottle shop set in the scenic city north of Guelph, Elora Brewing Company was founded by a diverse group of local friends, Matt Lawson, Jonathan Laurencic, Don Smith, Jim Murphy, and former head brewer of Barley Days Brewery Alex Nichols. Having set up shop in the summer of 2015 on historic Geddes Street in the downtown area, Elora Brewing Company's large space includes beer-inspired comfort food and in-house butchery by chef Ben Sachse, with a focus on local and seasonal dining.

———

THREE FIELDS, a triple-grain lager that utilizes barley, wheat, and rye, has many of the characteristics of a light beer in terms of mouthfeel, resulting in very thin biscuit flavours along with a distinctive earthy bitterness toward the end (2.5). **LADY FRIEND IPA** has a surprisingly light mouthfeel with large caramel and pine notes rounded out with a roasted cereal character (3). **ELORA BOREALIS** is a Citra pale ale with a whole whack of grapefruit and lime (3.5). **WANDERING MONK** has sweet mango and guava highlighting this Belgian IPA (3).

EVERGREEN CRAFT ALES

  36 Evergreen Drive, Nepean

🐦 @evergreenales

🌐 evergreencraftales.com

Probably Ottawa's (and possibly the province's) smallest brewery, Evergreen is named after the residential street that the garage it occupies is located on. Owners Chris and Jen Samuel have taken nanobrewing to its logical conclusion, operating out of their home garage with a brewing system that creates a tiny number of litres per batch. While the volume may be low, it does allow for a certain amount of variety, and Evergreen tries to have four different beers on at all times. The brewery does not keep conventional retail hours but tries to be open six to eight hours a week so that customers who have ordered online can find a convenient time to pick up their orders. The brewery has managed to seek funding through a subscription model, and those who join the Evergreen Club receive perks for their involvement, including first access to the brewery's seasonal beers.

MAIDEN VOYAGE is a pale ale that features pineapple, passionfruit, and grapefruit rind ahead of a heavily bitter finish (3). **RASPBERRY GOLDEN SOUR**, a collaboration with Small Pony Barrel Works, features a vibrant raspberry aroma that recedes into a slightly bitter, tannic palate and proceeds to a tart finish (3). **AROUND THE CORNER IPA** is a light, smooth take on the American IPA, with notes of pine and grapefruit (2.5). **DARK IS THE NEW LIGHT** is a fairly light-bodied stout with a small roast character and bitterness that might well be considered high for the style (2).

THE EXCHANGE BREWERY

📍 7 Queen Street, Niagara-on-the-Lake

📞 (905) 468-9888

🐦 @TheExB

🌐 exchangebrewery.com

🕐 Tue–Thu 2p.m.–9p.m., Fri 12p.m.–9p.m., Sat–Sun 11a.m.–9p.m.
   Tours Sat–Sun 3p.m.–4p.m.

Located on the downtown strip of Niagara-on-the-Lake, the Exchange is the first brewpub to inhabit this traditionally wine-friendly town. Taking its name from the telephone exchange that the building previously housed, the unifying concept here is the telephonic branding of each beer on the menu, a touch that extends right down to rotary trays for tasting flights. The modish black-and-white interior is pervasive rather than minimalist and fits in with Niagara-on-the-Lake's tourist appeal. The glassed-in brewery allows for observation of the brewing team at work from a comfortable seat at the tasting bar. The second floor features a large, comfortable seating area and a small but charming patio overlooking a residential street. A small selection of snacks is always available at the bar, while external catering is less frequently available.

ONTARIO CRAFT BREWERIES

Overseen by brewer Sam Maxbauer (formerly of Michigan's Jolly Pumpkin), the Exchange features a 10-BBL brewhouse and a cellar with two Hungarian oak foeders. A promising barrel program has started, with fifty French oak wine barrels from down the road in Jordan. While this suggests that long-term planning will focus on complex, sour offerings, for the time being the range of beers on offer is admirably diverse and rotates relatively frequently.

––––

WITBIER leans heavily on citrus presence, bringing lemon to the fore and settling into a light herbal interest in the mid-palate, bolstered by an oaky roundness. It develops orange notes and citric acidity as it warms (3). **DUNKELWEISS** is a restrained take on the style, eschewing the typical banana esters in favour of grain depth (3.5). **AMBER ALE** is full of specialty Chilean crystal malts, which provide a long, round caramel core that suggests but falls short of butterscotch (3.5). **PEPPERCORN RYE SAISON** has a dry, spicy body with a minty herbal complexity and bubble gum ester on the nose; a pleasant early standout (4.5).

GRAPEFRUIT PALE ALE fulfills its promise, with a massive aroma of juice and pith in a nicely balanced body (4). **IPA** is squarely in the Pacific Northwest style, with a sweet body and big pine aromas (3.5). **WHITE IPA** leads with peach, lychee, and mango on the aroma and refuses to be dominated by the Belgian character of its yeast (4). **PUMPKIN ALE** is in the Belgian style as well, playing clove and cinnamon over a body that remains full despite the dry finish (3.5).

FALCON BREWING COMPANY

📍 30 Barr Road, Ajax

📞 (416) 453-6120

🐦 @falconbrewingco

🌐 falconbeer.beer

Started in October 2012 by Bill Perrie and Jim Williamson, both long-time beer industry veterans, Falcon began selling their beer in August 2014 under the name of Stouffville Brewing Company. The initial product was contract brewed at Wellington Brewery and designed by Paul Dickey. Plans have been proceeding for some time, however, for them to open their own location, and the search for physical premises has led them to relocate southeast to Ajax. Falcon is notable for being one of very few contract-brewed beers to have launched their product directly into the Beer Store rather than the LCBO — a tactic that seems to be paying off due to their can's Euro-styled branding. Distribution has since expanded to the LCBO and a number of grocery locations.

Falcon plans to launch their brewhouse and tasting room in January 2017, with a patio to follow in the spring. The

5-BBL brewery will likely produce between eight and ten beers at a time, allowing for a certain amount of experimentation beyond the two core brands.

———

RED FALCON ALE is an Irish red with a sweetish grain and toffee aroma leading to a small amount of grassy hopping, which ends in a lightly roasty, dry finish (3). **LAGGAR FALCON** has a grassy, floral aroma that runs to a slightly metallic gyre in the mid-palate before finishing with a short, bitter dive (3).

5 PADDLES BREWING COMPANY

📍 1390 Hopkins Street, Unit 3, Whitby

📞 (905) 665-3042

🐦 @5PaddlesBrewing

🌐 5paddlesbrewing.com

🕐 Mon–Fri 11a.m.–7p.m., Sat 9a.m.–5p.m., Sun 12p.m.–5p.m.

Started in 2013 by a group of friends who come from home-brewing backgrounds, 5 Paddles has retained much of the experimentation that comes with taking that route into the industry. Originally starting out in a 950-square- foot brewing space, the brewery is now in the realm of 4,500 square feet, with enough of a capacity to regularly brew fan favourites and LCBO offerings while also maintaining the experimental beers the brewery has become known for. To date, 5 Paddles has produced well over 130 different recipes, with each of the owners focusing on a specialty area, be it English, Belgian, or dark beer. They have gained a reputation for outlandish beers with interesting ingredients.

The small and rustic taproom offers very reasonably priced flights of three or five beers in specially made canoe-shaped service trays. The discussion in the taproom frequently turns to the technical aspects of brewing, suggesting that the customers are as invested in brewing as the staff. 5 Paddles is one of the only breweries in the province to have hosted their own home-brewing competition.

The ratings and tasting notes included here are by no means extensive, as the selection changes frequently, and it is worth calling ahead to confirm stock.

——

HOME SWEET HOME is a honey vanilla wheat beer, as close as they have to a flagship. The flavour is citrus and wildflower on the palate, with an extremely light vanilla character on the finish that lingers beyond bitterness (3). **PADDLER'S PRIDE** has a light molasses Tootsie Roll character backing plum and quince on the palate and fading to a medium-length finish (3.5). **IN YOUR FACE IPA** is just that, with melon and passion fruit hitting first backed up by notes of lemon (3.5). **THE DOMINATRIX** is dank Cascade with orange and grass, hitting hard but tenderly with warming cocoa notes (4.5).

FLYING MONKEYS CRAFT BREWERY

📍 107 Dunlop Street E, Barrie

📞 (705) 721-8989

🐦 @FlyingMonkeys

🌐 flyingmonkeys.ca

🕐 Mon–Thu 11a.m.–7p.m., Fri–Sat 11a.m.–9p.m., Sun 11a.m.–6p.m.

Founded in 2005 and originally named after Barrie's first mayor, a complete rebranding from the traditional look and feel of the Robert Simpson Brewing Company to the outlandish and bizarre Flying Monkeys was implemented in 2009 to more properly represent the brewery's ethos of "normal is weird." While in the early years the brewery gained popularity through their core brands and unmistakable branding, they perhaps became best known for coming out with collaborations and esoterically flavoured one-offs concocted by founder and brewer Peter Chiodo. Recently, however, Flying Monkeys has found a firmer balance between their approachable and experimental offerings, providing a wide range of beers for all manner of drinker. Additionally, the brewery has fully converted their taproom into a brewpub that, with old Victorian-style couches, neon signs, and a bathroom library, fully embraces their uncompromising weirdness.

———

A more recent addition to the core brands is **MYTHOLOGY CANADIAN GOLDEN PILSNER**, an award-winning Czech pilsner that is remarkably true to the style, with a grassy character supported by a malt backbone and a lightly dry finish (4). **12 MINUTES TO DESTINY** is one of the best fruit beers out there, with deep notes of raspberry puree and earthy hibiscus tea in a crisp mouthfeel (4). **DEEP TRACKS** is an American brown ale with distinct northwest pine notes wrapped in malt character, which then leads to a roasted peanut character that hits toward the end (3.5). **SMASHBOMB ATOMIC IPA** contains distinct pine aroma and notes of mango, pineapple, grapefruit, and orange (3.5). **HOPTICAL ILLUSION ALMOST PALE ALE** has a smooth mouthfeel and flavours of grapefruit and pine wrapped up with creamy caramel (3).

Getting to the bigger and bolder, **SHOULDERS OF GIANTS** is a 10% imperial IPA with pine and cedar flavours kicking in fairly early, featuring a nice caramel base that leads toward the finish (4). **INVICTUS SOLERA-AGED RUSSIAN IMPERIAL STOUT** is a beast in nearly every aspect. Solera-aged for over a year in used bourbon or sherry barrels and sitting at 17.5%, this warm, boozy number with a sweet and creamy mouthfeel has stone fruits and vanilla as its prominent flavours (4.5). The ever-popular **CHOCOLATE MANIFESTO TRIPLE CHOCOLATE MILK STOUT** is by all accounts a Dufflet chocolate cake in a glass (4.5).

FOLLY BREWPUB

 928 College Street, Toronto
 (416) 533-7272
 @FollyBrewing
 follybrewing.com
 Mon–Fri 4p.m.–Late, Sat 1p.m.–Late

Folly Brewpub is the evolution of the former Habits Gastropub into a more beer-focused space, where there was originally only a small pilot system. Brewers Christina Coady and Chris Conway, former home brewers who were encouraged by Habits owners Michelle Genttner and Luis Martins to brew on their system, have interestingly taken a special focus on farmhouse ales, showcasing the wonderful changes farmhouse yeasts can produce in beer by consistently creating beers within the open-book definition of the style. The beers are paired incredibly well with the offerings of chef Anthony Santi and, should you wish for something stronger, Folly has the largest selection of whisky in the city.

The brewpub has seen significant growth in the past year, with the introduction of an often popular bottle shop, a large number of seasonal and limited edition offerings, and several barrel programs that operate on a year-round and one-off basis. Folly has also been known to host many unforgettable events throughout the year, from world-class collaboration beer dinners and concert screenings to International Women's Collaboration Brew Day and parties.

———

While Folly has a number of rotating beers available, they have four flagships that are year-round. **PRAXIS** "new world" saison hits hard with tropical notes before a mid-palate jab of bitterness takes it toward a note of fresh plum in the finish (4). **INKHORN FARMHOUSE BRUIN** is raspberry puree blending with a light coating of dark chocolate (4). **IMPOSTER SYNDROME FARMHOUSE IPA** is a hazy orange beer with incredible tropical fruit and citrus notes, and the brett steps in to make for a super clean finish (4). **FLEMISH CAP OLD WORLD SAISON** is a wonderful example of the effect a good yeast (in this case from Guelph's Escarpment Labs) can have on simple ingredients. The beer is crisp, with significant lemon notes with a balanced grain character that takes it in for an easy finish (5). **INVENTED TRADITION** is aged in Southbrook wine barrels and features deep wine and oak notes ending on a creamy oat finish (4.5). **LOQUACIOUS** is a beer brewed for Folly's first anniversary and spent a year in pinot noir barrels with Brettanomyces Lambicus yeast to give it a funky character. Notes of dark cherries, raisin, and plum hit nicely, going into a Flemish brown character as it warms (4). The seasonal barrel beer, **SHADOW PUPPETS**, is fairly light, with notes of pineapple, lemon, and cracked black pepper (4).

Of further note is Folly's **RHIZOME**, a rye-infused American farmhouse beer with a constantly changing hop lineup, which showcases the effects of the chosen hops nicely. As an example, the release made with Equinox and Mosaic hops was an overall bright and juicy beer, with a beautiful combination of melon, orange, and mango flavours (4).

FORKED RIVER BREWING COMPANY

📍 45 Pacific Court, Unit 4, London

📞 (519) 913-2337

🐦 @forkedriverbrew

🌐 forkedriverbrewing.com

🕐 Tours at 12p.m., 2p.m., and 4p.m. every Saturday.

🛒 Tue–Fri 11:30a.m.–6:30p.m., Sat 11a.m.–6p.m.

Although still a relatively young brewery, having poured its first beers in the summer of 2013, Forked River has quickly established a reputation in western Ontario and on tap in the GTA. Part of the reason is the backgrounds of owners Andrew Peters, David Reed, and Steven Nazarian, which include engineering and biotech, and the shared enthusiasm for home-brewing that prompted them to start the company. Each of them has won regional awards for their brews.

They also have a sophisticated understanding of their market. London has both a fanatical set of craft beer enthusiasts and a large number of beer drinkers who have not yet made the transition to more interesting offerings. Forked River's lineup includes two accessible standards, but also far more complex seasonal offerings and a highly impressive barrel-aging program with surprisingly positive results, given the short time frame during which it has existed. Forked River has recently undergone a 150-percent expansion (including a new retail store) after a social media campaign helped change provincial regulations.

———

CAPITAL BLONDE ALE has changed to become a core of lightly bready malt character accented by dank, resinous hops with notes of pepper and light berry (4). **RIPTIDE RYE PALE ALE** features a light-rye-toast spiciness in addition to toffee, and a light earthy bitterness and a retronasal hint of citrus (3.5). **MOJO CITRA RHUBARB WHEAT** approximates the summery flavours of lemonade and strawberry pie, slightly malic in sourness but quenching (3.5). **FULL CITY PORTER** features vibrant light roast coffee above a complex body of woody, nutty roast and chocolate, marshmallow, and subtle berry (4).

DYSANIA PALE ALE is a biscuit and caramel bodied American pale ale that supplants the typical C hop character with pineapple, passionfruit, and citrus (3.5). **QUEEN'S RANGER DOUBLE IPA** is similarly full of passionfruit, pineapple, and papaya maintaining a good balance while venturing over the 100 IBU threshold (4). **FLANDERS RED**, featuring the Vimy Memorial on the label, is a Remembrance Day tribute ale. Brewed in the Flanders red style, the barrel-aged beer develops an aroma of grape must and plum jam and proceeds to red fruit through the palate, rounding off the acetic character on the finish (4). **WEENDIGO IMPERIAL STOUT** takes on barrel and bourbon character courtesy of Wild Turkey, but features dark fruit in addition to the inevitable deep roast character (4).

4 DEGREES BREWING

📍 Smiths Falls

🌐 4degreesbrewing.com

Founded by four owners, Nick Ritchie, Andrew Howard, Joe Adams, and Chris Haines, 4 Degrees is intended to be a community hub in Smiths Falls. While the town suffered a loss of manufacturing industry in 2010 with the sale of the Hershey plant, 4 Degrees is part of a rebirth of local industry in the region, as much about creating local employment as creating good beer. The brewery's location in a now-vacated Staples is one of the cornerstones of the revitalization of the County Fair Mall and will help to anchor future development, with plans to employ as many as thirty people by the end of the decade.

While both of 4 Degrees' year-round offerings are currently brewed under contract at Taps in Niagara Falls, this is an example of a nearly immediate expansion to physical premises. With veteran Saskatchewan brewer Jay Cooke on staff to provide recipes and direction, the future is bright.

———

The beers are divided geographically by Highway 7 to appeal to rural and urban consumers, respectively. **TRUE NORTH OF 7** is an approachable take on a helles lager with a sweet grain character and a lightly peppery noble hop character on both the aroma and finish (2.5). **TRUE SOUTH OF 7** falls into the American amber range and has a grainy body dominated by caramel sweetness and a mild touch of roast (3).

FOUR FATHERS BREWING COMPANY

 Rockwood

 (226) 338-6028

 @4fathersbrewing

 fourfathersbrewing.ca

Operating out of the Wellington County town of Rockwood, Four Fathers Brewing is made up of Mike Hruden, John Kissick, Martin Castellan, and James Tyo, four devoted, beer-loving hockey dads with very diverse backgrounds, from fine arts professor at the University of Guelph to president of EB Games Canada. The four first met in the bleachers of their sons' hockey games, and that led to travelling to parts of the globe discovering new beers and getting into the world of home-brewing. After making note of the tremendous growth of craft beer in the province, the four decided to act and open their own brewery. Briefly enlisting the skill of Block Three brewer Kevin Freer and using the expertise all four have from their backgrounds, Four Fathers Brewing Co. was launched and has since gained a strong following. Indeed, the success has been so tremendous in their first year that the brewery is already looking to expand beyond their renovated barn brewing space to include a retail shop and tasting room.

Along with their beer, it must be noted that what sticks out for this brewery is their often fun and well-designed labels, which feature some outright hilarious descriptions.

———

THE STARTER is a session IPA with Galaxy hops, with lime and passionfruit hitting hard in the front and back of the palate (2.5). **HONEY BADGER** is a French saison made with locally harvested honey and freshly picked spearmint from a neighbour's garden. The honey makes a gentle presence mid-way, while the spearmint adds a light, refreshing, and not overpowering character that lingers in the aftertaste (4). The amusingly named **WEE GOBSHITE** red rye pale ale has light caramel notes starting to say something before getting a clattering by the more aggressive notes of melon, apricot, and citrus, with a spicy peppery note in the malt bitterness at the end (3.5). **SHEVCHENKO 9** is a solid dunkel, with dry, bready chocolate toffee notes (4).

FRANK BREWING CO.

📍 12000 Tecumseh Road E, Tecumseh

📞 (519) 956-9822

🐦 frankbeer.ca

🕐 Tue–Wed 11a.m.–11p.m., Thu 11a.m.–12a.m.,
Fri–Sat 11a.m.–1a.m., Sun 12p.m.–10p.m.

Located on a rejuvenating stretch of downtown Tecumseh at the west end of Lake St. Clair, Frank Brewing is best categorized as a brewpub with aspirations to greater things. Opened in late 2015 by Shane and Steve Meloche along with brewer Brad Wright, the brewery is bolstered by the ownership's experience in the local hospitality industry, since they also run Johnny Shotz just down the street.

In its first year, Frank is already nearing the limits of their capacity (although plans for expansion already exist), partially because of the popularity of their bar room. A peanuts-on-the-floor kind of place, they have a taplist that offers a large number of regularly available beers, while some experiments and one-offs occupy a small number of openings. The menu is straightforward, playing to the strengths of a limited kitchen by focusing on the pizza oven and sandwiches. In

ONTARIO CRAFT BREWERIES

the space of just under a year, Frank has become one of the most popular destinations for a night out in Tecumseh, and rightly so. Growlers are available for takeout through a bottle shop that adjoins the bar.

———

BOMBSHELL is a lightly sweet blonde ale; fairly clean and with minimal hop character, it serves as a gateway beer (3). **NO NONSENSE** is a lagered ale that has a nose of peach, with a light citrus and ginger hop interest on the back end (4). **SIMPLE MAN**, a solid oatmeal stout, has the lightly chewy texture and chocolate expected from the style (3.5). **OLD COMRADE** is a fairly fruity American amber with toffee and raisin in the body (3.5). **SMOOTH HOPERATOR** uses Citra and Vic Secret to effect a pineapple-accented American pale ale with a body that is dark for the style (3).

BIG HARVEST, a dunkelweizen with banana and clove on the aroma and a light toffeeish body and wheat tang, has proven to be an early experimental success (4). **DAY TRIPPER** is a comparatively lightly bitter IPA with a big pine scent and a small lemon zing (3.5). **HONEY HABANERO** is something of a rarity: a pepper beer in which the heat never becomes overwhelming. The habanero plays as peachy and fleshy across the roof of the mouth over a sweet, lightly grainy core (4).

FULL BEARD BREWING COMPANY

📍 219 Wilson Avenue, Timmins

📞 (705) 268-0444

🐦 @fullbeardbrew

🌐 fullbeardbrewing.com

🕐 Mon–Sat 12p.m.–9p.m., Sun 12p.m.–6p.m.

Timmins beer drinkers, bar owners, and festival organizers know Full Beard's owner Jonathan St. Pierre well, as his other business, Tap It Draft Services & Supplies, has been selling and installing draft systems in and around the area since 2005. With the help of his cousin, Ryan Farrell, the two set out to bring some true local beers to the folks of Timmins. While going through the initial stages of setting up their own facility, the pair started contracting out of Broadhead Brewing in Nepean, developing a presence in Sudbury and North Bay along with their hometown. Construction was arduous, but the brewery finally opened its doors to the public early this year.

———

ONTARIO CRAFT BREWERIES

5 O'CLOCK SHADOW PALE ALE makes for a solid flagship, with distinct grapefruit citrus character and a quick pine and spice kick in the finish (3).

GANANOQUE BREWING COMPANY

📍 9 King Street E, Gananoque

📞 (613) 463-9131

🐦 @GanBeerCo

🌐 ganbeer.com

🕐 Tours are available by appointment during the winter and daily at
1p.m., 3p.m., 5p.m., and 7p.m. in summer.

🛒 Summer: daily 12p.m.–9p.m.
Winter: Mon–Wed 1p.m.–6p.m., Thu–Sat 1p.m.–8p.m.,
Sun 1p.m.–6p.m.

Housed in a historic bell tower next to the Gananoque River, Gananoque Brewing strives to express the local terroir through the use of organic, locally sourced grains. The company, founded in 2011, went through an early period as a contract brewery before beginning to produce their own beers onsite in 2013. While their products are popular locally, a significant part of their success has to do with their early adoption of locally grown ingredients, helping to lead the way toward agricultural development in Eastern Ontario. Gananoque intends to introduce six to eight different beers in 2017 based on local terroir, acting as a showcase for what might be possible in the region's future.

———

Their flagship, **NAUGHTY OTTER LAGER**, leans toward the sweet end of the style's spectrum, with sweet grain body being the main attraction (2). **THURSTY PIKE PILSNER** is very light in body, with a grassy bitterness and fresh grain aroma (3). **COOPER'S HAWK AMERICAN PALE ALE** is lightly crackery with some small caramel and a grass and grapefruit aroma (3), while **BELL RINGER IPA** hits the C-hop trifecta in its malt-forward toffeeish body (3). **WHITE CALF IPA** is a white IPA that falls somewhere between witbier and Belgian IPA, featuring mild pineapple and mango hop character with a nose that suggests banana and a hint of clove (3.5). The pleasant surprise here is the full-bodied **BLACK BEAR BOCK**, an eisbock full of coffee, raisin, and lightly roasted grain (3.5).

GRAND RIVER BREWING

📍 295 Ainslie Street, Cambridge

📞 (519) 620-3233

🐦 @GrandRiverBeer

🌐 grandriverbrewing.com

🕐 Tours are available for groups of ten or more when booked in advance. Please call ahead.

🛒 Mon–Wed 10a.m.–6p.m., Thu–Fri 10a.m.–9p.m., Sat 10a.m.–6p.m., Sun 11a.m.–4p.m.

Housed in the shell of the Galt Knife Factory in Cambridge, Grand River Brewing was founded just before the current explosion of Ontario breweries in 2007. Grand River's initial focus was on brewing low-alcohol beers for those worried about overindulgence. While many of those initial beers were successful, such a project is limiting in scope and the focus has since broadened. The brewery's beers are frequently cited as an example of the qualities hard-water minerality can impart in brewing, and are noteworthy for their enhanced grain characters. In 2014, thanks in part to a sizeable government grant to promote expansion, the brewery grew in both manufacturing and distribution. In 2015 the

ONTARIO CRAFT BREWERIES

brewery underwent a large rebranding, moving to a more contemporary logo and selling their beers in cans. They also have recently started hosting events in their large, beautiful hospitality room.

———

The core products at the moment include **PLOWMAN'S ALE**, a rather floral amber ale with toffee notes and a sharp grain bitterness in the end (3.5), **TAILGATE**, a Munich helles that proves to be a light and accessible lager with light grassy notes accompanied by toasted grain and delicate pepper accents (3). **MILL RACE DARK** has a slightly roasty, husky grain, with notes of cocoa, raisin, dark berries, and roasted nuts (3.5). **RED TAIL** has sweet bready notes with caramel and an altogether muted hop character (3). **GALT KNIFE** is a lager that manages to strike a balance between sweet malts and floral, light citrus hop bitterness (3.5).

In season, you may find **CURMUDGEON IPA**, which leans on the English side of things, with a large malt presence and subtle yet distinct grapefruit and pine notes (3.5). **FARM GATE MALTED CIDER** has a significant toffee backbone supporting green apple flavours (NR). **RUSSIAN GUN IMPERIAL STOUT**, named for a local Crimean-era cannon, is deep dark roast with dried fruit, licorice, coffee, and chocolate (4).

GRANITE BREWERY & TIED HOUSE

📍 245 Eglinton Avenue E, Toronto

📞 (416) 322-0723

🐦 @GraniteBrewTO

🌐 granitebrewery.ca

🕐 Mon–Thu 11:30a.m.–12a.m., Fri–Sat 11:30a.m.–1a.m., Sun 11a.m.–12a.m.

🛒 Mon–Sat 11:30a.m.–11p.m., Sun 11a.m.–11p.m.

Started in 1991, the Granite is actually the second location of this brewpub originally from Halifax. Ron Keefe, with help from brother Kevin and legendary consulting brewer Alan Pugsley, has created one of Toronto's most enduring destinations for good beer. The Granite's open fermented ales are made with their house Ringwood yeast, which is especially good for producing cask-conditioned beers (a house specialty). It's an infrequently seen technique in Ontario and worth a look into the glass-walled brewing area. The brewpub has a cozy front room styled as a library; a large back room with fireplace, frequently used to host gatherings; and a patio that has become a popular venue for weddings in the summer months.

ONTARIO CRAFT BREWERIES

Change has occurred at the Granite leading up to their twenty-fifth anniversary, with Mary Beth Keefe, the landlord's daughter, taking over the majority of the brewing duties and adding newer styles of beer to a fairly traditional English lineup. Peculiar has become available at the LCBO because of an expansion of the brewery's cellar into the parking garage below the brewpub. The purchase of a small canning line has allowed for a limited number of canned products in the onsite beer store, in addition to 64-ounce returnable growlers, a packaging format in which the brewery led the Ontario market for years.

———

RINGWOOD is an English blonde ale with a pear and proofing-dough yeast character with earthy hops that come across as grass and apple-cured tobacco (3.5). **BEST BITTER** on tap is an English bitter, with twiggy tea-like hops, biscuits, and a touch of marmalade (3.5), while the cask version, **BEST BITTER SPECIAL**, has a fuller mouthfeel and a brighter dry-hopped character and should ideally be paired with the lamb curry (4.5). **HOPPING MAD** replaces some of the English hop character with Cascade, adding an orange peel and peppery bitterness to a full, grainy toffee body (3.5). **PECULIAR** is somewhere between a Northern English ESB and an old ale: deep fruity malts with red berries, mincemeat, and quince are balanced by chocolatey roast and a whiff of creosote (4). New for 2016 is the **GREAT NORTH MILD**, a complex dark mild that combines biscuit, treacle, chocolate, and coffee with a gentle bitterness; it's easy drinking and a great example of the style (4.5).

More recent additions to the lineup (those created by second-generation brewer Mary Beth Keefe) are **DARKSIDE BLACK IPA**, which leans heavily into the dark malt, playing almost as though it were a bitter porter (3), and **GALACTIC PALE ALE**, which uses Galaxy hops, developing pineapple, grapefruit, guava, and a mild touch of spearmint leaf (3.5).

GREAT LAKES BREWERY

📍 30 Queen Elizabeth Boulevard, Toronto

📞 (416) 255-4510

🐦 @GreatLakesBeer

🌐 greatlakesbeer.com

🕐 Mon–Thu 11a.m.–6p.m., Fri–Sat 10a.m.–8p.m., Sun 12p.m.–5p.m.

Originally opened in Brampton in 1987, Great Lakes found new life in 1991 under the ownership of the Bulut family in Etobicoke, with brewer Bruce Cornish. Back then, the sole offering was an all-malt lager, but in the intervening quarter century Great Lakes diversified their portfolio more than any other brewery in Ontario. In some ways the introduction of their Devil's Pale Ale, in 2006, signalled the beginning of a long-term change in the Ontario beer market.

Currently, Great Lakes is best known for their IPAs and innovative one-offs released under the Tank Ten label. Much of that success stems from the work of brewer Mike Lackey and the advent in 2009 of their Project X experimental beer series. Many of the Tank Ten recipes have been upsized from the hundred-litre pilot brewery and have earned the brewery serious credibility in the form of consecutive Canadian Brewery of the Year awards and a sweep of the Canadian Brewing Awards IPA category in 2014. The constant demand for these beers has seen the addition of numerous fermenters and new bottling and canning lines for the brewery, in addition to new brite tanks. The year 2017 will mark the brewery's thirtieth anniversary, and with that will come a series of celebrations. Potentially more important to beer drinkers in Ontario than that milestone is the addition of a 7-BBL copper brewhouse that will finally replace the original and well-worn pilot system.

While a large portion of the brewery's business is still based on their Blonde and Red Leaf lagers, they are not indicative of the likely future direction and are, therefore, not included here.

————

CANUCK PALE ALE is a fine example of a light-bodied West Coast American pale ale, with significant pine and grapefruit character (4). **POMPOUS ASS ENGLISH PALE ALE** has a nutty, light malt base featuring Special W malt for that raisin and licorice touch, supporting dank, earthy tea-like hops (4).

CORNISH BREAKFAST, named for the original brewer, is brewed with Station cold brew coffee designed to purpose and borrows a malt base from Pompous Ass, resulting in a bright, light roast and berry character in this coffee pale ale (4). **HARRY PORTER** is an extremely smooth-bodied American-style porter with a perfumey vanilla nose, a note that continues through the light roast and chocolate of the body (4).

SUNNYSIDE SESSION IPA, named for the lakeside pavilion on Toronto's west side, is a bright, summery session IPA that makes use of lemon, citrus, and grapefruit in a way reminiscent of Five Alive (4.5). **KARMA CITRA IPA**, redolent with exotic tropical fruits and exquisitely balanced, uses Citra hops to good effect (4.5). **THRUST! AN IPA** heavily features Nelson Sauvin hops, with a profile of white grape, mango, and stone fruit over a dank, resinous vegetation (4.5). The imperial IPA **ROBOHOP** is full of grapefruit, pine, and resin while retaining balance throughout the body despite its size (5).

HALF HOURS ON EARTH

📍 151 Main Street S, Seaforth

🐦 @hhoebrewery

🌐 halfhoursonearth.com

🕐 Sat 11a.m.–5p.m.

Located in Seaforth, Half Hours on Earth is a brewery that subverts a number of the expectations that people have of small-town Ontario breweries. Convention suggests that a brewery must make an approachable gateway beer for local consumption in order to succeed. Half Hours on Earth blew straight past gateway to cutting edge upon opening using methods that defy conventional wisdom.

The diminutive brewery produces a single hectolitre of beer at a time, although the scope of the brewhouse does allow for an enormous amount of variety. Instead of resting on previous successes, like his collaboration with Great Lakes, brewer Kyle Teichert's focus thus far is entirely on tart farm-house ales. The operating ethos of the husband-and-wife team is simply to make things they want to drink. Instead of a retail store, Half Hours on Earth operates through an online retail system, which allows consumers a single day a week to

ONTARIO CRAFT BREWERIES

pick up their orders. Instead of worrying about retail distribution, they ship orders across the province by Canada Post. This odd agglomeration of factors has resulted in one of the most exciting breweries ever to operate in the province.

———

Because of the frequent rotation of offerings, some beers noted here may be available more frequently than others. One series that seems to persist is the Yalla Yalla single-hop series, which extracts vibrant aromas rather than bitterness. **YALLA YALLA GALAXY** has a slightly muted fruit salad nose of mango, apricot, and peach (3.5), while **YALLA YALLA CITRA** is a firework of candied lemon that impacts gloriously before dissipating to nothing (5). **MINGUS DEW** is a table sour dry-hopped with Equinox, giving it a juicy melon rind and green-pepper punch over a lightly tart body (4). **GREEN MIND** explodes in mango and papaya with a light bubble gum ester before a finish that trails off quickly (4).

QU'EST-CE QUE C'EST is a Bière de Garde on Montmorency cherries that calls to mind the earthy, funky sweet-and-sour character of a cellar-aged cherry jam (3.5). **FUNK LAND III** is a blend of hoppy farmhouse (80 percent) and Flanders red (20 percent) that keeps the round acetic sourness of the latter style, while peach, plum, and red fruits play above musty vinous grape (4). **CONTROL BORED**, brewed with chamomile, shifts in drinking between bright, floral key lime yogurt custard and uncooked apple pie waiting for the oven (4.5). **TOTALLY** begins with a massive raspberry aroma, descending in the mid-palate to a jammy, vanilla biscuit middle, before vaporizing into a shower of hibiscus petals on the finish. A sour and sophisticated version of a Peek Freans Fruit Creme (5).

HALIBURTON HIGHLANDS BREWING

📍 1067 Garden Gate Drive, Haliburton

📞 (705) 754-2739

🐦 @HHBrewing

🌐 haliburtonhighlandsbrewing.ca

🕐 Thu–Sun 12p.m.–6p.m.

Husband-and-wife team Michael and Jewelle Schiedel-Webb opened up Haliburton Highlands in 2014 at the beautiful Abbey Gardens, which uses the brewery's spent grains as compost to enrich the soil. Brewmaster Michael Schiedel-Webb trained at the Siebel Institute's World Brewing Academy in Chicago, and developed his skills by working for Shades of Pale Brewing in Utah and Rahr & Sons Brewing in Texas. Paired with Jewelle's twenty-plus years of management and operations experience, their early years in operation have been a rousing success, showing that the demand for local beer is strong in Haliburton. So strong, in fact, that the brewery has already expanded from their small brewery and Mongolian yurt of a retail space into a significantly larger 4,500-square-foot building that has allowed them to increase production by more than fifteen times.

BLUELINE BLONDE is a fairly sweet beer with a distinct biscuity character and a quick finish (3.5). **INDIA PALE ALE** has lovely citrus notes that blend well with an evident malty backbone, making for an overall earthy flavour profile (3.5). The **IRISH RED ALE** is a very dark ruby, featuring bready toffee notes and a distinct dry note that welcomes a low-roasted finish (3). A strong local presence is evident in their **HONEY BROWN ALE**, which uses locally sourced honey to seamlessly blend sweetness with the roasted notes of the malt (4). **WEE HEAVY SCOTCH ALE** has a very sweet profile that hides its 7.5% alcohol content well; caramel and dried dark fruits throughout with a slight grape finish (3). The **BELGIAN RYE PORTER** brings forth notes of dried fruit blended with chocolate and pepper (3.5). Finally, the **COFFEE PORTER**, made with coffee from the Abbey Gardens' own County Coffee, celebrates the key ingredient wonderfully, with notes of cocoa and crunchy toffee (4).

HALO BREWERY

📍 247 Wallace Avenue, Toronto
📞 (416) 606-7778
🐦 @HaloBrewery
🌐 halobrewery.com
🕐 Tue–Fri 3p.m.–9p.m., Sat 11a.m.–9p.m.

Located directly across the street from Ubisoft Toronto, Halo Brewing are Eric Portelance and Callum Hay, two self-taught home brewers with backgrounds in digital product design and software engineering who took their devotion to home-brewing to the next step. Upon opening in the spring of 2016, the brewery received overwhelming support from local beer lovers and sold out of their initial offerings within the first week. Interestingly, one of the first things the pair insisted on was to make their brewery "open source," including the recipes for all of their beers on their website so they are free for anyone who wants them to use and alter, as a way to give back to the home-brewing community that taught the pair so much in their early years.

Halo makes a number of one-off and seasonal beers, and their overall quality improves batch to batch. As of writing, some of their oft-brewed selection includes the following. **HALF-TRUTH** is a session IPA with grapefruit and pine notes and a slightly sweet finish (3.5). **WHITE KNIGHT** is a weisse IPA with notes of passionfruit throughout (3). **CREATIVE DIFFERENCES** has distinct flavours of mandarin orange and lemon (3). A fan favourite, the **ION CANNON** is a gose made with strawberry and kiwi, with its primary ingredients well represented in this tart beer with notes of coriander (3.5). **MAGIC MISSILE** has distinct tropical melon notes with a light citrus undertone (3.5). Finally, the **DAY STAR** tart saison with apricots and lemon balances both fruits out nicely, with a dry finish (4).

THE HAMILTON BREWERY

 (905) 962-8294

 @hamiltonbrewery

 thehamiltonbrewery.com

The goal of the Hamilton Brewery is eventually to establish a bricks-and-mortar facility in Hamilton itself, but for the time being their beer is brewed at Railway City in St. Thomas. In a town with a history of workingman's beers like President's Choice, Laker, and Lakeport, it makes sense that the company's first beer should be called Blue Collar Pale Ale. As Hamilton continues its transition from steel town to hipster bastion, it's unsurprising that the utility lagers of the past should be replaced by a craft pale ale.

——

BLUE COLLAR PALE ALE is a standard American take on the style, with Centennial pine coming through heavily over a lightly buttery, cracker body (2.5).

HENDERSON BREWING COMPANY

📍 128A Sterling Road, Toronto
📞 (416) 863-8822
🐦 @HendersonBeerCo
🌐 hendersonbrewing.com
🕐 Daily 11a.m.–10p.m.

Founded in 2015, Henderson is the result of a partnership between Steve Himel and Mark Benzaquen, both of whom are beer industry veterans. The central conceit of the brand, demonstrated by bespoke decoration in the spacious taproom, is that the Henderson brewery has persisted throughout Toronto's history. Robert Henderson was the city's first brewer, and headlines, advertisements, and artifacts from some alternate reality demonstrate the way the brewery has changed over time.

The 9,000-square-foot facility is really most impressive for its taproom space, which features light snacks and large garage-style glass doors that roll up during the summer to create a fun industrial patio feel. In addition to the core brands Henderson produces year-round, the brewery has the

Ides series, which releases an experimental beer on the fifteenth of every month. The first Wednesday of every month, the brewery goes to the dogs with Doggie Night; take your pooch for a pint and some portraiture.

———

HENDERSON'S BEST falls somewhere between an amber ale and an ESB (and is advertised as either), with its pear ester and raspberry cane nose and a biscuit body that falls away into a gently coppery finish (3.5). **FOOD TRUCK** is lighter and designed to accompany food. Its light and corny aroma leads into a body that is somewhat reminiscent of buttered pineapple (1.5). Worth trying is the house root beer, which eschews the traditional sassafras in favour of cinnamon hearts.

HIGH PARK BREWERY

 @HighParkBrewery

 highparkbrewery.com

High Park Brewery was launched in 2015 by four old hockey buddies wanting to form a locally focused brewery named after the Toronto area they all lived in. Currently contracting out of Grand River with their own fermentation tanks, High Park Brewery are planning on opening their own space in the High Park area in the next year.

———

Their initial offerings include the **ACROSS THE POND** extra special ale, with heavy bready, toffee notes with hints of raisins and plums (3); the **OFF THE LEASH IPA**, which features grapefruit and lime citrus notes with a distinct malt backbone (3); and the **AGAINST THE GRAIN** golden lager, with a creamy mouthfeel and sweet oat note in a quick finish (2.5).

HIGH ROAD BREWING COMPANY

 @HighRdBrews

🌐 highroadbrewing.com

Currently contract brewed out of Niagara College in Niagara-on-the-Lake, High Road Brewing is the project of Rob Doyle and Curtis Bentley, two veterans of the Ontario brewing industry. Both attended Heriot-Watt University's brewing program in Edinburgh, and both are currently involved in teaching and production at Niagara College. One of the perks of brewing within that milieu is that both brewers have oversight on their production at all times, a condition few contract players in Ontario enjoy. While High Road has begun the search for funding and a physical location, their time has been put to good use refining and testing recipes against the day that they have expanded production and a facility of their own.

———

BRONAN is a Vermont-style IPA that runs the gamut of fruit flavours, from peach to dried apricot to gooseberry and grapefruit, deriving some of its stone fruit interest from the Conan yeast strain for a full-bodied, balanced hoppy beer (5).

CLOUD PIERCER is a New Zealand–style pale ale with a pronounced dragon fruit note backed up by the mildest hints of Douglas fir and spearmint; a truly interesting combination (4).

HIGHLANDER BREW COMPANY

📍 309B Highway 124, South River

📞 (705) 792-0808

🐦 @Highlanderbrew

🌐 highlanderbrewco.com

Started in 2009 by brewer Brian Wilson, Highlander has been successful in the face of difficulty for its hometown of South River. Because of a highway bypass that was completed in 2011, traffic through the town has markedly decreased. As a consequence, the brewery changed hands in 2012. Wilson has remained with the organization, but current owner Dwayne Wanner has provided additional expertise and ambition. One of the more interesting beers of note was a collaboration beer with Epitaph Records — the label could be peeled off and used as a playable record.

In an effort to help cultivate the town that's been so good to them, the brewery has recently expanded to a new facility, which they lease from South River itself. Their large event space, intended to be a place to promote the talent the community produces, is free to rent out for locals of the Almaguin Highlands region. As part of an understanding with Canadore

College, the brewery also plans to open a six-month course that would provide apprentices with a technical certificate and an understanding of the finer points of the brewing industry. Highlander is a textbook example of the potential of breweries to be part of the successful life of rural communities.

––––

LION GRASS, with the addition of lemongrass and dandelion leaves, is grassy and lightly weedy, emulating a freshly mown midsummer lawn (3). **SCOTTISH ALE** produces a milky note poured from the bottle ahead of deep caramel, granola, and a light floral bitterness (3). **BLACKSMITH SMOKED PORTER** is restrained to a light charcoal smokiness in a full body with bittersweet chocolate and a round graininess rather than full-on burning roast (3.5). **TWISTED SPRUCE**, formally known as Centurion, is made with spruce tips prominently featured as its primary ingredient, with honey and biscuit malts forming a base (3). **WEE HEAVY** is a Scotch ale that is deep and boozy, with plenty of helpings of creamy caramel and raisin (3.5). **RYE ROAD IPA** is on the side of an American pale ale, with rye malt and rye flakes included (NR). **PIPERS LOCH** is a brightly coloured beer with hints of citrus that is influenced by the West Coast (NR). **HIGHLANDER STOUT** is a deep and dark stout, with chocolate, coffee, and a slight note of orange in the finish (NR).

HOCKLEY VALLEY BREWING COMPANY

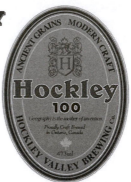

📍 25 Centennial Road, Orangeville

📞 (519) 941-8887

🐦 @Hockleybeer

🌐 hockleybeer.ca

🕐 Mon–Fri 9a.m.–5p.m.

Since 2002, Hockley has been offering a limited selection of beers in English styles that reflect the training of brewer Andrew Kohnen. What is truly impressive is the inroads they have made in the market, not only in Ontario but also in Manitoba and Alberta, with types of beer that are not currently in vogue: a sign that persistence and commitment to a model pays off. Since 2008, Hockley has been brewing slightly more mainstream beers under their Midland Beer Works label, which focuses on thematic elements related to Georgian Bay. In 2014, they announced a series of one-offs inspired by legends from the region.

———

HOCKLEY DARK is the brewery's most consistent and longest-serving offering. They describe it as being halfway between a northern English brown ale and a southern mild, which only means that it inhabits a realm between fruity, nutty toasted malt and darker chocolate and licorice flavours (3.5). **HOCKLEY AMBER** depends a great deal more on the mid-range, with deep toasted cereal and caramel playing off against spicy, grassy hops (3). **HOCKLEY CLASSIC** is the most recent addition to the core lineup and lighter than the others; a lager with a saltine cracker body and a light floral, apple aroma (2). **GEORGIAN BAY BEER** is a pale lager that fills the role of easygoing summer quaffer for a region-specific crowd. Its body is light cereal and a hint of corn with a light lemon hop character (2.5).

HOGSBACK BREWING COMPANY

📞 (613) 986-2337

🐦 @HogsBackBrewing

🌐 hogsback.ca

Named in reference to a prize-winning pig, and a term historically used to describe a portion of the Rideau River that resembled the backbone of a hog, HogsBack opened in 2010 and has contracted out to multiple breweries, including Big Rig, Wellington, and Broadhead Brewery. While for a brief time they did serve their beers on draft at several bars, they have since sold their beers exclusively at the LCBO and the Beer Store.

———

Their **VINTAGE LAGER** is very European influenced, with a distinct malt character featuring slight toffee notes and a slight earthy bitterness brought on by the Saaz hops (2.5). **ONTARIO PALE ALE** has a sweet honey and malt note with little bitterness (2). HogsBack's winter seasonal beer is the punny **APORKALYPSE NOW**, a very carbonated stout with notes of chocolate, cherry, and, you guessed it, bacon (2). Real smoked bacon does go into this beer, so vegans and vegetarians beware.

HOGTOWN BREWERS

 (416) 453-7557
 @HogtownBrewers
 hogtownbrewers.ca

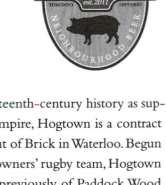

Trading on Toronto's late-nineteenth-century history as suppliers of pork to the British Empire, Hogtown is a contract brewery, currently produced out of Brick in Waterloo. Begun in 2012 with the input of the owners' rugby team, Hogtown quickly recruited Jay Cooke (previously of Paddock Wood and currently at District Brewing in Regina) for recipe design. Their porcine mascot has become a familiar sight on taps around the city of Toronto and goes by the name of Hogtown Hank.

———

The brewery's single offering thus far is **HOGTOWN ALE**, a light German hybrid ale in the kölsch style, pleasantly grainy with a hint of floral hop and a light metallic sting in the finish (3).

HOP CITY
BREWING CO.

 (905) 855-7743

 @HopCityBrewing

 hopcity.com

While many think of Hop City as simply a subsidiary of Moosehead, the history of the brewery is surprisingly complex and contains significant craft pedigree. The Hop City brand didn't exist until 2009, and the brewery wasn't located in Brampton until 2007. Prior to the name change and relocation, the company operated as Niagara Falls Brewing, famous for producing the first (and legendary) North American Eisbock and the immensely popular Gritstone Premium Ale.

Head brewer Kevin Gray has been with the company since 1991, which makes all the more impressive the amount of adaptability that Hop City has displayed in recent years. The rebrand coincided with the launch of a new line of products emphasizing a colourful cartoon style and stylistically updated beers that show a brewery holding their own in a marketplace obsessed with novelty. Production has recently expanded past the 10,000-hL mark, and several of their products are distributed in the United States.

The flagship brand, **BARKING SQUIRREL**, is an amber lager with a deep caramel body and a nose of dried fruit and wild grasses leading to a metallic bite on the finish (3). **LAWN CHAIR CLASSIC WEISSE** is mashed banana and pie spice on the nose, with a spiky carbonation leading to the tang of wheat and a hint of yogurt on the finish (3.5). **8TH SIN** is a roasty schwarzbier that drifts roast coffee and chocolate over the palate, while a medium body rushes beneath toward a clean finish. It develops a touch of apple as it warms (4). **HOPBOT** IPA has a wide aroma of pineapple, grapefruit, and mango with an underlying caramel body that fades into a perfumey herbal finish (4). The most recent addition to the lineup, **POLLY WANT A PILSNER**, is appropriately crackery and leans toward the German pilsner style with a round body and pleasingly dry finish (4).

HORSESHOE VALLEY BREWING COMPANY

 Oro Medonte

 (705) 816-2739

 @HVBrewCo

HVBrewCo.com

Located just north of Barrie, Horseshoe Valley Brewing Co. aims to be a locally focused brewery that introduces people to the wonderful world of better beer. To do so, they plan to take water from the Oro-Moraine Aquifer nearby. While their facility is still in the process of being completed, Horseshoe Valley is currently contracting out, releasing their flagship and the occasional seasonal to bars and stores.

Horseshoe Valley's first offering, **COLD WATER CLEAR LAGER**, is on par with a light beer, with floral notes and a slight cereal and corn sweetness that sets it above the mass-produced variety (3).

THE ONTARIO CRAFT BEER GUIDE

INDIE ALE HOUSE BREWING COMPANY

 2876 Dundas Street W, Toronto

 (416) 760-9691

 @indiealehouse

 indiealehouse.com

 Mon 5p.m.–Late, Tue–Sun 12p.m.–Late

 Mon 5p.m.–11p.m., Tue–Sat 12p.m.–11p.m., Sun 12p.m.–9p.m.

Opened in the autumn of 2012, the Junction's Indie Ale House has become one of Toronto's most successful brewpubs over the course of its short existence. Owner Jason Fisher is one of the Ontario brewing industry's most vocal proponents for change to alcohol retailing, periodically becoming down-right confrontational with government officials. Outspoken and unapologetic, this assertive character is also invested in the brewery, which specializes in larger-than-life flavours in their punchy ales.

The kitchen, under the direction of executive chef Todd Clarmo, has quickly gained a reputation for quality and gen-erous portions, which seem to increase in size at the Indie's almost legendary beer dinners. Indie Ale House produces

ONTARIO CRAFT BREWERIES

something like 1,500 barrels of beer a year at this point, thanks to an expansion of the brewery in 2014 that increased its size by 60 percent. Currently, they produce as many as fifty varieties of beer over the course of a year. The off-site barrel warehouse holds 120 barrels of various kinds, allowing brewer Jeff Broeders, an early graduate of Niagara College, plenty of room for experimentation. As of 2016, Indie is one of the smallest breweries in Ontario participating in a hop selection process. It's a subtle difference that has had an impressive effect on several of their products.

———

INSTIGATOR IPA is better integrated than in the past, with grapefruit and tropical notes on the aroma, a creamy rounded body, and pronounced bitterness (4.5). **LOVE TRIANGLE** is part of a series of treble-hopped IPAs; in this instance, it is made up of Ahtanum, Cascade, and Centennial, combining in a light body with bright pine and citrus over a spicy, resinous palate (4.5). **SPADINA MONKEY RASPBERRY** is a light sour beer not dissimilar to a Berliner weisse but bolstered by bright, tart raspberry throughout (4). **10-4** is a fourth anniversary beer, a barrel-aged Flanders red with grape must that features appropriate acetic tartness woven through with red fruit and a barky barrel character before its drying finish (4). **ZOMBIE APOCALYPSE** is an imperial stout. The 2016 version has roasted malt and a dark cacao character that plays across a dry body for the style (4). **ICONOCLAST** is an IPA finished with Brettanomyces, piney and drying throughout the body (3.5). **UNHEARD MELODIES** is a porter finished with Brettanomyces, funky with cherry and plum on the aroma through tobacco, roast, and chocolate on the body to a bone-dry finish (4). **FURLONG** is a Brettanomyces saison with a peach and lemon aroma and a deceptively round body that persists to a sharp dropoff (3.5).

INNOCENTE BREWING COMPANY

📍 283 Northfield Drive E, Unit 8, Waterloo

📞 (519) 725-1253

🐦 @Innocente_Brew

🌐 innocente.ca

🕐 Tours are available upon request. Please call ahead.

🛒 Mon–Wed 11a.m.–7p.m., Thu–Fri 11a.m.–9p.m.,
   Sat–Sun 11a.m.–5p.m.

When Steve Innocente started contract brewing under the Innocente name in Scotland in 2013, his focus was on hop-forward ales, a genre that wasn't widely available in Scotland at the time. Innocente was living there while completing post-doctoral work on ale-yeast strains in cancer research. Upon returning home to Waterloo, Innocente opened a brewery of his own with the help of his brother David. His focus has since shifted from the bitter profile of those early ales to a more balanced portfolio featuring diverse styles that appeal to a wider audience.

While this trend has continued in 2016 and the company is brewing more styles than ever, Innocente managed to take home a gold from the Canadian Brewing Awards for Two Night Stand (a double IPA), suggesting that his initial impulse may have been right after all. Regardless, the result is a brewery capable of producing quality beers in just about any style, a fact borne out by the popularity of the small tasting room among local drinkers.

———

The three core beers in the lineup are **FLING**, a take on a golden ale, with English and North American hops combining earthy, woody bitterness with citrus and toasted grain (3.5); **BYSTANDER**, an American pale ale with Galaxy hops, which express themselves as grapefruit and mango (3); and **CONSCIENCE**, an IPA which amps up the bitterness further and adds Ella hops to the mix for a hint of melon, grapefruit, and orange pith; really very bitter indeed (3.5).

PILS-SINNER is an updated take on a northern German pilsner using Waimea hops, with a leaf and tangerine note on the way to a crisp, bitter finish (4.5). **INN O'SLÀINTE** is an Irish red ale that leans squarely into toasted grain and caramel without becoming overly sweet (3.5). **CHARCOAL PORTER** is a light-bodied take on the style that nevertheless ventures just past roast into burnt-in smoky territory (4.5). **KITCHENER WEISSE** is a light, citrusy Berliner weisse with a pronounced wheat character and a gently bitter lemon sting (4).

JUNCTION CRAFT BREWING

 90 Cawthra Avenue, Unit 101, Toronto

 (416) 766-1616

 @junction_craft

 junctioncraft.com

🕐 Thu–Fri 4p.m.–9p.m., Sat 11a.m.–9p.m., Sun 12p.m.–5p.m.

Based in the Toronto area it's named after, Junction Craft Brewing is the handiwork of Tom Paterson, who has notably opened several longstanding Toronto venues such as the Paddock, and brewer Doug Pengelly, who owns Saint Andre Brewing in Etobicoke, which was a regular presence on the taps at the fully restored 1940s jazz bar. The two hit it off and over time decided to go into business together.

After over a year of brewing under contract at Guelph's Wellington Brewery, Junction Craft finally opened up their brewery, taproom, and retail space on Cawthra Avenue in 2012. They have been a constant presence at festivals and on retail shelves ever since. Visitors to the brewery will be treated to imagery showcasing the area's history. However, 2017 will see the brewery moving into their larger location, the historic building of the former Symes Road Incinerator. Expected features to the new location, located less than a kilometre away from the original, will be increased production, a larger tap room and event space, and more space for an exciting Destructor series barrel program.

———

Junction's initial offering and signature brew, **CONDUCTOR'S CRAFT ALE**, contains five malts and five hop varieties and is very malt-forward, with hints of stone fruit combined with an earthy bitterness in a slowly fading finish (3). The award-winning **BRAKEMAN'S SESSION ALE** has a distinctive biscuity malt presence with a light note of grapefruit (2.5). **LOCAL OPTION LAGER** has a very sweet aroma, with a significant amount of grain notes and a mild astringent finish (2). The star flavours of **STATIONMASTER'S STOUT** are without a doubt leather and dark-roasted coffee with a light wisp of cocoa (2.5). **ENGINEER'S IPA** is a West Coast IPA with mango and grapefruit leading the way to a very biscuity middle and a slightly honey-like aftertaste (2.5).

KAME & KETTLE BEER WORKS

KAME &
keTTLe
BEER WORKS

📍 25 Pelham Town Square, Fonthill

📞 (289) 273-2550

🐦 @kameandkettle

🌐 kameandkettle.ca

🕐 Thu–Fri 4 p.m.–9 p.m., Sat 1 p.m.–9 p.m., Sun 1 p.m.–6 p.m.

Named for local geological formations created by the last ice age, Kame & Kettle began brewing proper in the final days of 2015. The focus of owner Todd Barber and brewer Dave Beifuss, high school friends who have made good on their long-term desire to own a brewery, is on variety. Originally envisioned as a nanobrewing set-up, the single keg batch size ensures that there will always be a number of different beers on tap. The popular taproom features a glassed-in area from which one can watch the green glass fermentors bubble away. This popularity has meant that Kame & Kettle have had to contract some of their flagship brew, Minivan Kölsch, out to nearby Niagara's Best. Currently, plans are underway for a significant expansion that will double the size of the taproom, allow for a formalized patio, and increase production space. In the meantime, customers can purchase 950 mL Crowlers of the beers currently on offer for home consumption.

———

Due to the amount of variety, the beers included here are meant largely as examples, except for **MINIVAN KÖLSCH**, which has an apple and pear nose with a mild floral hop character that dips into a mildly souring trough in the mid-palate (3). **SCHWARZBIER** has a pine and Tootsie Roll nose that suggests something more like a Cascadian dark but drinks more sophisticated than that, with a touch of chocolate along with deep roast and a spicy hop note in the mid-palate (4). **PLUM DUBBEL** is less a dubbel than a Belgian-inspired fruit beer that takes on the light sourness of the titular fruit (2.5). **JACK O'LANTERN FIRE PUMPKIN** contains habanero peppers in such enormous quantity it may be best observed as a challenge rather than a quaff (2).

KATALYST BREWING COMPANY

 @KatalystBrewing

 katalystbrewing.com

Launched in the closing days of 2016, Katalyst is the project of long-time home brewer Mark Verok, who intends to use contract brewing to establish a presence in the Toronto market prior to opening a physical location for the brewery somewhere in the city's west end. Currently brewed out of Cool, the initial offering, Symington Saison, is a new-world take on the classic farmhouse style.

———

SYMINGTON SAISON conceals a juicy fruit nose in its hazy body, and while the Belgian ale yeast creates a certain amount of clove, it is subsumed by sweet pink grapefruit on the palate and through the finish (3.5).

KENSINGTON BREWING COMPANY

 156 Augusta Avenue, Toronto

 (647) 648-7541

 @drinkgoodbeer

 kensingtonbrewingcompany.com

Kensington Brewing Company was started in 2011 by Kensington Market resident Brock Shepherd. Originally running it from a single desk at the back of his previous business, the now-closed Burger Bar, Shepherd collaborated with brewer Paul Dickey (Cheshire Valley) to create Kensington's flagship beer, Augusta Ale. From its debut at the Burger Bar, distribution of Augusta Ale has expanded, as has the range of beers offered by the brewery. While Kensington is currently brewing their beers exclusively at Common Good in Scarborough, a brewery of their own at 299 Augusta Avenue has been under construction for several years and is expected to (hopefully!) open at some point in 2017.

———

ONTARIO CRAFT BREWERIES

Kensington's beers are all named after aspects of Kensington Market's geography and history. Their flagship, **AUGUSTA ALE**, is named after the street that Burger Bar called home. It pours a hazy, sunset orange, with flavours of tangerine and a delicate malt note (4). Named for the fish markets of the area, **BALDWIN FISHEYE PA** has a toffee-like aroma with notes of citrus backed by a strong malt character (2.5). **FRUIT STAND WATERMELON WHEAT** is a clean-tasting beer brewed with kölsch yeast, featuring the unmistakable and pleasant aroma and taste of watermelon (2.5). **MARKET PILS** has a bitter grassiness up front with a sweet orange and lemon peel note that moves in for a somewhat crisp finish (3.5).

KICHESIPPI BEER COMPANY

📍 866 Campbell Avenue, Ottawa

📞 (613) 728-7845

🐦 @kichesippibeer

🌐 kbeer.ca

🕐 Tours are available for groups of up to fifteen. Please call ahead.

🛒 Mon–Wed 10a.m.–5p.m., Thu–Sat 10a.m.–6p.m.

While Kichesippi only began producing beer in April 2010, the facility producing the beer has a longer history in the context of Ottawa's beer scene. Kichesippi's purchase of Heritage Brewing in late 2010 allowed them to make the jump from contracting out of the facility to owning it outright. While that deal did not initially include Perry Mason's popular Scotch Irish brands like Sgt. Major IPA and Stuart's Session Ale, Kichesippi was able to acquire them subsequently. Oddly, though, they have not produced them since. The brewery's vision was different from that of the brands that were previously produced out of the space, and the focus since has been on straightforward food-friendly styles of beer that are accessible to drinkers in all corners of the market. More recently, Kichesippi has begun introducing smaller-batch, seasonal products to complement their staple offerings, and the addition of a new canning line and some plans for facility expansion suggest that they have been very popular. They also produce a retro-branded range of excellent artisanal sodas under the Harvey & Vern's label.

———

1855 is an amber ale and the brewery's most popular year-round offering. It has a nutty body of toffee and toast that's well balanced by an appropriate bitterness and nearly ideal for pairing with pub fare (4). **NATURAL BLONDE** has a nose with a stone fruit character and an earthy, peppery spice on the finish (3.5). **HELLER HIGHWATER** has a soft, clean grain character with a gentle, lightly sweet body and a light wildflower and herbal spice aroma (4.5). **LOGGER PENNSYLVANIA PORTER** is a sort of American porter popularized by Yuengling that uses a lager yeast. The result is darker and nuttier than a Vienna lager, with a hint of molasses, and it is better integrated than in previous years (3.5). **DARTMOUTH COMMON** is a German hybrid–style dampfbier, a barley beer fermented with hefeweizen yeast that retains the clove and bubble gum notes of a hefe style, but with a fuller, less tart body (3). **BRISTOL STOUT** is a milk stout named for the family dairy farm in Bristol, Quebec; it's roasty and sweet with a spicy, grassy undercurrent that runs through it (3.5).

KILANNAN BREWING COMPANY

📍 103015 Grey Road 18, Owen Sound

📞 (226) 909-2122

🐦 @KilannanBrewing

🌐 kilannanbrewing.ca

🕐 Summer: Mon–Wed 12p.m.–5p.m. Thu–Fri 10a.m.–5p.m.,
Sat 9:30a.m.–5p.m.

Winter: Thu–Sat 10a.m.–5p.m.

This four-year-old brewery near Georgian Bay boasts a Siebel Institute of Technology–educated brewer in the person of Spencer Wareham. The German portion of that program is evident in the brewery's core offerings: accessible German-hybrid ales from Dusseldorf and Cologne on the Rhine. More recently, the brewery has begun to expand their offerings to include other styles, ones that more readily approach the expectations of the adventurous craft beer drinker. Kilannan is now brewing interesting one-offs with hops from New Zealand and branching out into more assertive styles of beer like IPAs and imperial stouts.

ONTARIO CRAFT BREWERIES

KÖLSCH is light bodied and fruity, with a white grape and wildflower aroma leading to a light, spicy bite on the finish (3). **ALT** sticks close to the altbier style, with an earthy topsoil aroma that leads into quite a mild body, with caramel and toasted nuts (3). **NEW ZEALAND RED ALE** plays light accents of passionfruit and pineapple against a deep biscuit and toffee background, leading to a dry finish (3.5). **THE MEN WHO STARE AT OATS** is an oatmeal stout with hints of tobacco and leather playing around something vinous in a cola-dark body with hints of leafy bitterness (3.5). **THE BEER FROM D.U.N.K.E.L.** develops a raisin and dark plum character in the aroma in addition to chocolate, toasted dark bread, and molasses, with a slightly warming finish (4).

KING'S TOWN BEER COMPANY

KING'S TOWN
BEER COMPANY

📍 3-675 Arlington Park Place, Kingston

📞 (613) 417-0375

🌐 kingstownbeerco.ca

🕐 Thu 4p.m.–8p.m., Fri 11:30a.m.–8p.m., Sat 11:30a.m.–5p.m.

Opened in the final days of 2016, just in time for Christmas, King's Town is located in Kingston's west end. The brewery currently operates on a growler-only retail system, designed specifically to avoid the necessity of competing in Ontario's retail channels. Featuring a 5-BBL brewhouse with an equal number of fermenters and brite tanks, they are fairly likely to be able to do just that, depending on the residents of Kingston for the majority of their sales. Brewer Mike Demmers has had twenty years of home-brewing experience leading up to this point and has crafted four year-round offerings with a series of one-offs that will be released with reference to Kingston's favourite historical figure, Sir John A. MacDonald.

————

KING'S TOWN ALE falls somewhere between northern English ESB and Ontario pale ale, with raisin, blackcurrant,

ONTARIO CRAFT BREWERIES

305

and mild coffee notes bolstering a light noble hop presence (3). **1840 STOUT** has a chocolate milk nose with a hint of snuffed candle somewhere in the background leading to a touch of roast barley astringency on the finish (2.5). **ISLANDER IPA** is bitter for a session IPA, but with a lingering pine and tangerine bitterness that works nicely despite outpacing the body considerably (3.5).

KINGSTON BREWING COMPANY

📍 34 Clarence Street, Kingston

📞 (613) 542-4978

🐦 @kbrew_pub

🌐 kingstonbrewing.ca

🕐 Mon–Sat 11:30a.m.–2a.m., Sun 11a.m.–2a.m.

Founded in 1986, the Kingston Brewing Company was the second brewpub opened in Ontario and is currently the longest lived. Housed in a nineteenth-century limestone building, the brewpub is a perennial Kingston hot spot, decorated in all manner of brewery memorabilia and especially festive at Christmas. The quality of the beer has had ups and downs over the years, but this is tied mainly to the popularity of the pub and the size of the onsite brewery; it has been hard to keep up with demand. For nine years (1992–2001), Dragon's Breath was produced by Hart Brewery in Carleton Place. It is currently served under the name Dragoon's Pale Ale and has been produced by a number of different breweries over the years, typically favouring those with Ringwood yeast to preserve that character. At the moment, it's Ashton Brewing Company from the Ottawa area.

In the wake of the retirement of long-time co-owner Van Turner, some improvements have begun to be made in the brewery. While the iconic red delivery van remains parked outside on Clarence Street, the bar has been replaced by a new surface, and the brewer is actively searching for a new all-grain pilot system in an effort to begin collaborative brewing with local home brewers, an act that should bolster Kingston's craft beer scene significantly.

––––

DRAGOON'S PALE ALE is distinctly English in style, with a fruity flavour and pronounced bitterness (3.5). **WHITETAIL CREAM ALE** is clean for a cream ale, lightly fruity with pronounced notes of grain (3). Of the beers produced onsite, the most successful are the **FRAMBOISE ROYALE**, whose aggressive raspberry presence sits somewhere between Chambord and Swedish Berries (2), and the **DRAGON'S BREATH REAL ALE**, a malty cask-only offering with tea-like hops (2–3, depending on cask condition).

LAKE OF BAYS BREWING COMPANY

📍 2681 Muskoka Road, Unit 117, Baysville

📞 (705) 767-2313

🐦 @LB_Brewing

🌐 lakeofbaysbrewing.ca

🕐 Hours vary seasonally; check website for updates.

Very few stories begin, "At one time, my father found himself the owner of a commercial property in Baysville," but that's just how Darren Smith's goes. With his father's property, Darren's dream of opening a brewery was realized, and Lake of Bays Brewing Company was opened in 2010. Originally, Smith was the head brewer, but he later handed over operations to experienced Danish brewer Dan "Dunk" Unkerskov.

Aside from their year-round offerings, Lake of Bays is perhaps best known for their limited partnership beers, most notably with the NHL Alumni Association. Past beers in the Alumni series have included tributes to Jacques Plante, Darcy Tucker, and CuJo (Curtis Joseph).

———

ONTARIO CRAFT BREWERIES

The **TOP SHELF VIENNA LAGER** is the year-round signature beer of the Alumni series. It is a rather light-bodied beer with a toasted malt backbone blended with very mild bitterness (2). **CROSSWIND PALE ALE** has a very strong biscuit-grain character with mild citrus and grassy notes (2.5). **SPARK HOUSE RED ALE** has warm toffee flavours accompanied by mild coffee in a subtle cocoa finish (2.5). **ROCK CUT BAYSVILLE LAGER** pours dark golden. With an overall bready flavour, there are grassy and candy-like properties that have also found their way in (2). **10 POINT INDIA PALE ALE** is an English-influenced IPA with a heavy caramel presence and a burst of grapefruit and pine (3).

LAKE OF THE WOODS BREWING COMPANY

 350 Second Street S, Kenora

 (807) 468-2337

 @lowbrewco

 lowbrewco.com

 Sun–Wed 11a.m.–11p.m., Thu 11a.m.–12a.m., Fri-Sat 11a.m.–1a.m.

 Daily 11a.m.–11p.m.

Lake of the Woods Brewing is a fine example of the way in which a determined brewer can help to revitalize a community. The signs of Kenora's industrial and geographical heritage are something that Lake of the Woods wears on its sleeve. Occupying a restored 1912 fire station that was gutted and rebuilt to purpose, the company brews beers named after a disused (ostensibly haunted) gold mine, a shuttered paper mill, and the firehouse itself. Additionally, the brewery often incorporates imagery reminiscent of late 1950s magazine ads for their beer labels. Owner Taras Manzie is doing his bit to help lead the tourism economy in the region by providing a 275–seat taproom, restaurant, and brewing facility that employs over one hundred people in the busy season. The taproom caters to wide-ranging tastes with specialty seasonal beers, a games room on the second floor, and a diverse selection of pub-grub favourites.

ONTARIO CRAFT BREWERIES

311

Thanks to funding from FedNor's Targeted Manufacturing Initiative for Northern Ontario, Lake of the Woods has further expanded its production and distribution access, introducing areas previously bereft of craft beer to a taste of something local. Considering the tremendous growth the brewery has seen in recent years, it is safe to say that Lake of the Woods does not suffer from a lack of ambition or ingenuity when it comes to problem-solving.

———

SULTANA GOLD is a North American–style blonde ale with hints of toffee and plum and a touch of pear in a light and creamy body (3.5). **HAPPY CAMPER** is a honey brown ale incorporating the key ingredient from nearby Manitoba. Despite its light body, the subtle notes of clove and chocolate come through, blending well with the sweet honey to make for an altogether warming campfire beer (4). **TIPPY CANOE** makes use of wild rice grown nearby in Shoal Lake, adding a pleasant, almost peppery character (3.5). **BIG TIMBER**, an American IPA, packs a punch with notes of grapefruit and lemon, and an assertive malt presence backing it up (4). **FIREHOUSE** is an English nut brown ale, gently flavoured with caramel, biscuit, and chocolate, with a light, almost almond-like finish (3). **FORGOTTEN LAKE** is a strong fruit beer, tart and lightly herbal with hints of caramel. Brewed with wild blueberries, the fruit imparts a pinkish hue and the flavours of both berry and stem to the beer (3).

LAKE ON THE MOUNTAIN BREWING COMPANY

📍 11369 Loyalist Parkway, Prince Edward County

📞 (613) 476-1321

🌐 lakeonthemountainbrewco.com

🕐 Fri–Sun 12p.m.–6p.m., or by chance if brewers are working during the week.

Situated just walking distance from the Glenora Ferry and facing one of the most beautiful lakeside views in Ontario, Lake on the Mountain Brewing first came into the public eye in 2007, setting up a small extract brewing facility in Lake on the Mountain Resort and offering their beers to the hosting establishment's two local venues, The Inn and The Miller House. Things changed, however, in the fall of 2016 when the brewery moved to a much larger facility away from the resort. Now boasting a full-scale brewing facility, bottling line, retail shop, and spacious tasting room that makes for a homey, comfortable place when night falls, Lake on the Mountain has undergone a significant transformation in terms of quality. Some things, however, never change. As with their previous location, the view just outside the brewery is a breathtaking one.

———

The brewery currently has a number of one-offs and seasonals available on tap, but the frequently found offerings include the **CREAM ALE**, displaying a slight berry note in the beginning, which makes its way to light caramel and a coppery dry finish (3.5). The **ONOKENOGA PALE ALE** has a note of pine up front that makes way for honeydew melon, resulting in an altogether sweet finish (4). **COUNTRY BROWN** is medium roast coffee and nice nutty backing, with a gentle hint of chocolate toward the end (3.5). **CITRA IPA** contains, rather unexpectedly, a whole whack of grapefruit notes from the Citra hops, subdued slightly by the sweet malt backbone (3.5)

LAKE WILCOX BREWING COMPANY

📍 3-1033 Edgeley Boulevard, Vaughan

📞 (647) 749-0489

🐦 @WilcoxBrewery

🌐 lakewilcoxbrewing.com

🕐 Mon–Wed 11a.m.–6p.m., Thu–Fri 11a.m.–9p.m., Sat 11a.m.–5p.m., Sun 12p.m.–5p.m.

Behind Lake Wilcox Brewing Company are David De Ciantis and Ray Nicolini, who also own Lake Wilcox Canning, a canning facility that operates out of the U-Brew facility at the Brew Kettle of Richmond Hill. While originally brewing out of Railway City Brewing in St. Thomas, De Ciantis and Nicolini moved to their own bricks and mortar brewery in Vaughan last year. A 6,500-square-foot building with a 20-hL brewing facility all under the supervision of brewmaster Aaron Martin, Lake Wilcox produces several mainstay and small-batch beers and operates as a contract facility for new breweries.

———

Their first beer is the **MAD QUACKER AMBER LAGER**, a Vienna-style amber with a light mouthfeel and hints of caramel and berries, leading toward a quick finish (3). **LAKE HOUSE CRAFT LAGER** is light and sweet, with grassy character and a note of white bread toward the end (2.5). **BANDIT AMERICAN PALE ALE** is quite sweet and bready, with notes of grapefruit making a brief appearance (2). **BLACK HOPS BLACK IPA** has prominent flavours of tangerine and pine that cut off mid-way to make way for cocoa (3).

LAST CASTLE BREWING COMPANY

LAST CASTLE
— *brewing co.* —

📍 286 Bridge Street, Port Stanley

🐦 @LastCastleBrew

🌐 lastcastlebrewing.com

🕐 Tue–Sun 12p.m.–5p.m.

Last Castle is the brewery side of The New New Age, a herb farm and apiary located in the Otter River Valley. Owners Stephen and Katie Hotchkiss, originally from Los Angeles, take inspiration from Druidry, permaculture, and green wizardry. The storefront in Port Stanley is a testament to their commitment to the appreciation of nature, magic, and locally sourced commodities, showcasing local art and many of their own products, which include honey, body care products, and a wide variety of teas. The store also houses their own organic farm-to-table bistro, where different Last Castle beers are poured on an almost weekly basis.

———

While Last Castle's beer is under constant rotation because of their small size, their one mainstay, **FIELD MAGICK**, features floral and tropical fruit in the aroma and a delicately spicy and tart flavour with a dry finish (NR).

LAYLOW BEER BAR & EATERY

📍 1144 College Street, Toronto

🐦 @laylowbarTO

🌐 laylowto.ca

🕐 Mon–Thu 5p.m.–12a.m., Fri 5p.m.–2a.m., Sat 11a.m.–4p.m. and 5p.m.–2a.m., Sun 11a.m.–4p.m. and 5p.m.–12a.m.

Opened in September 2016, Laylow is really more neighbourhood hot spot than brewpub. You won't see gleaming tanks lining any of the walls. Instead, Laylow is all ambient lighting and relaxed hip hop music, featuring a massive bar as a centrepiece. For the most part, owners Dan Boniferro and Colin Weadick are content to serve other people's beer, with a focus on quality rather than quantity of options. The same can be said of the tightly selected food menu, which features cheese and charcuterie in addition to some more robust fare. The brew system must be one of the smallest going in the province of Ontario, and brewer Brandon Judd has designed a number of recipes on their pico-size system.

––––

The beers borrow their names from the bar's soundtrack. **GHOST IN A SHELL** purports to be a traditional saison, although the unconventional spice melange of coriander, white peppercorn, and curry leaf throws a kink in that claim. A light–bodied, refreshing beer, the palate is slightly muddled (3.5). **BLACK ON BOTH SIDES** is a deeply roasty stout with a small apple ester in the middle of the aroma that is supported by husky cocoa and chicory, with a body so dark that it leads a small astringency into the finish (3.5).

LEFT FIELD BREWERY

📍 36 Wagstaff Drive, Toronto

📞 (647) 346-5001

🐦 @LFBrewery

🌐 leftfieldbrewery.ca

🕐 Daily 11a.m.–9p.m. Tours are available on Saturday and
Sunday at 2p.m.

Situated in one of the few remaining industrial zones in the
Greenwood-Coxwell corridor, Left Field Brewery is run by
husband-and-wife baseball fans Mark and Mandie Murphy.
Starting out as home brewers, they soon moved to contracting out of Grand River Brewing and Barley Days Brewery
before finally opening their own facility on Wagstaff Drive.
The Murphys have developed a reputation in the beer community of Toronto as a local team that made it to the big
leagues through a combination of talent and hard work.
Since opening, the brewery has gained popularity as a community hub, with patrons from the neighbourhood and
beyond congregating at the taproom to refill their bottles,
sample new releases, and watch the game on the big screen.
Over the last year Left Field has expanded production

significantly while also taking advantage of the LCBO to widen their distribution.

———

With few exceptions, Left Field's beer names are based around their baseball theme. **EEPHUS OATMEAL BROWN ALE** takes its name from a kind of slow pitch. Left Field's first beer, it has cocoa and coffee notes and a creamy mouthfeel (4). **MARIS* PALE ALE** features light ruby red grapefruit and orange rind notes with a slight hint of pine (4). A recent addition to the lineup, **LASER SHOW** is an intensely hopped and juicy Vermont double IPA that has beautiful tropical fruits blending with grapefruit and orange juice (5). Seasonals include the **SUNLIGHT PARK SAISON**, made with grapefruit zest (4). Additionally, every year Left Field does a collaborative coffee porter, incorporating roasts from their neighbour Pilot Coffee Roasters. The 2016 version of **BRICKS & MORTAR COFFEE PORTER** features Ana Sora Ethiopian coffee beans, which are incredibly well represented in this full-bodied beer without being overbearing or too acidic. Milk chocolate and vanilla are prominent, with a light strawberries and cream presence near the end (5).

LIBERTY VILLAGE BREWING COMPANY

📞 (647) 618-8059

🐦 @LibertyVilBeer

🌐 libertyvillagebeer.com

Liberty Village Brewing Company is the creation of long-time friends Cassandra Campbell, Steve Combes, Kosta Viglatzis, and brewmaster Eric Emery, whose home-brewed beers inspired his friends to start a brewery in 2012. While their initial foray into large-scale brewing was at Junction Craft Brewing and Cool Beer Brewing in Etobicoke, they are now contracting out of Brunswick Bierworks, with upcoming plans to open their own physical location.

———

Their mainstays include the classic **504 PALE ALE**, named for the streetcar that serves their neighbourhood. It features a mild peach aroma with distinct lime and orange flavours that come together with a slight dry note, finishing well (4.5). The **BLACK BLESSING CHOCOLATE STOUT** has a distinct, creamy-chocolate tone with a touch of warming coffee flavours (3). The **GOSEBUSTER** is an excellent gateway beer to the gose style, with grapefruit notes, a delicate tartness, and a very subtle salt presence (3.5).

THE LION BREWERY RESTAURANT

📍 59 King Street N, Waterloo

📞 (519) 886-3350

🌐 huetherhotel.com

🕐 Mon–Fri 11a.m.–1a.m., Sat–Sun 10a.m.–1a.m.

Opened as a brew pub in 1987 by the Adlys family, the Lion Brewery Restaurant at the Huether Hotel has to be seen to be believed. Although the beer is now brewed next door at the Gold Crown facility, which doubles as a brew-on-premises facility for area home brewers, the Lion Brewery's beers are served throughout the Huether Hotel complex.

The Lion Brewery Restaurant houses a cellar in which some of the first lager-style beer was stored in Ontario and a private room that was part of the nineteenth-century brewery's maltings. Upstairs, the Billiards Room possesses a down-at-heel charm and a selection of vintage pinball and arcade machines. The compound also contains an upstairs bar called Barley Works and a 280-seat outdoor patio for summer revelry. For an accurate sense of early brewing in Ontario both in the nineteenth century and the 1980s, it is impossible to do better than this national historic site, now in its thirtieth year of operation.

———

Although many beers are offered on a seasonal basis that reflect highlights from the tastes of the last twenty years, the best offerings are in classic styles. **LION LAGER** is an amber lager light on caramel with a distinct grassiness in the aroma and a reasonably bitter finish (3), while **WUERZBURGER** is lighter in malt character and more approachable to new converts (2.5). The **IPA** is British in style, with notes of blackcurrant and lemon and a balanced sweetness (3). **ADLYS ALE** is a straightforward full-bodied red ale with caramel and bready grain punctuated by a note of tart berry, not unlike a jam roll (2.5).

LOCK STREET BREWING

📍 15 Lock Street, Port Dalhousie,
St. Catharines

🐦 @LockStreetBrew

🌐 lockstreet.ca

🕐 Mon–Tue 12p.m.–6p.m., Wed–Sun 11a.m.–9p.m.

Set up in the historic Lion Tavern building, Lock Street Brewing was founded by Darryl Austin and Wolfgang Guembel, who hoped to breathe new life into the small St. Catharines community. While a soft launch of their beers was held in January 2016, the beers, developed by brewmaster Sarah Casorso, were brewed sporadically on a contract basis while the team navigated the red tape that comes with renovating a historical building. The brewery finally opened their doors in late 2016, with an absolutely packed launch event.

————

INDUSTRIAL PALE ALE is Lock Street's first beer to arrive in LCBO stores shortly after it's launch. The beer features delicate notes of citrus and a mildly bitter grain characteristic that makes itself the star of the show (3).

LONDON BREWING CO-OPERATIVE

 521 Burbrook Place, London

 @LondonBrewingca

 londonbrewing.ca

This small London-based brewery is organized as a worker's co-operative. Operating since 2013, they are focused on brewing with local and organic ingredients. The co-op has been pouring their beers on a pop-up basis exclusively through the Root Cellar Organic Cafe, another co-operative business, which, along with food delivery service On The Move Organics, is partially owned by some of the owners of the brewery.

Recently, the co-op has moved out of their nano-sized space near the Root Cellar to a 15-BBL system on Burbook Place, literally around the corner from fellow London brewery Anderson Craft Ales.

————

While the majority of the London Brewing Co-operative's beers are one-offs, more regular offerings are the **TOLPUDDLE**

PORTER, which has a rather light mouthfeel with chocolate and coffee flavours, finishing very quickly and leaving a slightly bitter aftertaste (3). **NORFOLK RED** has very sweet, creamy caramel flavours (2).

LONGSLICE BREWERY

🔎 259 Lansdowne Avenue, Toronto

📞 (647) 479-2469

🐦 @LongsliceBrews

🌐 longslice.com

Started in 2014, Longslice is a Toronto-based contract brewery currently producing beer out of the Cool facility in Etobicoke and the Collective Arts facility in Hamilton. The Peat brothers had success as home brewers during their high school years and decided to start their own company after placing second in the IPA category of the Toronto Beer Week Homebrew Contest. Longslice's beer has become popular in bars across the GTA largely because of the variety of formats in which it's offered. The brightly coloured tallboy cans display several visual puns and the brewery's fun-loving character. Their website reflects this too, with old school 8-bit graphical artifacts out of a LucasArts game.

———

As of 2016, Longslice has two offerings, one designed by each of the Peat brothers, a system that allows them each to express themselves and provides a small amount of fraternal competition. **HOPSTA LA VISTA** (Jimmy's beer) is a hybrid of English- and American-style IPAs, malt-dominant with a wide range of hop characters, from pine and mango to vanilla notes. The bitterness is relatively mild behind honeyed malts (3). **LOOSE LIPS** (John's beer) is a Vienna lager with a lightly floral, soapy European hop character, a toffeeish middle, and a dab of candied fruit on the finish (3).

LONSBERY FARMS BREWING COMPANY

 @LonsberyBeer

 lonsberyfarms.beer

Founded by Karl Lonsbery, a seventh-generation farmer from near Harrow, Lonsbery Farms is intended to be a farm-to-table brewing experience, growing its ingredients as locally as possible. Lonsbery has substantial experience in the beverage alcohol world, having been a winemaker for the Mastronardi Estate Winery for the last decade. While plans for opening the physical plant have been delayed into 2017, experimental batches are being brewed under contract at Windsor's Craft Heads and are periodically available on tap at that location.

––––

LONSBERY CREAM ALE is the initial offering and promises to be an approachable choice to display the farm's produce (NR).

LOST CRAFT BEER

 (416) 271-5980

 @LostCraftBeer

 lostcraft.ca

Brewed under contract by Common Good Beer Company in Scarborough, Lost Craft is unique in Toronto in that they actively court a more urban market than the majority of the city's contract-brewed beers. While the beer itself certainly does not break any new ground, the success of Lost Craft is down to the ability of founder Shehan De Silva, who has positioned the company as a kind of geographical gateway brewery. Rather than introducing drinkers to a more adventurous style of beer, he's introducing craft beer to entire new sections of the 905 and having a certain amount of success downtown at the same time.

———

REVIVALE is brewed in the kölsch style, with a pear and banana nose and some light floral and woody hop interest that doesn't quite manage to balance the residual grainy sweetness of the finish (2.5). **CRIMZEN** is a fairly basic red ale, and as such features a certain amount of caramelly malt sweetness (3).

LOUIS CIFER BREW WORKS

📍 417 Danforth Avenue, Toronto

📞 (647) 350-5087

🐦 @LouisCiferBW

🌐 louisciferbrewworks.com

🕐 Mon–Wed 11:30a.m.–12a.m., Thu–Fri 11:30a.m.–2a.m., Sat 11a.m.–2a.m., Sun 11a.m.–12a.m.

🛒 Mon–Fri 11:30a.m.–11p.m., Sat–Sun 11a.m.–11p.m.

Located on the Danforth between Chester and Pape subway stations, Louis Cifer has become a popular destination in a bustling neighbourhood full of young families because of their extensive pub menu and family-friendly atmosphere. Opened in 2014, the bar continues to retain an equal number of high-quality local craft beers on tap as a complement to their own house beers. While some of the earliest batches of Louis Cifer's beer were produced off site, production has been consolidated within the glassed-in brewing facility under the watch of Connor Deuchars. The range of house-made products continues to gradually improve as he gains additional experience and ventures further into experimental territory with bolder flavours.

ORIGINAL SIN BLONDE ALE has pronounced orchard fruit esters on the nose and a lightly sweet body of arrowroot and barley grain (2.5). **COCONUT LEMONGRASS THAI-PA** was originally made for International Women's Day and contains coconut paste, creating a pervasive impression of a holiday on a tropical beach (3.5). **EXTRA SPECIAL BITTER** has apple esters ahead of a nutty toasted malt body that contains a hint of cocoa (3). **GATES OF ALE IPA** is a curious combination of New Zealand and West Coast hopping that comes across as apricot and bright lemon on the aroma (3.5).

DRY IRISH STOUT expresses a dry-roasted character with a smoky finish but without much depth (3). **GOTHIC AMERICAN BROWN ALE** is front loaded, packing a piney wallop on the aroma before receding through toasted malt on the second half (2.5). **STRAIGHT OUTTA CONVENT WEST COAST IPA** is chock full of tropical fruit, with mango, passionfruit, and grapefruit leading a relatively light, bitter body (4). **DARK HORSE ESPRESSO APA** does what it says it's going to, but with a sophisticated coffee character and a bitter light roast with a touch of earthy, peppery vegetation leading to a complex, bitter finish (3.5).

LOWERTOWN BREWERY

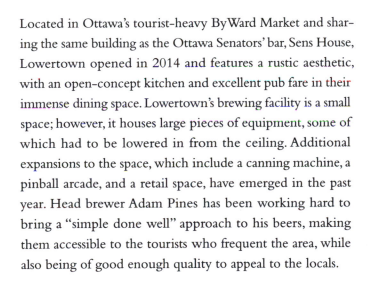

 73 York Street, Ottawa

 (613) 722–1454

 @LowertownOttawa

 lowertownbrewery.ca

 Mon–Fri 11a.m.–1a.m., Sat–Sun 9a.m.–2a.m

Located in Ottawa's tourist-heavy ByWard Market and sharing the same building as the Ottawa Senators' bar, Sens House, Lowertown opened in 2014 and features a rustic aesthetic, with an open-concept kitchen and excellent pub fare in their immense dining space. Lowertown's brewing facility is a small space; however, it houses large pieces of equipment, some of which had to be lowered in from the ceiling. Additional expansions to the space, which include a canning machine, a pinball arcade, and a retail space, have emerged in the past year. Head brewer Adam Pines has been working hard to bring a "simple done well" approach to his beers, making them accessible to the tourists who frequent the area, while also being of good enough quality to appeal to the locals.

———

The four core Lowertown offerings are **LOWERTOWN LAGER**, which features a light mouthfeel with a pleasant biscuity character brought on by the German malts (3); **DARK LAGER**, which pours a deep copper and has a molasses aroma with roasted–nut malt flavourings and a caramel sweetness (3.5); the award-winning **PALE ALE**, which is well balanced, with a distinct citrus and earthy hop character and a biscuit presence that is rather inviting for newcomers to the style (4); and **RED FIFE**, which has a very toffee-like malty twirl levelled out with a slight coppery dry finish (3.5). **TIMBER SLIDE IPA** has a strong, fairly bitter malt backbone balancing out notes of citrus (3). **NITRO DRY STOUT** is a classic Irish dry stout served on nitro, with coffee, chocolate, and heavy cream notes all throughout in an appropriately dry finish (4).

MACKINNON BROTHERS BREWING

MACKINNON
BROTHERS
BREWING
C⁰.
/ | \

📍 1915 County Road 22, Bath

📞 (613) 777-6277

🐦 @MacKinnonBrew

🌐 mackinnonbrewing.com

🕐 Tours available. For groups larger than five, the cost is
$10 per head.

🛒 Summer: Wed–Sun 11a.m.–5p.m.
Winter: Thu–Sat 11a.m.–5p.m.

Located outside Bath, MacKinnon Brothers has the longest
historical legacy of any brewery in Ontario despite being
founded in 2014. The family has been on the farmland the
brewery occupies since 1784. Between them, Ivan and Dan
MacKinnon possess all of the skills needed to run a brewery.
Ivan is a mechanical engineer, while Dan is a Heriot-Watt–
trained brewer. The time spent learning about beer in Scotland
has created the happy result that their malt-driven beers are
very like those their ancestors might have enjoyed in early
Ontario. The brewery itself is ingenious in design and possesses
one of the province's only subterranean cellars.

ONTARIO CRAFT BREWERIES

In 2015, the brewery produced hops, wheat, and barley on their own land and held the first annual Back to the Farm Beer and Music Festival, which drew nearly one thousand people and is poised to become an important community tradition. In the autumn of 2016, MacKinnon became the first modern-era brewery in Ontario to produce a single-estate beer with barley and hops grown on their own land. In many ways, the brewery leads the Ontario market in terms of interest in local ingredients and foreshadows in some ways what may be possible within the province as they begin to substitute their own malt in their year-round lineup.

———

CROSSCUT CANADIAN ALE has a somewhat misleading name — it is in fact an amber lager, not a pale ale. With its slightly Grape-Nutty toasted grain flavour and a healthy, full body, it's very popular locally (3). **8 MAN ENGLISH PALE ALE** is modelled after northern English cask ales and features a significant toasted grain and toffee sweetness in balance with orange and faint licorice on the aroma (4). **BROTHERS HOUSE ALE**, brewed for Kingston's Red House pubs, is a light sessionable ale with El Dorado hops and so much like a radler it might be mistaken for Five Alive (3). **RED FOX**, the summer seasonal, features Citra hops and is coloured by beets. The aroma is of zested lemon rind and healthy beetroot sugar, though that is balanced on the palate by a dry finish (3.5).

The winter seasonal, **WILD PEPPERMINT STOUT**, has its namesake catered by Roots Down Organic Farm just down the road and drinks like a sophisticated York Peppermint Pattie, the mint properly spicy rather than simply mentholated as the grain core rolls by below (4).

2016 HARVEST ALE, inspired by German marzen lagers, is revelatory. Brewed with estate-grown Newport and Vojvodina hops and AC Metcalfe 2 row barley malted by Barn Owl Malt in Hastings County, it succeeds by simply respecting the ingredients. A subtle citrus and cedar aroma leads to a lightly toasted barley character that continues through a full, round mouthfeel to a gently spicy herbal finish (5).

MACLEAN'S ALES

📍 52 14th Avenue, Hanover

📞 (519) 506-2537

🐦 @macleansales

🌐 macleansales.ca

🕐 Tours are available by appointment.

🛒 Mon–Thu 11a.m.–4:30p.m., Fri 11a.m.–7:30p.m., Sat 11a.m.–4p.m.

Charles MacLean has been present through every stage of Ontario's brewing renaissance and is at least partially responsible for the early popularity of cask ale in the province. Breweries like Wellington and StoneHammer still display his influence in their recipes decades later. MacLean's Ales is the project he has chosen for the fourth decade of his career. For those familiar with his work, the range of products from the new brewery will not come as a shock. The specialization is in traditional English styles. The attraction here is the quality, subtlety, and balance that come from a long career of trial and error.

———

FARMHOUSE BLONDE, made with Ontario hops and barley, features a gentle biscuit character and a floral nose with light sweetness in a soft finish (4). **LOW GEAR** is a sessionable golden ale down below 4% with mild citrus and grassiness from the hops and a light strawberry maltiness (3.5). **ESB** is a big, spicy take on the style, with pungent twiggy hops that seem to linger indefinitely (4.5). **PALE ALE** is lively and toffeeish with a distinct orange-pekoe hop aroma (3.5). **INDIA PALE ALE** breaks slightly from the English mould to feature pine and marmalade aromas and an assertive bitterness (3). **LUCK & CHARM OATMEAL STOUT** is a complex brew. Its smooth body displays notes of coffee, tobacco, licorice, and molasses (4). **ARMCHAIR SCOTCH ALE** is a boozy fireside sipper lodged deep in caramel with a small wildflower nose (3.5). **OLD ANGUS ALE** is a fruit-and-nut bar in a glass: raisin, plum, and dried stone fruit meet toasted cereal, chocolate, and toffee (4.5).

MAGNOTTA BREWERY

📍 271 Chrislea Road, Vaughan

📞 (905) 738-9463

🌐 magnottabrewery.com

🕐 Mon–Fri 9a.m.–9p.m., Sat 8:30a.m.–6p.m., Sun 11a.m.–5p.m.

Founded in 1997 in a then recently expanded Magnotta facility in Vaughan, Magnotta Brewery is an offshoot of the main business at Magnotta Winery. The company rose to prominence selling grape juice to home winemakers under the Festa Juice name before becoming a winery in their own right. Magnotta has not left behind its roots in the realm of home production. The Festa Juice label has been joined by Festa Brew, high-quality pre-produced wort in a variety of styles for use by home brewers. In fact, Magnotta's various locations sell all the home-brewing equipment a novice brewer might need at very reasonable prices.

Over the years, the instinct in both the wine and beer sides of the business has been to provide high-quality product at very reasonable prices, an instinct that has garnered Magnotta's True North beers something of a cult reputation at the Beer Store. The brewing facility has a reputation for being one of the cleanest in the province, going as far as having positive pressure filtered air pumped in to reduce the number of variables that might affect the beer in production. The Vaughan location has recently added a growler station and a series of adventurous one–off brews created by their brewing team.

———

TRUE NORTH BLONDE LAGER has a full mouthfeel with a sweet, Grape–Nuts malt character and a wildflower and under-growth hop aroma (3). **TRUE NORTH COPPER ALTBIER** leans toward the Dusseldorf version of the style, with a waft of com-posting leaves complementing deep bready malt and light chocolate tones (3.5). **TRUE NORTH CREAM ALE** is practically chestnutty in its toasted grain, with a mellow sweetness and a touch of leafy herb on the finish (3). **TRUE NORTH STRONG ALE** is a full on take on the English style. The malt is dark and contains deep toast, raisin, and caramel in addition to some light chocolate. The hops are twiggy and floral, while the entire affair has a hint of Lyle's Golden Syrup (3.5). **TRUE NORTH INDIA PALE ALE** is properly English as well, with woody orange pekoe aromas and a hint of chrysanthemum (3.5). **ORIGINAL CRAFT LAGER** displays a strong herbal hop aroma over a gentle grain body with a slightly metallic finish (3.5).

MANANTLER CRAFT BREWING COMPANY

 18-182 Wellington Street, Bowmanville

 (905) 697-9979

 @manantler

🌐 manantler.com

🕐 Tours are available through a booking form on the website.

🛒 Mon–Wed 4p.m.–7p.m., Thu–Sat 11a.m.–11p.m., Sun 1p.m.–6p.m.

Since opening its doors in early 2015, Manantler has proven to be a pleasant surprise for the brewing scene in Bowmanville. The brewery houses a popular taproom with a speakeasy vibe that frequently acts as a live music venue. Manantler has produced a large number of different beers in its first year, including a highly publicized collaboration with the Eagles of Death Metal, which had part of its sales going to benefit victims of the Paris terror attacks. While some appear more frequently than others, the appeal here is novelty. Their Lollihop series, for instance, uses single-hop pale ales to highlight different hop characters. Notable in all offerings, however, be they one-offs or collaborations, are the whimsical artistic labels that highlight the brewery's fun-loving nature.

ROBERTA BLONDAR, one of Manantler's most frequent issues, is named for the Canadian astronaut, although the hops used are down-to-earth. The blonde ale possesses a subtle grapefruit aroma grounded by dirty, spicy bitterness in a lightly cereal-sweet body (3.5). **LIQUID SWORDS** is a massive American IPA that combines a number of different citrus characters. Grapefruit, tangerine, and blood orange vie for superiority above a sticky-sweet caramel body while retaining balance (4). **SEISMIC NARWHAL** is aptly named for its enormity. Resin, pine needles, tangelo, and pineapple combine in a practically overwhelming aroma. It has a hugely bitter body to match. Guaranteed to break the ice (4.5). **THE DARK PRINCE** is a black IPA that verges into stout territory. Very smooth drinking, with chocolate and medium roast coffee notes complementing the citrus hops in bitterness (4). **STEADY HORSE** is a session ale with light and bright grapefruit and lemon citrus, with a sharp jab of tropical notes in a quick and light ending (4).

MANITOULIN BREWING COMPANY

 43 Manitowaning Road, Highway 6, Little Current

 @manitoulinbrew

 manitoulinbrewing.co

Manitoulin Brewing got its start when friends Blair Hagman and Nishin Meawasige, visiting Guelph for the Hillside music festival, were inspired by the demand and popularity of local beer evidenced by the lines at the festival's craft beer tent. Such a view led the pair to bring that enthusiasm for local beer to their home on Manitoulin Island. Currently brewed out of Collingwood Brewery under the expertise of brewer Mark Lewis, Manitoulin's beer is available in many places on the island, including the MS Chi-Cheemaun ferry, which connects the island to Tobermory.

Those looking for growler fills and selected merchandise are in luck, though, as their own facility on Manitowaning Road in Little Current is now under construction, with an estimated completion time of late 2017.

Manitoulin Brewing's focus on local extends beyond just the name of the brewery. The branding makes use of the region's locally grown hawberry, and current and future beer names incorporate a destination or reference within Manitoulin Island. Their flagship beer, **SWING BRIDGE BLONDE ALE**, named after the iconic bridge in Little Current that acts as a gateway to the mainland, is a rather solid and somewhat bitter blonde, with low caramel and biscuit character, a slight peppery hop note, and an apricot and berry sweetness in a dry, piney finish (3).

MASCOT BREWERY

MASCOT — BREWERY

📍 31 Mercer St, Toronto

📞 (416) 979-0131

🐦 @mascotbrewery

🌐 mascotbrewery.com

🕐 Restaurant: Tue–Sat 5p.m.–2a.m.
Beergarden: Mon–Fri 4p.m.–2a.m., Sat 12p.m.–2a.m.,
Sun 2p.m.–9p.m.

Mascot Brewery is a brewpub and beer garden located in Toronto's entertainment district. The space opened up in several phases starting in the spring of 2015, and is the work of long-time entertainment and dining industry veteran Aaron Prothro, previously the owner of noted nightclubs Nyood and F-Stop. While the tap and bottle selection includes a curated list of local beer, house beers designed by long-time brewer Michael Duggan are available. Mascot had previously been contracting their beer through Duggan's, with an onsite facility opening up this year.

———

Mascot Brewing has two initial offerings. The **MASCOT HEFEWEIZEN** features a large presence of banana, both in aroma and taste, in an approachably light body with a crisp and delicately dry finish (3.5). The **MASCOT PILSNER** has a sweet, dry, biscuity grain note and a long finish (3).

MASH PADDLE BREWING COMPANY

📍 111 Sherwood Drive, Unit 3A, Brantford

📞 (289) 253-8157

🌐 mashpaddlebrewing.com

🕐 Sat 11a.m.–7p.m.

Located in Brantford's resurgent Artisan's Village, Mash Paddle is the creation of husband-and-wife team Teddy and Nicole Scholten and head brewer Matty Buzanko. While the brewery was initially planned for Hamilton, the decision to settle in Brantford has proved to be a productive one for Mash Paddle, who now enjoy a certain amount of cachet locally. While production capacity was initially a struggle, volume doubled and then tripled over the course of 2016, and the brewery now has the ability to supply both of their flagship products in addition to occasional one-offs.

Mash Paddle's beer is infrequently available on tap in Hamilton and Kitchener, making the brewery the best place to get it. Currently the retail side of the business is only open on Saturdays, but that will likely expand as the business continues to grow in popularity and size.

UNNAMED PALE ALE is a full-on tropical assault, with distinctive melon, mango, and lemon notes and a subtle, biscuity finish (3.5). **DUTCHMAN'S ALT** is a take on the standard Dusseldorf specialty hybrid beer and is named for Teddy Scholten's Dutch heritage (NR).

MERCHANT
ALE HOUSE

📍 98 St. Paul Street, St. Catharines

📞 (905) 984-4060

🐦 @merchantale

🌐 merchantalehouse.ca

🕐 Daily 11a.m.–2am.

Nestled on St. Paul Street in St. Catharines, Merchant Ale House opened its doors in 1999. Friends John Tiffin, Iain Watson, and James Vanderzanden wanted to bring the difference of house-made beer to a downtown restaurant scene that was starting to grow its vibrant nightlife. Since then, the "Merch" has been a favourite destination for families, friends, and students.

Murray Street Brewery, the official name of the brewing side of the pub, has gone from serving two house beers to eleven year-round, including a rotating seasonal offering as well as several quality guest taps. Food served is traditional pub fare, including nachos, an exceptional reuben sandwich, and world-class sweet potato fries. Especially of note, however, is the Merchant's atmosphere. The building itself is a beautifully restored historical structure, with much of the stone foundation and wooden flooring still intact.

The two original beers first poured at the Merchant are by far the most popular. The **OLD TIME HOCKEY ALE** is an amber ale with a slight hint of brown sugar (3) and the **BLONDE BOMBSHELL** has a floral aroma and a light, dry body with grassy and subtle apple notes (2).

Among the brewery's other offerings is the **DRUNKEN MONKEY OATMEAL STOUT**, with a medium body and roasted–coffee notes complemented by a hint of cocoa and a slight creamy mouthfeel (3). The **EXTRA SPECIAL BITTER** is actually bitter, featuring an aroma of molasses and distinct notes of English hops (1.5). **BLUEBERRY WHEAT** is served with fresh blueberries in the glass, containing a dry, biscuity mouthfeel with sweet blueberry throughout (3). The **IPA** is bitter all across the board, with orange peel, sweet grapefruit, and pine flavours (3). Finally, the **PORTER** is on the sweet side of the style, with notes of milk chocolate, coffee, and tobacco with a quick finish (3.5).

MIDIAN BREWING

📍 1335 Wyandotte Street E, Windsor

📞 (519) 257-0327

🐦 @MidianBrewing

🌐 midianbrewing.com

🕐 Mon–Wed 4p.m.–9p.m., Thu–Sun 3p.m.–10p.m.

Located on a resurgent strip of Wyandotte just west of Walkerville, Midian Brewing opened officially on Thanksgiving 2016 after several years of planning, having initially been incorporated in 2013. While beer has only recently begun flowing out the front door on a regular basis, the parent company, Northern Wolf Fermentation Technologies, has been busy creating batches of gourmet malt vinegar in the interim. The brewery's focus is on technical mastery and lab QC, which has seemingly slowed their progress toward opening as they strive to perfect their recipes.

BLACK PRINZ DARK ALE is an English-style dark ale that leans toward porter in style thanks to the inclusion of cocoa nibs as an ingredient. The smoothly textured beer is also used

THE ONTARIO CRAFT BEER GUIDE

in a line of chocolates as an example of the brewery's vertical integration (2.5). **OLD STYLE ENGLISH BARLEYWINE** aims for a significant depth of Maillard malt character, practically evoking roast chicken skin on the palate, although without much hop interest (2).

MILL STREET BREWERY

MILL STREET BREWHOUSE

- 125 Bermondsey Road, Toronto
- (416) 759-6565
- @MillStreetBrew
- millstreetbrewery.com

MILL STREET BREWPUB (OTTAWA)

- 555 Wellington Street, Ottawa
- (613) 567-2337
- @ MillStBrewPubOT
- millstreetbrewery.com/ottawa-brew-pub
- Mon—Tue 11a.m.—11p.m., Wed 11a.m.—12a.m.,
  Thu 11a.m.—1a.m., Fri 11a.m.—2a.m., Sat 10:30a.m.—2a.m.,
  Sun 10:30a.m.—10p.m.

MILL STREET BREWPUB (TORONTO)

- 21 Tank House Lane, Toronto
- (416) 681-0338
- @ MillStBrewPubTO
- millstreetbrewery.com/toronto-brew-pub
- Mon 11a.m.—10p.m., Tue—Wed 11a.m.—11p.m.,
  Thu 11a.m.—12a.m., Fri 11a.m.—2a.m., Sat 10:30a.m.—2:00a.m.,
  Sun 10:30a.m.—10p.m.

BEER HALL AT MILL STREET BREWPUB

📍 21 Tank House Lane, Toronto

📞 (416) 681-0338

🐦 @millstbeerhall

🌐 millstreetbrewery.com/toronto-beer-hall

🕐 Sun–Wed 12p.m.–9p.m., Thu 12p.m.–1a.m.,
Fri–Sat 12p.m.–1a.m.

Mill Street Brewery was founded in 2002 by Steve Abrams, Jeff Cooper, and Michael Duggan and set up shop at 55 Mill Street in Toronto's historical Distillery District. The area that housed the former Gooderham & Worts distillery has a rich history that dates to the 1830s and to this day stands as an example of the city's Victorian-era industry. In its first seven years, Mill Street won multiple awards, including Best Microbrewery in the Greater Toronto Area at the Golden Tap Awards from 2004 to 2008 and Canadian Brewery of the Year at the Canadian Brewing Awards from 2007 to 2009.

In 2005 Joel Manning was brought on as brewmaster, a position he has kept to this day. Manning originally got his start in 1986 as a trainee at Amsterdam Brewery, taking courses to expand his knowledge until his departure in 2004. His biggest task in the early years of Mill Street was overseeing the move of large-scale brewing to a much larger facility in Scarborough, while the original brewery location was converted into a brewpub.

Since then, Mill Street has become a national giant, and were once one of the breweries where young brewers could earn their stripes before moving on to another brewery or even starting their own. Further growth came in 2011 with the leasing of two additional locations: a historic grist mill located near Chaudière Falls in Ottawa, which became a brewpub; and a location at Pearson International Airport, which made Mill Street the first craft brewer to open shop in a Canadian airport. In 2013 the original location in the Distillery District saw an expansion in the form of a beer hall opening adjacent to the brewpub, which features a fully operational still that makes "bierschnaps," a spirit made with Mill Street's house beers.

In October 2015 Mill Street announced that they had been purchased by Labatt Brewing Company for an undisclosed amount, and have since expanded significantly, increasing distribution, acquiring Brickworks Ciderhouse, and opening brewpubs in St. John's, Newfoundland, and Calgary, Alberta.

————

Mill Street makes many year-round beers that are available in stores and one-offs available exclusively at its brewpub locations or in their famous seasonal box sets. The original offering from Mill Street, **ORIGINAL ORGANIC LAGER**, has a slightly sweet bready character to it, with a very subtle citrus note wrapped in rough, grainy mouthfeel (2.5). The **100TH MERIDIAN ORGANIC AMBER LAGER** is the best of the lager offerings, bringing in notes of berries, dried fruit, and a hint of lemon with a mildly dry finish (3.5). **TANKHOUSE ALE** defines the Ontario pale ale style, with a slight toffee sweetness flowing nicely with notes of citrus and pine (4). **COBBLESTONE STOUT** is Toronto's answer to Guinness in that it is exclusively served on nitro in cans and on draft, giving it a smooth, creamy mouthfeel (4.5). Likewise, the **VANILLA PORTER** also has a creamy texture because of being served on draft or in cans on nitro, and its light mouthfeel with distinct vanilla notes makes it a good winter warmer (4.5). The **STOCK ALE** has a light body with a slight sweet lemon taste mixed with graham cracker and tied together with a crisp finish (3.5). The **BELGIAN WIT** is a fairly light-bodied beer with a touch of coriander and bready notes (3). The more recent addition to the lineup, the **WEST COAST STYLE IPA**, is for all intents and purposes a glass of freshly squeezed juice one might have for brunch. Grapefruit and tangerine are the strong notes, with a slight hint of pine toward the end (3.5).

MOTOR CRAFT ALES

motor
CRAFT ALES

📍 888 Erie Street E, Windsor

📞 (519) 252-8004

🐦 @motorcraftales

🌐 thisismotor.com

🕐 Mon–Thu 11:30a.m.–9p.m.,
Fri 11:30a.m.–10p.m.,
Sat 12p.m.–10p.m., Sun 12p.m.–8p.m.

Perhaps it's the proximity to Detroit or perhaps it's the flatness of Windsor's streets (which seem almost tailor-made for drag racing), but there's something of the home mechanic–DIY ethos about Motor. Part of the larger brand that includes Motor Burger (noted itself for having some of the best burgers in western Ontario), Motor Craft Ales is heavily invested with automotive symbolism. From the racing stripes and chalk-drawn schematics on the walls of Motor Burger to the piston-head tap handles and machined sample trays, down to the names of each brand, it's vastly successful thematically.

At the moment, the entire brewing set-up is housed in the basement of Motor Burger, with fermentation taking place in glass carboys. Given that brewer Donovan McFadden graduated from customer to brewer only four years ago, it's a format that would have proven limiting for a less driven company, but it has not stopped Motor Craft Ales from opening a small bottle shop at their front door. An expansion of brewing facilities into another location in Ford City is expected to happen over the course of 2017, and it should continue the momentum the brewery has brought not only to their own products but to the brewing scene in Windsor. Motor has also expanded their reputation with international collaboration; they infrequently brew with Detroit's Batch Brewing.

———

C-HOP TOP IPA is built on a solid chassis of bitterness, closer after revision to a classic American IPA with a classic pine and citrus aroma (3.5). **MODEL A** is an amber ale that comes across in the body like apple butter on brown toast (2.5). **DRAGULA** is a slightly roasty schwarzbier, with licorice, chocolate, and a tarry whiff that finishes cleanly (3.5). **RIDER CREAM ALE** is a straight-ahead cream ale, lightly toasty with orchard fruit — really suited to the pub fare the brewpub excels at (3.5). **FAST EDDY'S GOLD** is an apple core of an altbier, with peel and herb, a hint of earthy humus, and an outsize bitterness (2.5). **TURKEY CAR** is an American pilsner brewed with rice for a light body that features Wild Turkey hops from outside of Collingwood, possibly the best use of those hops in the province thus far (4).

ONTARIO CRAFT BREWERIES

MUDDY YORK BREWING COMPANY

📍 22 Cranfield Road, Toronto

📞 (416) 619-7819

🐦 @MYBrewingCo

🌐 muddyyorkbrewing.com

🕐 Tue–Wed 11a.m.–4p.m., Thurs–Fri 11a.m.–7p.m., Sat 11a.m.–4p.m.

Muddy York Brewing Company is the first professional venture of multiple award–winning home brewer, BJCP-certified beer judge, and author of the blog *Hoptomology* Jeff Manol. Borrowing the moniker given to the settlement of York in the late 1700s on account of its unpaved streets, Muddy York has adopted historical elements in its branding and in its bottle shop. Located in the East York area of Toronto, the brewery has achieved a reputation for helping the local brewing community and for being in high demand. Since opening there has been a sizeable expansion for the brewery, with increased tank space, a shop that opens regularly, and several collaborative and special beers.

During a period where IPAs were the standard introductory beer for a new brewery, Muddy York chose to offer a beautiful, traditional porter as its first beer. **MUDDY YORK PORTER** has a nice cocoa flavour, with subtle coffee notes and a smooth, marshmallow-like finish (4.5). **MAJOR SMALL BEST BITTER** has chewy toffee notes with light berry sweetness and a creamy mouthfeel (4). Finally, and most impressively, is the **GASLIGHT HELLES**, with its light caramel and brown sugar flavours, delicate bitterness, and beautifully dry finish (4.5).

MUSKOKA BREWERY

📍 1964 Muskoka Beach Road,
   Bracebridge

📞 (705) 646-1266

🐦 @MuskokaBrewery

🌐 muskokabrewery.com

🕐 Tours Fri—Sat at 12:30p.m., 1:30p.m., 2:30p.m.
   Large groups please call ahead to book.

🛒 Mon—Thu 9a.m.–5p.m., Fri 9a.m.–6p.m., Sat 10a.m.–5p.m.

Folks with long memories might remember the brewery's original name of Muskoka Cottage Brewery. When it was opened under that name in 1996 by Gary McMullen and Kirk Evans, it quickly became a destination for visitors and locals of the town of Bracebridge. Many, however, will remember Muskoka more for its extensive rebranding effort in 2011, which opted for a more rustic and wood-cut look, with the original tagline, "The taste of cottage country," being replaced by "Venture off the beaten path." This rebranding followed on the tails of the release of Mad Tom IPA. Originally marketed as the first in the Cabin Fever series of one-offs, Mad Tom quickly replaced Muskoka's

Cream Ale as its best-selling beer and helped set the scene for what would become the province's growing obsession with hop-forward beers.

In 2012 Muskoka grew out of its original location in downtown Bracebridge and made the move to a much larger facility, one definitely more "off the beaten path." The space allowed for increased distribution of their beers, the ability to function as a contracting facility for other brewers, and enough space to brew a number of collaborations and special monthly one-off beers under the Moonlight Kettle series.

———

The signature **CREAM ALE** is a fantastic representation of the style, worthy of the best-seller title. It has a light caramel sweetness making way for hints of orange zest in a smooth mouthfeel and finishes on a dry note (4.5). **CRAFT LAGER** has some sweet, slightly grassy notes with a jab of citrus before the biscuit character takes the wheel (4). **DETOUR** is one of the earliest beers in the province marketed as a session IPA and includes notes of melon, lemon sherbet, and pine, with an airy finish (4). **KIRBY'S KÖLSCH** was originally part of the Moonlight Kettle series. Sweet notes of citrus hit first, with a fairly dry body and just the slightest hint of peach in the end (3.5). **MAD TOM IPA** features distinct notes of grapefruit and pine with a touch of pepper at the tail end (4). Mad Tom's stronger sibling, **TWICE AS MAD TOM**, is rather heavy on notes of marmalade, with a pronounced pine bitterness in the end (4). The latest beer in their catalogue, **SHINNICKED STOUT**, is made using the Lumberjack medium roast blend by coffee producers Muskoka Roastery and has warming notes of chocolate and coffee throughout (3.5). **WINTER BEARD DOUBLE CHOCOLATE CRANBERRY STOUT**, their much-loved winter seasonal, is commonly sold in bottles that have been aging in the brewery's cellar for fourteen months. Expect to find heavy cocoa notes in there, with very little in the way of cranberry (3).

NAPANEE BEER COMPANY

📍 450 Milligan Lane, Napanee

📞 (613) 409-2337

🌐 napaneebeer.ca

🕐 Tue–Thu 1p.m.–6p.m., Fri 1p.m.–8p.m., Sat 12p.m.–6p.m., Sun 12p.m.–5p.m.

One of a handful of breweries to start up in eastern Ontario in 2016, the Napanee Beer Company's story has an element of the prodigal to it. While working at a marketing career in Toronto, Napanee-born brewer Geordan Saunders received a home-brewing kit for Christmas and pursued this hobby for nearly five years prior to opening his own company in his hometown. Accolades followed in competitions, including a Toronto Beer Week–awarded collaboration with Toronto's Amsterdam Brewery in 2013. For the most part, Napanee focuses on lagers and Belgian-style beers but is likely to expand their repertoire through seasonal releases and their Redacted series, which will focus on complex small-batch offerings available only through the brewery.

———

DEADLINE is a premium lager with a small amount of corn in the grist to lighten the body and a lightly melony hop character (3). **BLACKLIST** is a schwarzbier with a dry body and roasted character that plays as light chocolate with a faint wisp of smoke (4). **MAYDAY** is a Belgian pale ale that manages to keep the clove and spice of its yeast character in check, with a floral and lemony hop character remaining balanced and gentle (3). **EXTREMIST** is a Belgian IPA that uses West Coast American hops to bolster an orange peel character that plays with a gentle yeast character (3.5). **DEVILISH** is a spiced black saison with organic vanilla and Saigon cinnamon subtly balanced against a light roast character, a clever alternative to an autumnal pumpkin beer (4).

The original Bank Street location of Ottawa's Clocktower Brew Pub is considered the city's oldest brewpub, having opened in 1996.

Ottawa's Big Rig Brewery, with a wide distribution presence and three locations, owes much of their success and growth to their brewmaster, Lon Ladell.

Junction Craft Brewing's signature beer is the Conductor's Craft Ale, containing five malts and five hop varieties.

London's Toboggan Brewing Co. is a large and welcoming brewpub, offering a number of Ontario beers including their own made by brewer Tomas Schmidt.

Cask Days, held every year in Toronto, is perhaps the largest cask beer festival in North America.

Toronto's Muddy York Brewing Co.'s first offering, the Muddy York Porter, is a traditional take on the style, with notes of coffee and chocolate.

One of the key ingredients of beer is its grain, which provides fermentable sugars and adds to the colour of the beer.

Ontario is now home to dozens of hop growers, each with their own unique varieties.

Housed in a decommissioned elementary school near Simcoe, the family-run New Limburg Brewing Co. serves a number of quality beers in the traditional Belgian styles.

One of Ontario's few brewery farms, Ramblin' Road is run by John Picard of Picard's Peanuts fame. The brewery is a multi-purpose facility that also makes potato chips.

NEUSTADT SPRINGS BREWERY

📍 456 Jacob Street, Neustadt

📞 (519) 799-5790

🐦 @NeustadtBeer

🌐 neustadtsprings.com

🕐 Tours are available during the summer for $7 by advance booking. Group tours are available by special arrangement.

🛒 Daily 10a.m.–6p.m.

One of the few success stories of the second wave of Ontario's brewing renaissance, Neustadt Springs Brewery was founded by Val and Andrew Stimpson. Transplants from Lancashire, England, the pair had worked there as licensees for Daniel Thwaites PLC, a brewery that thrives on tradition. This must have had an impact, as they chose to situate their own brewery in Neustadt's picturesque Crystal Springs Brewery, originally founded in 1859. When Neustadt launched in 1997, it was so popular locally that the first batch of beer sold out in five hours.

The range of beers that they offer tends to adhere not only to traditional English styles, but also to the lower alcohol templates of that pub culture. This does make Neustadt's offerings somewhat niche in terms of the current craze for experimentation with new hop varietals, but no less impressive in terms of quality or international recognition. Several of the couple's products have routinely made a strong showing in the U.S. Open Beer Championship, and the brewery holds the distinction of being Ontario's most internationally awarded brewer. The year 2016 has seen the completion of a tasting room so that customers can sample their wares prior to purchase, and plans are afoot for a small kitchen that will allow patrons to enjoy light meals.

———

10W30 is a complex English mild, though it has a slightly exaggerated strength. Tasting notes are of pear, dark-bread rusk, dusty cocoa, woody hops, and dried fruit before a medium-length roasty finish (3.5). **MILL GAP BITTER** is a sessionable pint with a pronounced bready malt and fruity, tea-like hop character shining through (4). **SCOTTISH PALE ALE** is a sweeter, deeply malty number with a mellow, woody hop character, suitable for pairing as a chaser with whisky (3.5). **BIG DOG BEAUJOLAIS PORTER** replaces 3 percent of its volume with Pelee Island wine in order to emulate the sour, vinous character of traditional London-style porters (3.5). **NEUSTADT LAGER** is brewed in a northern European style, meaning that the bitterness is somewhat light, leaning toward floral and metallic (3), while **SOUR KRAUT** is a raspberry-flavoured light lager — tart yet moderately subtle (3.5). **456 MARZEN LAGER** is a richly malty Oktoberfest-style beer, bready and nutty with earthy hops and a small whiff of smoke balancing out the finish (3.5).

NEW LIMBURG BREWING COMPANY

📍 2353 Nixon Road, Simcoe

📞 (519) 426-2323

🐦 @NewLimburg

🌐 newlimburg.com

🕐 Wed–Sun 1p.m.–10p.m.

🛒 Daily 1p.m.–10p.m.

Located in a decommissioned elementary school near Simcoe, New Limburg is a unique story in the Ontario brewing landscape. The Geven family, who own the brewery, are transplants from Holland by way of Limbourg, Belgium. Perhaps due to the focus allowed by the fact that their home is in one half of the school and their business is in the other, the brewery has improved dramatically in nearly every conceivable way over the course of a year. Initial pilot batches have given way to a larger, 2-BBL system that is just barely keeping up with local demand. The taproom has been transformed into a kind of chalkboard-walled salon complete with a baby grand piano, while the frontage of the building has become a spacious patio. One of a very small number of breweries in

Ontario to bottle condition their beers, New Limburg has appropriately repurposed the school library for this task.

As a result of Jo Geven's nostalgia for the beers of Wallonia, the majority of the beers brewed by son Mischa at New Limburg are in Belgian styles. The ingredients used are traditionally Belgian, although the candi sugar is no longer manufactured on site. Daughter Milou is in charge of the brewery's lab, while mother Yvonne designs the artwork for the labels and handles the branding. The entire family works the taproom, interacting with customers and serving locally made bitterballen as a snack. It is a slice of Belgium transported to rural Ontario.

———

BELGIAN BLOND is a brightly carbonated take on the style. Fairly high in alcohol, it has an aroma of poached pear and peppery spice through its sweet, grainy body (4.5). **PETIT BLOND** is in the pale ale style, incorporating American hops in the form of Crystal and Cascade. There is a light lemon-drop and orange blossom character, bolstered by lightly peppery spice and a mildly grainy body with significant effervescence (4). **WIT** is light and floral, expanding on the traditional orange and coriander profile of a witbier with chamomile, producing a complex medium-bodied version of the summer favourite (4). **BLACK SHEEP MILK STOUT** is full of cocoa, light roast coffee, and vanilla, with a lightly creamy body from the lactose that sweetens the pot (4).

BELGIAN DUBBEL has become lighter in profile over the last year, with dried fruit character now leading the aroma. There is significantly more cherry and plum, and a nuttier malt mid-range balancing cane sugar depth (4). **TRIPEL** has a boozy pear and clove nose, with the slightest whiff of spearmint and eucalyptus herbal character ahead of a big fruity body that dries out hot on the tongue (3.5). **ST. ARNOLDUS** muddles sassafras, plum, pear, cherry pit, light molasses, honey, and chocolate in its big, dark body (3.5).

NEW ONTARIO BREWING COMPANY

 1881 Cassells Street, North Bay

 (705) 707-1659

🐦 @NewOntarioBrew

🌐 newontariobrewing.com

🕐 Sun–Mon 11a.m.–9p.m., Tue–Sat 11a.m.–11p.m.

New Ontario Brewing Company is the first brewery to open in North Bay since the original brewery of the same name began selling beer over one hundred years ago. Opened in the summer of 2015, the brewery has seen high success, in part by being an active member of their community, sponsoring local events, and supporting North Bay businesses. Traffic is very consistent at their space, with the retail shop and tasting room acting as a watering hole for locals and visitors of all ages, who stop by for a few pints before picking up a few growlers. The trio who run New Ontario Brewing Company, cellarman and operations manager Dan Delorme, along with long-time friends and military comrades front-of-house and business manager Ron Clancy and brewmaster Mike Harrison, have been doing their bit in bringing good beer to northern

Ontario and beyond, thanks to a recent expansion into LCBO distribution. By making use of Escarpment Lab yeast and constantly refining their beers while coming out with new releases, New Ontario is a must-visit in northeastern Ontario.

———

New Ontario's first LCBO release is the **BEAR RUNNER BLONDE**, which has a touch of biscuit sweetness up front in a fairly dry body and a sweet drifting finish (3.5). **FRISKY PETE'S ENGLISH PALE ALE**, named in honour of the chipmunk that lives under the brewery, and made with yeast from Escarpment Labs, is a solid English pale, featuring a swirl of sweet caramel and earthy hop character (4). **TREE TOPPER RED ALE** contains a healthy dose of floral and citrus from the Amarillo hops and leads into a warming, roasty finish (3.5). **CLOTHING HOPTIONAL** is an India session ale, with deep earthy flavours mingling with toffee, roasted malts, and a bright, somewhat piney jab of bitterness (4).

In addition to their regular beers, New Ontario frequently releases special beers from their Voyageur series. An example of one of the beers to come out of this series is the **101 CENTENNIAL IPA**, a triple IPA that commemorates the anniversary of the burning down of the original New Ontario Brewing 101 years ago. Honey, toffee, and dates are prominent in the beer, with light hints of dark fruits in a sweet, but not overly syrupy, finish (4).

NIAGARA BREWING COMPANY

📍 4915-A Clifton Hill, Niagara Falls

📞 (905) 374-4444

🐦 @NiagaraBrewCo

🌐 niagarabrewingcompany.com

🕐 Mon–Thu 12p.m.–8p.m., Fri 12p.m.–1a.m., Sat 11a.m.–1a.m., Sun 11a.m.–11p.m.

Fronting directly on Clifton Hill, this brewery is a somewhat surprising addition to the street of fun. One might not have high expectations of a brewery neighbouring two wax museums, but the Niagara Brewing Company caters to the parents taking (or possibly sending) their children to those attractions. The brewery is open-concept, providing visitors with an inside look at the function of a brewhouse from their tables. The food menu is tight and focused (as it ought to be, having been designed by Jamie Kennedy), featuring local ingredients where possible and including spectacular cheese and charcuterie boards. A spacious patio to the side of the brewery provides some respite from the bustling main drag. As of 2016, the original brewer, Gord

ONTARIO CRAFT BREWERIES

Slater, has been replaced by Rick Neheli, originally of the Niagara Falls Brewing Company.

––––

For the most part, the offerings on tap are straightforward representations of popular styles, while the addition of seasonal products has continued into the brewery's third year. **NIAGARA PREMIUM LAGER** is soft bodied, leaning toward being a Munich helles with a light, clean grain sweetness and a hint of citrus (3.5). **AMBER EH!** is a toasty caramel amber ale with a spicy hop bite (3.5), while **HONEYMOON PEACH RADLER** does exactly what it's meant to: bring peach nectar to the party in a light-bodied summer quaffer (3). **BEERDEVIL IPA** is a throwback to early craft IPAs, with caramel malts slightly overwhelming the bitterness, leaving a sweet finish (2.5).

WHITE CANOE is a light and refreshing American wheat, focusing on the wheaty tang the ingredient provides (3.5). **CREAM ALE** has a stone fruit and garden greenery nose with a core of toasted barley grain (3). **PUMPKIN PIE ALE** has a range of pie spice character leaning toward barky cinnamon and a hint of woody hop above a straight-ahead barley sugar body (3). **HENNEPIN STOUT**, named for the first European to write about the falls, is a very dark stout with lightly smoky roast character and accents of chicory and anisette (3.5).

NIAGARA COLLEGE TEACHING BREWERY

nc **Teaching Brewery**
AT NIAGARA COLLEGE

📍 135 Taylor Road, Niagara-on-the-Lake

📞 (905) 641-2252 x 4099

🐦 @NCTBrewery

🌐 firstdraft.ca

🕐 Summer: daily 10a.m.–6p.m.
Winter: Mon–Fri 11a.m.–5p.m., Sat 10a.m.–5p.m., Sun 11a.m.–5p.m.

The NCTB is likely the most influential brewery in Ontario at the moment, given that their primary product is not beer but graduating brewers. The teaching brewery, ably headed since 2010 by Jon Downing (himself with a brewing pedigree stretching back to the opening of Ontario's first brewpub in 1985), is staffed by students with varying levels of experience and ability. As the goal of the program is to transform students into professionals with hands-on brewing experience, the quality of the standard beers can differ slightly from batch to batch. The real highlight here is the ability to taste some of the over 250 beers designed by the students each year before they are employed by breweries across the province, as well as to taste those designed by Downing himself. There is a reason the school won Best Brewing Program in North America at the U.S. Open Beer Championship in 2016.

As of this year, the NCTB's offerings have mostly been rebranded into the brightly coloured, academically themed Beer 101 series. This is meant to impart both students and beer drinkers with the understanding of classic styles of beer from across the world, and it might teach you a little about brewing geography. This effort has been assisted by a facility expansion and the enlargement of the brewing and instruction staff.

———

For the purposes of this entry, all beers listed are part of the 101 series except for the final listing. **WHEAT** falls somewhere between a hefeweizen and a kristalweizen in character, with a slightly clovey nose and a lasting sweetness in body (3). **LAGER** is a European/North American hybrid with Canadian malt and German hops. There is a slight souring yeast character in the highly carbonated body (2.5). **PALE ALE** is in the Burton-on-Trent style, with apple and pear esters up front and a lightly chewy biscuity body with complementary bitterness (3.5). **STOUT** has a smooth creamy body with a solid roast character (4), while the **IPA** is a contemporary Vermont style with a big fruity nose of orange and apricot and a fairly light bitterness (4). The

STRONG ALE, full of nuts and toffee on the palate, is more of a northern English expression of the style (3.5).

Their most commercially successful beer thus far has been **1812 BUTLER'S BITTER**, which balances toasted malt with subtle floral aromas (3).

NIAGARA OAST HOUSE BREWERS

📍 2017 Niagara Stone Road,
   Niagara-on-the-Lake

📞 (289) 868-9627

🐦 @OastHouseBeer

🌐 oasthousebrewers.ca

🕐 Public tours and tastings Sat–Sun 11:30a.m. and 3:30p.m.
   Patio open on summer evenings.

🛒 Mon–Thu 10a.m.–5p.m., Fri 10a.m.–12a.m., Sat 10a.m.–7p.m.,
   Sun 10a.m.–6p.m.

Situated among vineyards on the way into the village of
Niagara-on-the-Lake, Niagara Oast House is an instance of
geography dictating the character of a brewery. The brewery,
housed in a bright red barn, crafts beers in the Belgian style
and captures the farm-to-table ethos that the Niagara
Peninsula has come to embody in recent years. An expansion
of the brewery in 2014 created more fermentation space and
room for barrel aging. An immaculate taproom clad in barn
board, and the Hayloft, a special-event space for live music
and the occasional wedding reception, were also added at this
time. The brewery expanded their patio in 2016, creating an

ideal stop for travellers through wine country looking for refreshment. The terrace overlooks row upon row of grape vines and a small hop trellis, which provides a small amount of Oast's annual volume.

———

Year-round offerings include **SAISON**, a spritzy, bottle-conditioned affair with a bright lemon–drop character and a slightly soapy, herbal accent. It has improved vastly since its introduction (4). **BIERE DE GARDE** features a loamy, earthy approach with dried berry and fruit notes in the mid-palate (3.5). **BARN RAISER** is a hybrid pale ale with citrus, orchard fruit, and lychee and a full, toasted malt mouthfeel (3.5).

Occasional specialties include the standout quaffer **OOST INDIE BIER**, a rare interpretation of a Dutch koyt with an aroma of steel-cut oatmeal and a lightly fruity herbal character (4); **BIERE DE MARS,** which runs sweet and sour, with dried fruits and vanilla playing off a souring grain character with touches of vanilla and yogurt on the way to a tart finish (3); and **KONNICHIWA PEACHES**, a firm and fruity oak–aged hefeweizen that uses locally grown peaches to fantastic effect (4). **DUNKEL** is a straightforward version of the German favourite that snuck in among a more esoteric lineup, with a full malt body accented by chocolate, molasses, raisin, and plum (4). **OL' FARMER BROWN'S DARK-ASS**

ALE is a brown ale aged in a cabernet franc barrel and refermented with Brettanomyces. Red fruit and chocolate meet in the mid-palate on the way to a bone dry finish that displays grape must retronasally (3.5).

NICKEL BROOK BREWING COMPANY

NICKEL BROOK
TRADE **BREWING** MARK
C°

📍 864 Drury Lane, Burlington

📞 (905) 681-2739

🐦 @NickelBrookBeer

🌐 nickelbrook.com

🕐 Mon–Tue 11a.m.–6p.m., Wed–Fri 11a.m.–9p.m., Sat 9a.m.–5p.m., Sun 12p.m.–4p.m.

Nickel Brook originally came into existence in 2005, intending to be an impressive addition to Better Bitters Brewing Company, a brew-on-premises business that brothers John and Peter Romano have been operating since 1991. Named after John's children, Nicholas and Brooke, the brewery began thriving on its own almost immediately, with several award-winning beers hitting the market.

Popular success for Nickel Brook began in early 2010, when Ryan Morrow became brewmaster after spending four years climbing the ranks. Since then, Morrow has been providing unique and often critically celebrated beers to the public. This embrace of innovation is highlighted by a rebranding effort implemented to more

ONTARIO CRAFT BREWERIES

accurately reflect Nickel Brook's modern approach to brewing.

Much of Nickel Brook's volume is produced by Morrow, who does double duty as brewer for Collective Arts, at Arts & Science Brewing in Hamilton, where the two breweries share a space. In 2016 the original Burlington location was relaunched as the Funk Lab, a space devoted to brewing funky, sour beers with rare or wild yeast strains. Through the work in the Funk Lab, Nickel Brook has been able to create a number of one-off special beers alongside some very interesting year-round offerings.

———

CAUSE & EFFECT BLONDE contains a lot of citrus, backed up with hints of honey, ginger, and flowers (3). **CONTINENTAL DRIFT** hits tropical notes nicely, with a honeydew melon twirl midway, finishing on distinct notes of pine (4). **NAUGHTY NEIGHBOUR** is an American pale ale with a crisp and refreshing mouthfeel, and grapefruit zest, orange, pineapple, and honey notes (4). **HEAD STOCK** is a rather high ABV IPA at 7%, containing flavours of mango, lychee, lemon, red grapefruit, and pine, with a slight caramel flavour (4.5). **EQUILIBRIUM ESB** has a lot of sweet bready notes and sticky toffee, reminiscent of bread pudding with a citrusy bitterness toward the end (3.5). **OLD KENTUCKY BASTARD** is a bourbon barrel aged variation of the brewery's Bolshevik Bastard imperial stout and arguably the most popular of the bastards, with 2015's version effectively being Ontario's answer to Goose Island's Bourbon County Stout. Deep and boozy, it has hints of rich espresso and creamy vanilla with a milk chocolate sweetness in the finish (5).

The first year-round offering from the Funk Lab, **UNCOMMON ELEMENT**, is a brett pale ale that is best sipped on over time, for as the beer warms slightly, flavours of mango, plum, pear, pineapple, and dark cherry blossom out (4.5). **RASPBERRY ÜBER BERLINER STYLE WEISSE**, made with Ontario raspberries and a sour German wheat beer base, is an explosion of raspberry (4).

NITA BEER COMPANY

📍 190 Colonnade Road, Unit 17, Ottawa

📞 (613) 688-2337

🐦 @nitabeerco

🌐 nitabeer.com

🕐 Wed–Fri 11:30a.m.–7p.m., Sat 11a.m.–5p.m.

Situated in a Nepean industrial park, the Nita Beer Company is named for its founder and chief beer officer, Andy Nita. Beginning production in January 2015, the brewery is a DIY affair with most of the work done by the seven investors in the business, all of whom come from technical professions. The event space at the front of the building is clad in barn-board from a structure they personally demolished, and the beer labels utilize some of the tremendous talent of local artists of the area.

———

TEN12 is a lightly floral, slightly berry-sweet blonde ale, accessible to mainstream beer drinkers (2.5). **PERFECTUM** is a dry stout that takes on a heavy cocoa and dark-roast character to complement its thick, chewy body (3). **EL HEFE** is a lightly

THE ONTARIO CRAFT BEER GUIDE

tangy hefeweizen, with accents of banana, vanilla, and matchstick (3). **OPA** is a heavily herbal take on the IPA that is slightly overbalanced by malt sweetness (3). **LONE WOLF MCALE** is a pale ale with a healthy dose of raw ginger and caramel (3). **5 FINGERS BROWN ALE** is a pretty solid take on the style, with toffee and deep roasted flavours in a quick finish (3).

NORSE BREWERY

📍 11 Ritchie Drive, Nobel

📞 (705) 345-0274

🐦 @Norsebrewery

🌐 norsebrewery.com

🕐 Tue–Sat 10a.m.–6p.m. Sun 10a.m.–3p.m.

Having opened at the end of November 2016 just north of Parry Sound, Norse Brewery is completely run by the Rogozhkin family. The idea came to form a brewery in 2012 and, after settling on Seguin for a home, the family got to work acquiring a 20-BBL facility and spending nearly a year perfecting a recipe that was up to their standard. While several brewers may scoff at such caution, the practicality has clearly paid off in this small brewery. The beer itself, inspired partly by the drinks the family enjoyed in their travels to such places as the Czech Republic, Germany, and the U.K., are doing quite well locally, with some bottles available wrapped in a classic rope puzzle, which adds an element of fun.

The mix of a shared family passion, forward and practical thinking in terms of development, and unique takes on simple styles will no doubt make Norse's retail space a must-visit.

—

NORSE ALE UNFILTERED, the brewery's debut beer, is a dark ale with a Belgian/Scottish influence and a complex malt character. It's rather light bodied, with slight cocoa up front that moves into coffee, which sticks around after the crisp, refreshing finish (3.5). **NORSE ALE RED** has delicate caramel and molasses notes but a significant flavour of honey that makes it stand out (4).

NORTHERN SUPERIOR BREWING COMPANY

📍 50 Pim Street, Sault Ste. Marie

📞 (705) 450-5468

🐦 @northernsuperio

🌐 northernsuperior.org

🕐 Wed–Sat 3p.m.–8p.m.

Many folks from northern Ontario get a touch nostalgic when Northern Breweries is mentioned, and for good reason. For nearly one hundred years they were a dominating force in the region, with locations in such places as Sudbury, Timmins, and Sault Ste. Marie. Northern Superior Brewing opened with the intent of educating and following in the footsteps of the northern Ontario giant, often consulting with former brewers of the now-closed brewery and creating beers modelled on their releases. After three years of planning, the brewery finally opened in a 3,200-square-foot retail space by the waterfront.

The brewery's flagship, **NORTHERN SUPERIOR LAGER**, is an American-style amber lager with a slight jab of bitterness up front followed by notes of caramel (NR).

NORTHUMBERLAND HILLS BREWERY

- 📍 1024 Division Street, Cobourg
- 📞 (289) 435-2004
- 🐦 @TheNHBbrewpot
- 🌐 nhb.beer
- 🕐 Wed–Sat 12p.m.–6p.m.

Located close to the 401 in Cobourg, Northumberland Hills is the result of fifteen years of home-brewing on the part of brewer and co-owner Rick Bailey. Taking inspiration from Whitby's 5 Paddles, this nanobrewery has aimed not for a flagship brand but for a variety of styles over the course of its first year of operation. The brewery exudes a DIY ethos, from its carefully organized and scrupulously clean brew-house to its repurposed flat-bottomed wine fermenters. Northumberland Hills may lay claim to the province's coolest delivery vehicle, with its recently repurposed El Camino.

———

The beer for sale at their retail store changes frequently, but these brands are reliably available. **SUPER CONTINENTAL** is a malty take on the Ontario pale ale, with a significant orange

THE ONTARIO CRAFT BEER GUIDE

394

and pine aroma well balanced by caramel and chocolate malts (3.5). **KODIAKS LACROSSE LAGER**, inspired by the local team, is an American adjunct lager with a gentle barley and cooked-rice body and a hit of lemony hop just mild enough to let you know it's there (3.5). **PROJECT 22** is a dark lager, light in body for a dunkel, with a small amount of raisin and bready crumb (3). **MK. X** is a brown ale in the southern English style, somewhat thin bodied, but with aromas of fruit-cake, vanilla, and a wisp of smoky dark roast coffee (3).

NORTHWINDS
BREWERY
LIMITED

📍 499 First Street, Collingwood

📞 705-293-6666

🐦 @Northwindsbeer

🌐 northwindsbrewery.com

🕐 Mon–Tue 11:45a.m.–10p.m., Wed–Thu 11:45a.m.–11p.m.,
Fri–Sat 11:45a.m.–12a.m., Sun 11:45a.m.–10p.m.

Collingwood's first brewpub, Northwinds, succeeds in equal parts because of the strengths of both kitchen and brewery. Head chef Travis Barron, late of Oliver & Bonacini's Blue Mountain location, oversees a dining room that proudly displays the locations of local food suppliers on an outsize map. The menu combines detail and rusticity; farm-to-table ethos and beer-friendly favourites integrate seamlessly, as in the case of their housemade chicharron. Northwinds also enjoys a reputation for having some of the best barbecue in the region.

All of the servers at Northwinds are trained through the Cicerone program and have attained the rank of Certified Beer Server. This fact ensures that guests will always be shown brewer Bryan Egan's work in its best light. Egan's tenure, beginning in late 2015, has seen the lineup of core offerings alter gradually, including some impressive new brews in the fourteen-tap rotation. This activity comes at a point in time when Northwinds is transitioning to include a second location in the Blue Mountain Village (which ought to be open for spring 2017).

———

WEE WILLI WINKELS is the local bestseller, a light German-style helles with melon and candied berry notes in among light grain (2.5). **THREE STAGE XTRA PALE ALE** is a lightly bitter blonde ale with honeyed malt presence and apricot highlights (3), while **ROOSTER TAIL AMERICAN PALE WHEAT** features a bright burst of clementine from an Amarillo dry hop before falling away toward the finish (3.5). **CANNONBALL BLACK SAISON** delivers a clever twist on the farmhouse ale, as a core of dark malt roast runs through its centre without becoming cumbersome (3.5). **GATEKEEPER BELGIAN IPA** is an assertive take on the concept, with bright Southern California–citrus and tropical-fruit hopping and a hint of astringency (3).

Newer offerings include **LOST CABIN VIENNA LAGER**, a heavily nutty version of the style with a pronounced sweetness (3), and a revamped **HACKY SACK KETTLE SOUR,** which features tart raspberry and blackberry and a sharp acidic kick from a *lactobacillus* blend (4). Last but not least, the **ANNIVERSARY BLONDE STOUT** packs cocoa, coffee, and a hint of sweetness into a velvet-textured blonde beer, a truly creative oddity (4).

OLD CREDIT BREWING COMPANY

 6 Queen Street W, Port Credit

 (905) 271-9888

 @OldCreditBrew

 oldcreditbrewing.com

 Tours available daily. Book groups larger than four in advance.

Mon 1p.m.–7p.m., Tue–Sat 10a.m.–7p.m., Sun 12p.m.–5p.m.

Founded in 1994, Old Credit are situated in Mississauga next to the mouth of the Credit River and owes their nautical theme to the presence of nearby Snug Harbour. The brewery occupies the original site of the first-wave craft brewery Conner's. The original brewmaster, Orrin Besco, had been a Molson employee for fifteen years prior to the advent of Old Credit and formulated the recipes, which have not changed substantially these two decades. The brewery employs an interesting technique after fermentation. Beer is held for eight weeks of maturation at -3.5 Celsius, a process which they refer to as "ice-aging."

_____

PALE PILSNER has a malt and honey aroma with a light floral hop and a corny mid-palate that leads to slight bitterness (2). **AMBER ALE** is Grape-Nut and granola throughout its light body, with a slight herbal tang on the finish (2). **HOLIDAY HONEY** is in the honey brown style and has a floral aroma, with a thin body and hints of chocolate and toasted bread that disappear on the finish (2.5).

OLD FLAME BREWING COMPANY

 135 Perry Street, Port Perry

 (289) 485-2739

 @OldFlameBrewery

🌐 oldflamebrewingco.ca

🕐 Tours Tue—Fri 12p.m., 2p.m., 4p.m., Sat 2p.m., 4p.m., Sun 12p.m.

🛒 Mon 11a.m.—6p.m., Tue—Sat 11a.m.—9p.m., Sun 11a.m.—6p.m.

Located a mere block from Lake Scugog, Old Flame has helped Port Perry reclaim some of its heritage. The 130-year-old building that houses the brewery was originally the Ontario Carriage Works, but more recently it spent a significant amount of time as an LCBO outlet. The 2013 renovations have restored the building's original brick façade, which features carriage windows. The brewery has a 15-hL brewhouse manned by Niagara College graduate Scott Pautler and a brewery store that's open seven days a week. Featuring a thematic motif of lost romantic love, Old Flame is about drinking to remember rather than drinking to forget.

———

The year-round selections from Old Flame are all lower-alcohol-style lagers, while the Brewer's Discretion series allows for experimentation in other directions. **BLONDE** is a helles–style lager with a soft grain mouthfeel, a whiff of sulfur, and a vinous, herbal hop character that ends abruptly (3). **RED** is a candy-apple-coloured Vienna lager that leans malt-heavy for the style, with notes of toffee, raisin, and chocolate complementing a slightly coppery hop bite (3.5). **BRUNETTE** is the star of the show, with toasted grain and bittersweet chocolate riding the roundness of a creamy mouthfeel (4). **DIRTY BLONDE** is in the kellerbier style, an unfiltered lager with a lightly bready malt character and floral herbal hopping that has a pleasantly lingering bitter finish (3.5).

OLD TOMORROW BEER

📞 (416) 792-6553

🐦 @OldTomorrowBeer

🌐 oldtomorrow.com

Founded by the Toronto-based mother-and-son team Pat and Ian MacDonald and assisted by consulting brewer Jamie Mistry, Old Tomorrow is a contract brand that leans heavily on Canadian history for their appeal — their bottles are emblazoned with the silhouette of John A. Macdonald. Old Tomorrow is brewed at Big Rig in Ottawa.

Offering perhaps the most variety of any of Ontario's contract brewers, Old Tomorrow maintains a significant presence at festivals, frequently demonstrating many of the recipes found on their website. Credit is certainly deserved for the dedication to continued discovery of culinary applications for their beer. The authors recommend the Maple, Cheese, and Bacon Dip.

———

The core beer is billed as a Canadian pale ale and features a small amount of spicy character from the Canadian rye that is used as part of the grist. **ORIGINAL CANADIAN PALE ALE** has a soap and pepper aroma with a spicy citrus mid-palate and a dry finish (3). **MONTY'S GOLDEN RYED ALE**, a collaboration with *Amazing Race Canada* host and Olympian Jon Montgomery, takes on the flavour of rye whisky and oak. Rye spice and orange zest are highlights on the nose but are encased on the palate by the deep woody character, lingering after the swallow (3.5). **TRACK 85 LAGERED ALE** is perhaps light for the altbier that it claims to be, but it possesses a nutty barley and pear aroma that follows on to a spicy, practically leathery mid-palate (3.5). **HONEY GINGER SHANDY** fulfills its boast of containing both ingredients, but in the process leans more toward the territory of an herbal soft drink than a traditionally balanced shandy (2.5).

THE OLDE STONE BREWING COMPANY

📍 380 George Street N, Peterborough

📞 (705) 745-0495

🐦 @OldeStoneBrew

🌐 oldestone.ca

🕐 Mon–Thu 11:30a.m.–12a.m., Fri–Sat 11:30a.m.–1a.m., Sun 12p.m.–12a.m.

Founded in 1996, the Olde Stone brewery actually caters to two separate on-premise restaurants: the Olde Stone Brewpub, which specializes in typical pub fare, and Hot Belly Mama's, a Cajun-inspired restaurant. Until 2015, the brewer was Doug Warren, who started with Upper Canada in Toronto, but the duty has been assumed by Aaron O'Neill, who was previously the assistant brewer. What has not changed are the recipes brewed in the basement of the building, all of which use whole cone hops.

The brewpub reflects Peterborough's Irish heritage and displays a tasteful minimalist appearance of dark wood, exposed brick, and high ceilings, without garish branding. A cozy elevated snug in the middle of the room provides a quiet space for small groups. The kitchen makes the majority of the food items from scratch, including house-made beer pickles and stout mustard. Seasonal beers are brewed at the brewer's discretion, and the cask rotates depending on what's available.

————

RED FIFE is an American wheat beer that uses Red Fife wheat (originally developed as a crop near Peterborough) as a specialty ingredient. Its aroma resembles nothing so much as a wheat cracker with a heavy dash of black pepper. The body is light, dry, and refreshing (4). **PICKWICK'S BEST BITTER** is a biscuity, cookieish take on a Yorkshire bitter, with an earthy, spicy hop aroma and appropriate lightly buttery mouthfeel (4). **WILDE OLDE ALE** has a light coffee aroma with a touch of raisin and plum brightened up by mild pine bitterness (3). **OR DUBH** is a dry Irish stout served on a nitro tap. The whole cone hops are noticeable here, lending a round spiciness to the body, which is full of coffee, chocolate, and lightly smoky roast (4).

ORANGE SNAIL BREWERS

📍 295 Alliance Road, Unit 16, Milton

📞 (289) 270-1680

🐦 @OrangeSnailBrew

🌐 orangesnailbrewers.ca

🕐 Wed 12p.m.–5p.m., Thu–Fri 11a.m.–9p.m., Sat 11a.m.–6 p.m.,
Sun 12p.m.–4p.m.

Located in a small industrial unit, and visible due to the words CRAFT BEER chalked in foot-high letters on the wall outside the taproom, Orange Snail is the first brewery based near Milton in over a hundred years. The brewers are mindful not only of their heritage but also of their place in the community. Black-and-white pictures of the previous brewery are featured on the walls of the gift shop, and all of the beers in their regular lineup are named for landmarks and personages from the Milton area. Currently, they are working with a 3-BBL system and fermenting in plastic equipment in temperature-controlled cold rooms; however, demand for their beer locally suggests that they will shortly be forced to look into a larger facility.

IRON PIG PALE ALE is moderately sweet, with a combination of Hallertau and Cascade hops that create a pithy, refreshing orange and spice character (3). **RATTLE 'N' NEMO**, named for two local conservation areas, is halfway between an amber ale and an Irish red ale. The balance and depth of chocolate and toffee-malt notes with piney Cascade shows good judgment (3.5). **16 JASPER IPA** is an American-style IPA that begins with a Douglas fir sting in the aroma and follows on with a lightly fruity minerality before crashing into a wall of berry bitterness (3.5).

OUTLAW BREW COMPANY

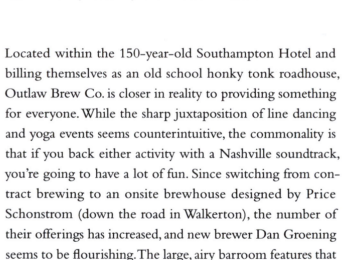

📍 196 High Street, Southampton

📞 (519) 797-1515

🐦 @outlawbrew

🌐 outlawbrewco.ca

🕐 Hours vary seasonally. Check website for details.

Located within the 150-year-old Southampton Hotel and billing themselves as an old school honky tonk roadhouse, Outlaw Brew Co. is closer in reality to providing something for everyone. While the sharp juxtaposition of line dancing and yoga events seems counterintuitive, the commonality is that if you back either activity with a Nashville soundtrack, you're going to have a lot of fun. Since switching from contract brewing to an onsite brewhouse designed by Price Schonstrom (down the road in Walkerton), the number of their offerings has increased, and new brewer Dan Groening seems to be flourishing. The large, airy barroom features that high-ceilinged Ontario tavern feel, a standard menu of pub favourites, and a games room with pool and Buck Hunter.

———

BRONCO COPPER ALE delivers a medium toasted malt character with a slightly floral, coppery hop bitterness and a moreish finish (3). **21 LAGERED ALE** has an apple and peach nose that leads into a semisweet creamy body with a jagged sting of bitterness (2.5). **SOUTHERN LASS** is a blonde ale with heather tips and local wildflower honey, and it features an apricot and roadside grass nose through its sweet body (3.5). **2 MOON JUNCTION BLUEBEERY WHEAT** uses organic blueberry juice in order to bolster a wheat body with subtle sweetness and tartness (2.5). **BANDIT DARK** is a lightly smoky old school dark ale that leans right into chocolate and coffee (3). **THE SHERIFF IPA** is sweet for the style but makes up for that with a cartoonishly bright fresh-squeezed orange presence (3).

OUTSPOKEN BREWING

📍 350 Queen Street E, Sault Ste. Marie

📞 (705) 206-2858

🐦 @OutSpokenBrew

🌐 outspokenbrewing.com

🕐 Thu 1p.m.–7p.m., Fri 1p.m.–9p.m., Sat 1p.m.–7p.m.

Opened in 2014, OutSpoken Brewing is the first operating brewery in Sault Ste. Marie since the famous Northern Breweries closed in 2006. For over two years, partners Vaughn Alexander and Graham Atkinson have been cutting through red tape and restoring the eighty-year-old building's original elements, creating a rustic, historical feel. Their opening is one of several examples of the rise of good beer in northern Ontario.

———

OutSpoken's flagship is **RABBIT'S FOOT IPA**. This warming ale has a spicy tangerine and pine bitterness blending with rich caramel (3). **ANVIL RED ALE** has deep caramel with dark fruits and a slightly bready mouthfeel (2.5). A notable seasonal is **FIRESTOKER PUMPKIN SPICE ALE** for autumn. Naturally, pumpkin pie spices provide the main flavour here. The brew has a dry mouthfeel and a somewhat clean finish (2.5).

PARSONS BREWING COMPANY

📍 876 County Road 49, Picton

📞 (613) 929-3789

🐦 @parsonsbrewing

🌐 parsonsbrewing.com

🕐 Fri–Sun 11a.m.–6p.m.

Located just off County Road 49 in Prince Edward County, Chris and Samantha Parsons's brewery has a lot going for it that makes them stand out. There's Indy, the bernese mountain dog that acts as official greeter when you pull up to the driveway. There's the beautiful sunlit bottle shop and event space with a 180-year history as a blacksmith shop and, fittingly, a parsonage. And there's also the coffee beans on sale, grown by Samantha's father, Grandpa Miguel's farm in Guatemala. Indeed, it's interesting to see so much history and deep geographic and family roots in a brewery that only opened in the fall of 2016.

Chris and Samantha, who originally came from the banking and marketing worlds, have worked hard to make the brewery as locally focused as possible, using nearby resources from Barn Owl Malt to locally carved tap handles from the Red Barns nearby. Unsurprisingly, the authentic local focus has been a huge appeal to the folks within the county. The demand is so high that the family has found themselves making more deliveries than they thought they would in their bright orange 1972 Volkswagen Westfalia. For now, the Parsons's focus is to keep up with demand while making the space ready to be a tied-house brewery, serving local food and playing host to events. Additionally, staying true to the County's main export, the brewery is set on a small estate vineyard with pinot and Chardonnay grapes, which the family plans to cultivate for a house wine.

———

WESTY PALE ALE is the brewery's flagship, named in tribute to their van. Grapefruit notes are prominent throughout, with a slight hit of orange rind and a sharp, slightly abrupt finish (3.5). **CRUSHABLE PILSNER** is in the German style, with sweet biscuit character and a dry finish (3.5). **GRANDPA MIGUEL'S COFFEE STOUT**, made with the family's Guatemalan beans, is rather light in colour but full of dark flavours of espresso, rich cocoa, and dark cherry (4).

PEPPERWOOD BREWERY & CATERING

BREWERY & CATERING

📍 1455 Lakeshore Road, Burlington

📞 (905) 333-6999

🐦 @pepperwoodgroup

🌐 pepperwood.on.ca

🕐 Mon—Thu 11:30a.m.—10p.m., Fri 11:30a.m.—1a.m., Sat 10:30a.m.—1a.m., Sun 10:30a.m.—10p.m.

With the space living previous lives as Suds International Brewpub and one of the Luxembourg chains before its current resident, Pepperwood had a small selection of beers that was greatly improved on in 2000, when new offerings were conceived and brewed in-house by Paul Dickey before he left in 2009 to start Cheshire Valley. Along with its beers, the bistro also developed a fine dining atmosphere offering a selection of tantalizing dishes and a brunch experience that has made the establishment famous city-wide. After a long hiatus from brewing, Pepperwood began putting focus on its house beers in recent years, using its onsite facility to brew and making slight adjustments to the recipes while still retaining the original concepts of Paul Dickey's beers.

MONKEY BROWN ALE has a deceptively thin mouthfeel when compared to the intense roasted grain character the aroma advertises (3). **PEPPERWOOD PALE ALE** is a very well-balanced beer, featuring lovely hints of mango, pineapple, and lemon zest, with a roasted malt profile evening out in a dry finish (3). The **PEPPERWOOD RED ALE** has a slight nutty caramel flavour, with a quick dry note in the end leading to a rather clean finish (2.5). The **PEPPERWOOD CREAM ALE** has a candy-like aroma that makes way for a creamy sweet mouthfeel with a slight earthy bitter finish (2.5). Finally, the **FRAMBOISE** showcases raspberry notes, even finishing off with the fruit's characteristic dryness (3).

PERTH BREWERY

📍 121 Dufferin Street,
   Highway 7, Perth
📞 (613) 264-1087
🐦 @PerthBrewery
🌐 perthbrewery.ca
🕐 Mon—Thu 9a.m.–7p.m., Fri 9a.m.–8p.m., Sat 9a.m.–5p.m.,
   Sun 12p.m.–4p.m.

Started in 1993 during the brew-on-premises craze that gripped the province, Perth Brewery made the transition to brewing commercially in late 2013. It is for this reason that the facility still allows customers to package their own beer in cans and wine in bottles. The more important story here is the size and speed of the transition they have made. During the summer, the busiest season in the beer industry, the brewery has twenty full-time employees. Their 15-BBL brewhouse has allowed them to increase their volume significantly, and new fermenters installed in the spring of 2015 allow for additional variety in terms of beer styles offered. A canning line added even more recently has helped increase the consistency and variety of the brews available through their retail

ONTARIO CRAFT BREWERIES

store. The taproom has also been remodelled with a twenty-five-foot granite bar, allowing visitors to sample their wares in a more comfortable environment.

Although they do not advertise it on their packaging, Perth Brewery uses a product called Brewer's Clarex as part of their filtration regime. A product which denatures gluten, Brewer's Clarex guarantees that any beer produced by the brewery will be reduced in gluten content below 10 PPM, well below guidelines for gluten-free diets in Canada. This means that Perth brews the widest selection of reduced gluten beer styles in Ontario, a fact that will bring joy to sufferers of gluten intolerance looking for something other than a light commercial lager.

———

OH CANADA MAPLE ALE comes across as banana pecan pancakes drenched in syrup, both in aroma and on the palate (2.5). **BONFIRE BLACK LAGER** has a waft of beechwood smoke across the nose, followed by dark rye bread, bitter chocolate, and an off-dry finish in the throat with a hint of ash (3.5). **EASY AMBER** has a light toffee malt sweetness that fills in around the edges of a relatively sweet body (2.5). **EURO PILSNER** is a good example of the style, with a properly sharp grass-and-weed herbal bitterness supported by a lightly sweet mid-palate and mildly sulfurous yeast character (3.5).

121 LAGER falls closest to a commercial American lager, with a light orchard fruit and corny grain nose and a slightly drying finish (3). **BACK 9 LAGERED ALE** is a good example of a cream ale, with notes of peaches and cream in the aroma before a fairly full body (3.5). **MOCHA STOUT** has coffee, roast, and a touch of lactose sweetness, representing the mocha concept nicely (3.5). **HOPSIDE IPA** is a straightforward Pacific Northwest IPA of the old school, striking immediately out for a pine forest. Potentially the best gluten-reduced IPA in Canada (4).

PINT PURSUITS BREWING COMPANY

📞 (289) 776-6374

🐦 @pintpursuits

🌐 pintpursuits.com

After a long period of time creating test batches of beer on his 50-litre home-brewing system, brewer Matt Cummings teamed up with his business-savvy uncle Larry Titchner to found Pint Pursuits. Cummings, who fell in love with the simple-done-well styles of Germany when he was studying there, aims to make beers that pay tribute to the old styles many Ontario beer drinkers love while also adding a personal twist to set them apart. For the time being they are contracting out of Wellington Brewery in Guelph while they scout for their own physical location in Toronto.

———

Pint Pursuit's first commercial offering, **LORD OF LUPULIN**, came out late last year and is made with Vermont Ale yeast and Mandarina Bavaria, Azacca, and Centennial hops. The result is a beer with rather bright notes of lemon and grapefruit peel, with an astringent grain character in the end (2.5).

PITSCHFORK BREWING COMPANY

 @Pitschfork

 pitschforkbrewing.com

Founded in 2015, Pitschfork is a contract brewery headquartered in midtown Toronto but brewing out of the Stratford Brewing Company. Out of the gate, owner Mike Schroeter is attempting to emulate the drinkability of the dry, crisp pilsners of the Rhineland-Palatinate, Bitburger being a prime example. Pitschfork's products are largely available in bars across the city of Toronto. At present the brewery is working on developing an LCBO presence.

———

PITSCH PERFECT PILSNER is a northern German–style pilsner with a spicy, herbal noble hop character due to the Spalter hops, although mildly metallic on the soft palate (3). **FISTFUL OF FESTBIER** is an Oktoberfest marzen with a hint of Grape-Nut aroma and a metallic hop bite (2).

PLAN B BEER WORKS

 174 St. Paul Street, St. Catharines

 (905) 688-2253

 @PlanBBeerWorks

 planbbeer.ca

 Wed–Thu 3p.m.–9p.m., Fri–Sun 2p.m.–10p.m.

The task of starting one's own brewery is fraught with unforeseen circumstances. Because of that, it's always wise to have an alternative plan in your back pocket just in case. That lesson definitely applied for founders John Coates and Neil Wood, who had originally planned their brew space to be in Pelham under the name Short Hills Brewing Co. After months of red tape and realizing some of the near insurmountable troubles that come with opening such a space, they went with Plan B and worked out a lease in downtown St. Catharines, just a short walk away from the Merchant Ale House.

The area is comfortably small, with local art adorning the walls and plenty of space for live musical shows and events throughout the year. At their tasting bar, you'll find a number of one-off brews by Coates in constant rotation and beer to go in the increasingly popular Crowler can.

For the most part Plan B will be making use of their small-batch facility and primarily brewing one-offs. **1ST WORLD LUXURY** is a blonde ale with an upfront astringency making way for notes of berry and cracker leading into the finish (2). **BREAKFAST STOUT** is rather light in body, but quite heavy in sweet chocolate and cocoa, with a tang of leather and a dry finale (2.5).

THE PUBLICAN HOUSE BREWERY

📍 300 Charlotte Street, Peterborough

📞 (705) 874-5743

🐦 @PublicanHouse

🌐 thepublicanhouse.com

🕐 Mon—Thu 11a.m.—11p.m., Fri—Sat 10a.m.—11p.m.,
   Sun 11a.m.—11p.m.

Founded in 2009, Publican House helped to fill the void left in Peterborough's local brewing scene by the purchase of Kawartha Lakes Brewing by Amsterdam Brewing in 2003. Impressively, the brewery has made an impact across the province. It gained an almost immediate presence in Toronto pubs upon opening but owes a great deal of its success to local consumption and cottagers. Publican House has been constantly expanding since its inception. The original space housed a brewery and a retail store, which has subsequently moved into the storefront next door. Further expansion in 2016 will take annual production to just under 4,000 hL annually. Plans to convert the Peterborough Arms next door into a brewpub should be complete by spring 2017, adding a second brewpub to the Peterborough area. Currently, the retail store sells cans and growlers. There is a tasting room, as well as an outdoor beer garden in pleasant weather.

———

PUB HOUSE ALE is a take on a kölsch, with meadow grasses in the aroma, a light-bodied corny grain character, and a reedy, bitter finish (3). **SQUARE NAIL PALE ALE** is a quality example of a West Coast pale ale, with pine and citrus over a light toffee malt body (4). **HENRY'S IRISH ALE**, named for nineteenth-century Peterborough brewer Henry Calcutt, is ruby in colour with a sweet, toasty malt character and very low bitterness, and is moreish and popular locally (3). **HIGH NOON** is a light, summery apricot grenade of a wheat beer, fruity and refreshing with the wispiest hint of matchstick (3.5). **EIGHT OR BETTER** falls somewhere between Belgian abbey styles, although advertised as a tripel. The esters split between pear and plum and the sweet body has a touch of spicy hop leading to a lip-smacking finish (3.5).

RADICAL ROAD BREWING CO.

📍 1177 Queen Street E, Toronto

📞 (647) 794-7909

🐦 @RadicalRoadBrew

🌐 radicalroadbrew.com

🕐 Wed–Thu 5p.m.–10p.m., Fri–Sat 12p.m.–10p.m.

🛒 Tue–Thu 11a.m.–11p.m., Fri–Sat 11a.m.–12a.m.,
   Sun 11a.m.–11p.m.

Jon Hodd and Simon Da Costa, two brewers from Etobicoke's Black Oak Brewing, announced plans to start their own label in 2013. Initially operating out of Black Oak, the two made a big and bold first impression with bottled offerings such as Canny Man, a 9.1% wee heavy beer aged for seventy-one days in Speyside Scotch whisky barrels and The Wayward Son, a 7.5% Belgian-style golden ale aged in Ontario Pinot Noir barrels. With impressive and elaborate packaging that matched their creative ambition, Radical Road's beers definitely stood out on LCBO shelves.

After a prolonged hiatus, the pair announced plans in early 2016 for their own facility, with partners Julian Holland and Steve Davis putting their respective backgrounds of sales and branding to use. In the summer of that same year, Radical Road opened the doors of their Leslieville brewpub. The small space features a beautiful rustic interior, food by chef Kyle McClure, and a bottle shop.

———

The beers on offer at Radical Road have stepped away from the original "go big or go home" ethos and are instead more on the approachable side (with an obvious creative flair). The brewery's signature beer, **SLINGSHOT CALIFORNIA COMMON**, is one of the better examples of the style, featuring a distinct coppery character that makes way for a mildly grainy and soft finish (3.5). **SHORELINE SAISON** is more in line with a hefeweizen, prominently featuring the traditional notes of banana and clove, with a slight Belgian candi swirl and a dry finish that lingers (2.5). **GO FOR BROKE KELLERBIER** has a lot of tropical fruit notes for the style with a slight note of astringency in the finish (2.5). **8 TRACK IPA** has a lot of mango backed with pine and a strong malt backbone (3.5). **YUZU PALE ALE** is one of Radical Road's more adventurous offerings, with a sharp acidity cutting into the palate and the distinct flavours of the Japanese yuzu adding a level of complexity that makes this beer stand out (4).

RAILWAY CITY BREWING COMPANY

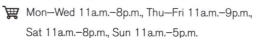

- 📍 130 Edward Street, St. Thomas
- 📞 (519) 631-1881
- 🐦 @Railwaycity
- 🌐 railwaycitybrewing.com
- 🕐 Tours Mon–Wed 4p.m.–6p.m., Thu–Fri 4p.m.–7p.m.,
  Sat 12p.m.–6p.m., Sun 12p.m.–3 p.m.
- 🛒 Mon–Wed 11a.m.–8p.m., Thu–Fri 11a.m.–9p.m.,
  Sat 11a.m.–8p.m., Sun 11a.m.–5p.m.

Founded in 2008, Railway City borrows its identity from the legacy of St. Thomas as an important rail junction in the development of the province in the nineteenth century. This even affects the name of their IPA, Dead Elephant, which commemorates the unfortunate collision between a locomotive and P.T. Barnum's star attraction, Jumbo.

The brewery has changed significantly in recent years, altering its core lineup of beers, undergoing a significant rebranding effort, and releasing special beers from their Barrel Reserve and Side Show series. The brewery also underwent a significant expansion to a new location five times the size of the original site. Because of this expansion, they have been able to produce brands for contract brewers, a business plan that has seen Railway City's reach grow significantly.

———

BLACK COAL STOUT has a medium body with notes of milk chocolate and light roast coffee (3). **DEAD ELEPHANT** has dank resin, apricot, and grassy characters jousting for dominance in the aroma, with the malt bitterness contributing more to the taste (3). **THE WITTY TRAVELLER**, a witbier that uses orange peel, coriander, white pepper, and Belgian yeast, strains to create a refreshing and lightly peppered quencher (4). **HONEY ELIXIR**, with over 20 kilos of honey added to each batch, has primary ingredient that provides a lovely sweet swirl to the roasted malt notes found within (3.5). **CREW CRAFT** is a lager that features dry biscuity notes moving toward a quick, snappy citrus bite in the finish (3). The India session lager, **EXPRESS**, is rife with lemon and orange peel, with a touch of pineapple in the dry finish (3).

Less frequent offerings include **ORANGE CREAMSIC ALE**, a beer that by all accounts tastes like an orange creamsicle, perfect for a hot and nostalgic summer day (NR); and **DOUBLE DEAD ELEPHANT**, a more gigantic variation of the original with notes of pear, apricot, and pine in an assertive bitter finish (3).

RAINHARD BREWING COMPANY

 100 Symes Road, Toronto

 (416) 763-2337

 @RainhardBrewing

 rainhardbrewing.com

 Wed–Thu 12p.m.–8p.m., Fri–Sat 12p.m.–9p.m., Sun 12p.m.–5p.m.

Tucked away in a 1940s industrial building in the Stockyards neighbourhood near St. Clair and Keele, Rainhard Brewing is one of a number of promising Toronto breweries founded in 2015. Brewer Jordan Rainhard spent the better part of a decade as a home brewer before deciding to take on the challenge of opening his own brewery.

Rainhard initially specialized in North American styles, but this became less true as the brewery entered their second year. The appearance of a number of lager-style beers has considerably diversified the brewery's range of products, and Jordan Rainhard's development as a brewer has led to less esoteric ingredients and techniques as his ability with professional-scale equipment has improved. Rainhard has doubled their production capacity in 2016 to over 1,400 hL, and during this period of expansion they have become something of a trendsetter, bringing customers to the taproom and patio and other brewers to the neighbourhood. Perhaps most impressive were a duo of medals in two of the most hotly contested categories, IPA and Double IPA, at the Canadian Brewing Awards.

―――

The core lineup includes the lightly funky farmhouse ale **TRUE GRIT**, which features crackery wheat, lemon, and pepper (3.5); **DAYWALKER VERMONT SESSION IPA**, which has changed completely this year, now lower in alcohol and featuring Conan yeast and Hallertauer Blanc and Mosaic hops, creating an aroma of grapefruit, cantaloupe, and stone fruit with a fuller body (4); **ARMED 'N CITRA AMERICAN PALE ALE**, which has changed as well, with Citra, Galaxy, and Simcoe providing mango and passionfruit on the nose (3.5); and **LAZY BONES**, a familiar and comforting American IPA with a light, sweet body and tropical fruit aroma overlying a Douglas fir bitterness (4.5). **UNFILTERED PILSNER** is chock full of woody, spicy noble hops with a peppery Saaz bite; it receives six weeks of conditioning, ensuring a round mouthfeel (4). **BROGGEN DREAMS** is a roggenbier with a sharp rye spice and citrus nose that leads to a smooth, round body (4). **HOP CONE SYNDROME** is an enormous pine and lemon double IPA that is apparently a blend of an even stronger double IPA; the candy sweet malt body just barely prevents the balance from going off the rails (4.5). **HEARTS COLLIDE**, a bourbon barrel–aged version, develops a dried cherry depth as the malt and bourbon character play off each other, resulting in a round body and warming finish (4.5).

RAMBLIN' ROAD
BREWERY FARM

📍 2970 Swimming Pool Road,
   La Salette

📞 (519) 582-1444

🐦 @RamblinRoadBeer

🌐 ramblinroad.ca

🕐 Mon—Sat 10a.m.—5p.m., Sun 11a.m.—4p.m.

As one of Ontario's few brewery farms, Ramblin' Road owes a great deal of its success to the food industry experience of owner John Picard. The Picard's Peanuts chain currently has four locations and, while Picard may have begun life as a peanut farmer, the decision to branch out into hop production in 2007 led toward the vertical integration of beer and snacks under the same roof in 2012. The fertile land and dry, loamy soil of Norfolk County is practically ideal for both peanuts and hops, making the pairing a simple one.

The brewery is a multi-purpose facility that houses not only a 25-hL brewhouse, but also a large production space for a number of flavours of potato chips. Just across the parking lot is a two-acre hop garden that provides a significant portion of the hops for Ramblin' Road's beers and helps educate visitors. The brewery draws spring water from its

ONTARIO CRAFT BREWERIES

own well, which aids in giving the beer a sense of terroir. As of 2016, the brewery has opened The Roost on the second floor, which serves a limited lunchtime menu of hamburgers and has proven to be very popular locally.

———

Ramblin' Road has six beers available. The three originals include **COUNTRY LAGER**, which is dry and crisp, with a colour that resembles orange blossom honey (2.5); **COUNTRY PILSNER**, which has a spicy noble hop character in the mid-palate and a pronounced crackery grain character ending with a dry finish (3.5); and the **COUNTRY CREAM ALE**, which is a fantastic representation of the style, showcasing the characteristics of the grains well while remaining smooth in texture and fairly light in citrusy hop bitterness (4.5).

Other beers include the **PUREBRED RED ALE**, which has a strong bready and toasted malt backbone accompanied by toffee and fruit notes in the finish (2.5); **IPA UNLEASHED**, which incorporates a rich, malty depth with strong grapefruit notes and a complex hint of blackcurrant (3); and, most interestingly, the **DAKOTA PEARL ALE (DPA)**, which is beer that has washed the Dakota Pearl potatoes that Picard's uses to make their Extreme Style Kettle Chips in its beer-bathed flavour. It pours a golden colour with a smooth, potato note that adds a creamy mouthfeel (3). Unsurprisingly, it pairs very well with the kettle chips it helped create.

REDLINE BREWHOUSE

📍 431 Bayview Drive, Units 8 & 9, Barrie

📞 (705) 881-9988

🐦 @RLBrewhouse

🌐 redlinebrewhouse.com

🕐 Tue—Wed 11a.m.—10p.m., Thurs—Fri 11a.m.—11p.m., Sat 10:30a.m.—11p.m., Sun 10:30a.m.—9p.m.

Redline Brewhouse, a family-owned pub and brewhouse, can best be described as a fully realized dream. After decades of living the corporate life, Doug Williams made the change to starting his own heavy-equipment sales and rental house, but he and his wife, Kari, often found themselves daydreaming about starting a brewery and bar, which they nicknamed "Our Bar." After some encouragement from their son, Devon, they set to work creating their huge space that has further room for expansion despite already containing a brewery, retail shop, office space, and restaurant. Staying true to what they'd dreamed of for "Our Bar," Doug and Kari have made sure that the letter *R* is prominent in all of Redline's branding, and the name of the brewery itself is a testament to the Williams family line.

Redline focuses on serving locally grown food; the beer is made by award-winning brewer Sebastian "Seb" MacIntosh, who most notably won the Cask Days IPA Challenge in 2013. The eye-catching cans of Redline beers are often seen in LCBOs and are fairly standard in many bars.

———

Redline's offerings include a variety of beers. The **5:01 GOLDEN ALE** has a refreshing mouthfeel, with peppery, orange sweetness, and a dry, biscuity finish (3.5). **CLUTCH AMERICAN PALE ALE** has hints of tropical fruit, with kiwi in the aroma and mango in the taste (4). **DOUBLE CLUTCH** double IPA has lots of grapefruit zest and mandarin oranges (2.5). **CHECK ENGINE** is an American amber ale, with bready toffee and caramel notes with a light fruity sweetness toward the end (3). **AIR RIDE IPA** has pineapple notes prominent all throughout, with a biting, bitter finish (3.5).

REFINED FOOL BREWING CO.

📍 137 Davis Street, Sarnia

📞 (519) 704-1335

🐦 @refinedfool

🌐 refinedfool.com

🕐 Mon–Thu 11a.m.–11p.m., Fri–Sat 11a.m.–12a.m.,
   Sun 11a.m.–11p.m.

🛒 Daily 11a.m.–11p.m.

Prior to Refined Fool's advent in 2013, there had not been a brewery in Sarnia for at least eighty years, and even that brewery was designed to surreptitiously provide beer to Michigan. Refined Fool is more focused on bringing craft beer to Lambton County and is one of very few breweries in Ontario that operates in a co-op ownership structure. It is the result of a group of ten friends coming together to realize their goal of opening a nanobrewery. Growth has been rapid. The brewery's lively taproom features a patio in summer and has begun to host live music. Occasional beer dinners are very well attended, with mouth-watering recipes to pair with the beers listed on their website. The playful branding, featuring a top hat and colourful stripes, renders their beer visually distinct, while the massive assortment of offerings available over the course of the year rivals any brewery in Ontario for variety. The year 2016 has seen a temporarily thwarted attempt at expansion, which clearly suggests the direction of the brewery's future.

———

POUCH ENVY, an Australian pale ale, is a very gently bitter and lightly acidic beer, presenting most of its tropical fruit character in the aroma (3.5), while **QUIET DOWN, I'M DOING CARTOGRAPHY** seems a more robustly malty take on the same beer, with much of the same pineapple character benefitting from the support of malt in the mid-palate (4). **NOBLE OAF** is an effervescent rye saison with a light, spicy body and a peppery finish that hides its higher alcohol content (4). **SUBURBAN MENACE** is an outsize American amber ale with a berryish floral character coming from the Mosaic hops playing over a toasted grain body (3.5).

    BLACKWATER resides at the high end of the breakfast stout category, with coffee from Blackwater Coffee & Tea as an assertive portion of the aroma over a chewy oatmeal body (4). **MURDER OF CROWS** is one of Ontario's best black IPAs, with roasted barley, coffee, chocolate, pine, and citrus bitterness coming through in an immense and balanced body (4.5). **ILLITERATE LIBRARIANS** is a grapefruit IPA that leans right into white grapefruit pith and stays there; a Floridian vacation in a bottle (3.5). **SHORT PIER, LONG WALK** is a double IPA that packs a punch like a pine cudgel, slightly overbalancing its caramel malt body (3.5).

RHYTHM & BREWS BREWING COMPANY

 100 Symes Road, Toronto

 (416) 268-9916

@RhythmBrewsTO

rhythmandbrews.ca

Launched at the end of January 2016, Rhythm & Brews are a contract brewery that operates around the conceit of supporting not only quality beer, but also Toronto's music scene. Brewer Andrew Byer is currently producing their beer out of Rainhard Brewing and has developed a great deal of experience as both a home brewer and a nationally ranked beer judge. While the company produces a single offering on a year-round basis, there are also a number of beers brewed collaboratively, including Never Wanna Die.P.A., made to support local rockers Diemonds.

———

VINYL TAP is a reddish-hued lager somewhere between a Mexican Vienna lager and a new world pilsner, with lemon and pepper above a medium malt body (3.5). **NEVER**

WANNA DIE pale ale is a relatively juicy classic pale ale with a pine and grapefruit character (4). **ANARCHY IN THE 6IX** is largely about mocha, with roast and chocolate character playing over a smooth, chewy body that finishes in a wisp of smoke (3.5). **SET THE WORLD ON FIRE** is a smoked cherrywood English ale that relies on woody smoke and sweet malts for its interest (3.5).

ROUGE RIVER BREWING COMPANY

ROUGE RIVER
BREWING COMPANY
MARKHAM ❖ ONTARIO

📍 50 Bullock Drive, Unit 8, Markham

📞 (905) 209-1236

🌐 rougeriverbrewingcompany.com

🕐 Thu–Fri 5p.m.–9p.m., Sat–Sun 12p.m.–6p.m.

Although it was opened to the public in the closing months of 2016, Rouge River has been a project in development since 2010. Partners Stephen Barato, Aldo Scopazzi, and Jordan Mills have been working on the premises (which used to be a brew-on-premises) for the better part of a year. Mills, the brewer, not only holds the designation of Advanced Cicerone, but is also one of a very few people to have worked previously in both brewing and marketing capacities for Mill Street. While the recipes have been in development in some cases since 2012, the focus of the brewery is on novelty. The 10-BBL system and plastic fermenters are given over to the production of pale ales and IPAs, which change with the season. The front room of the brewery houses comfortable seating and a stage for musical performances.

PLANET OF THE APAS is a straight-ahead modern American pale ale featuring Mosaic and Amarillo hops for a bouquet of apricot, pineapple, and tangerine in a lightly honeyed body that lingers bitterly (3.5). **AUTUMN PALE ALE**, included here as an example of experimentation, features Loral (or HBC 291) hops with their practically sandalwood-y spice and citrus and floral tones (3). **WINTER IPA** features a significant depth of rye spice and caramel balancing punchy bitterness with toasted bread, licorice, and a note of dark chocolate (4).

ROYAL CITY BREWING COMPANY

📍 199 Victoria Road S, Unit C8, Guelph

📞 (888) 485-2739

🐦 @RoyalCityBrew

🌐 royalcitybrew.ca

🕐 Mon 12p.m.–6p.m., Tues–Wed 12p.m.–7p.m., Thurs–Fri
12p.m.–9p.m., Sat 11a.m.–9p.m., Sun 12p.m.–5p.m.

Royal City is the project of Russell Bateman and brewmaster Cameron Fryer, two long-time friends and home brewers, both of whom have a passion for beer and an optimistic outlook in regards to the thriving scene in Guelph. Fryer is a self-professed beer geek, having first found his love of craft beer while drinking brews from Wellington Brewery during his time as a student at the University of Guelph. He gained further experience in the employ of Great Lakes Brewery in Etobicoke. After honing their skills by focusing on a core lineup of beers, they finally opened their space on Victoria Road in early summer 2014. The taproom and retail space is a notable stop for locals and visitors to Guelph, and flights of their seasonal and one-off beers are practically mandatory drinking.

The **DRY HOPPED PALE ALE** has distinct notes of citrus and pine while being backed by a subtle malt character (3). **SUFFOLK ST. SESSION ALE** is a special bitter with distinctive honey and caramel notes followed by a moderate earthy hop presence (4). The **HIBISCUS SAISON** has a sweetly floral aroma that makes its way into the taste, ending with a dash of peppercorn in the dry finish (4). **SMOKED HONEY** is a brown ale that features leather and tobacco notes accompanied by a subtle note of local honey, all tied together with a coffee finish (3). **100 STEPS STOUT** contains a smoky note blended well with light roast coffee and a ping of molasses (3).

RURBAN BREWING

📍 416 Cumberland Street, Cornwall

📞 (613) 360-0661

🐦 @RurbanBrewing

🌐 rurbanbrewing.com

🕐 Mon—Tue 1p.m.–5p.m., Wed—Thu 12p.m.–5p.m.,
Fri 12p.m.–6p.m. Sat 11a.m.–4p.m.

Before Rurban Brewing's opening in April 2016, there had not
been a brewery in Cornwall for nearly one hundred years. So
it wasn't before time when retired high school science teacher
A.J. Roraback and his wife, Karen, also a teacher, announced
plans for an upcoming brewery in 2013. The beers at Rurban
(a combination of "rural" and "urban") are brewed by A.J., previously an active member of the Ottawa-area Members of
Barleyment home-brewing club with over ten years' brewing
experience. Since its opening, the brewery has been something
of a social hub for the people of Cornwall, with folks stopping
by the welcoming taproom and retail space to sample the beers
and restock their supply.

———

PALATINE PALE ALE is distinctly sweet, with caramel notes not leaving much in the way of bitterness (2.5). **LATE AMERICAN PALE ALE** combines pine, melon, and mango with a pronounced toffee background and a lightly peppered finish (3.5). **STOPS AND GOES** is a gose-style beer with sweet ginger notes and a dry wheat finish (2.5). **NEW JOHNSTOWN'S BEST BITTER** has a candied banana character and a coppery finish (2). **19TH STRONG SCOTCH ALE** is rife with grape, plum, and a molasses backing (3). The amusingly named **MORE PORTLY THAN STOUT** is indeed more on the robust porter side of things, with a nice medium body, notes of roasted coffee and hot cocoa, and a creamy finish (3.5).

SAINT ANDRE

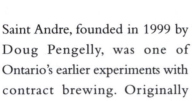

Saint Andre, founded in 1999 by Doug Pengelly, was one of Ontario's earlier experiments with contract brewing. Originally brewed at Guelph's F&M before making the transition to its current home at Cool Brewing in the early 2000s, the brand first made its debut at Toronto's Festival of Beer back when it was hosted by Fort York. Perhaps most memorable about the brand, though, was its initial method of delivery, a Citroën 2CV truck driven by Pengelly himself.

———

Although Pengelly has shifted his focus to Junction Brewing (in which he is a partner), **SAINT ANDRE VIENNA LAGER** can still be seen scattered throughout bars around Toronto and in a few select Beer Store locations. The beer contains biscuit flavours, a delicately sweet malt body, and a grassy, somewhat peppery bitter note (3.5).

SANDWICH BREWING COMPANY

📍 3230 Sandwich Street, Windsor

📞 (519) 555-1212

🐦 @SandwichBrewing

📘 Sandwich-Brewing-Co-313341135522289

Located next door to the perennially popular Sandwich Towne hot spot the Rock Bottom Bar and Grill, Sandwich Brewing is in some ways an expansion of that business. Sibling owners Nicole and Jason Sekela and brewer Scott Black have undertaken the major part of the renovation of the nineteenth-century structure that houses the brewery themselves. The result is a thoroughly modern brewery with state-of-the-art equipment that is nonetheless housed among exposed brick and beam and perfectly preserved tin ceilings. In addition to a first floor taproom, Sandwich features an upstairs gallery with a commanding view of the brewhouse. The copper-clad exterior is designed to wear over time, allowing the brewery to replicate the feel of the neighbourhood, making the entire venture something of a showpiece for visitors.

The first two offerings are, at time of writing, ready for release. They are a pale ale hopped with Amarillo (NR) and a smooth chocolate porter (NR).

SAWDUST CITY BREWING COMPANY

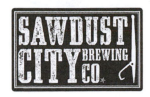

📍 397 Muskoka Road N, Gravenhurst

📞 (705) 681-1100

🐦 @sawdustcitybeer

🌐 sawdustcitybrewing.com

🕐 Daily 11a.m.–11p.m.

🛒 Daily 9a.m.–11p.m.

Sawdust City is a testament to the phrase "patience is a virtue," as it took over three years of battling red tape and overcoming logistical problems to go from brewing their beer out of Etobicoke's Black Oak to realizing their dream of running a brewery, saloon, and retail space. Now the dream is a reality, and all of it is housed in what was once a Canadian Tire in Gravenhurst. The spacious location has become a central destination in the community, being the chosen spot for parties, concerts, game nights, and gatherings for locals and tourists alike. It was also the hosting location of Funk Fest, Canada's first ever sour beer festival that attracted people from all over to the small town in order to sample some of Ontario's best sour offerings.

ONTARIO CRAFT BREWERIES

Much of Sawdust's success lies with the creativity of their offerings, which run from unique core brands for all levels to special series releases and experiments in barrel aging and wild yeast cultivation. Led by head brewer Sam Corbeil, a student of VLB in Berlin and former instructor at Niagara College's Brewmaster and Brewery Operations Management program, the skill and creativity found in the award-winning Sawdust City's beers have made the province, and northern Ontario, all the better.

————

Many of Sawdust City's beers are named after aspects of life in Gravenhurst, though the connection is often subtle. **GOLDEN BEACH PALE ALE** is a brightly flavoured beer, with notes of pineapple, passion fruit, mango, and lemon dancing around together with a slight grain note to make up a refreshingly light body (5). **LONE PINE IPA** is the beer that effectively put the brewery in the mind of the public. A very hop-forward beer — expect notes of grapefruit and pine, with a touch of malt quietly hiding (4). Its conceptual sibling, **TWIN PINES IIPA**, is a monster of orange peel citrus and resinous pine notes, with a dry finish (5). **LITTLE NORWAY PALE LAGER** is light and grassy, with a comfortable bitter character that makes a smooth landing into the finish (4.5). **SKINNY DIPPIN' STOUT** is a smooth oatmeal stout featuring notes of black coffee, chocolate, and a plum-like sweetness that ends on a nice bitter note (3.5). The cheekily named **LONG, DARK VOYAGE TO URANUS** is an imperial stout that is almost deceptive in flavour for a 9.5% ABV beer. It contains a sweet aroma and has cocoa and espresso flavours, with a rich, creamy body (4.5). **THE O.D.B.** is a much-loved imperial brett saison aged in Gamay barrels, making for a beer with a very dry, honeyed, wooden profile with distinct tart flavours (4). A Halloween collaboration with Toronto's Bar Hop, **BLOOD OF CTHULHU** is an imperial stout brewed with a maddening amount of raspberries, cranberries, and tart cherries, resulting in notes of chocolate and spiced coffee with deliciously tart notes of all three of the key ingredients (4.5).

SECOND WEDGE BREWING COMPANY

📍 14 Victoria Street, Uxbridge

📞 (905) 852-3232

🐦 @Thesecondwedge

🌐 thesecondwedge.ca

🕐 Tue–Sat: 11a.m.–9p.m., Sun 12p.m.–6p.m.

Located in Uxbridge, Second Wedge Brewing is a result of the efforts put in by husband-and-wife team Rob Garrard and Joanne Richter, who were originally granted $12,000 to lease a retail space thanks to the Uxbridge BIA's innovative "Win This Space" contest. Since announcing their opening, the pair have been overwhelmingly supported by businesses in the community. Restaurant Urban Pantry, for instance, was the first place to serve the brewery's beer and additionally deliver food to customers visiting the brewery. The building includes a fairly spacious tasting area complete with tables, bottle shop, and a beautiful outdoor patio with a herb garden adorning its borders.

Further adding excitement for folks in Uxbridge and beyond is the hiring of long-time brewer Doug Warren as brewmaster, who has over twenty-five years of experience in the industry, getting his start at the Upper Canada Brewing Company and moving on through the years to Kawartha Lakes, Church-Key, Mill Street, and Olde Stone Brewing Company, where he was brewmaster for eight years.

———

ELGIN BLONDE has a light smoky character upfront that transforms into a soothing, creamy biscuit flavour that lasts well after the finish (4). **3 ROCKS IPA**, named after a bike trail in nearby Glen Major Forest, has floral, peppery notes in the aroma and a distinct pine bitterness in its taste (3). **RAIN MAKER PORTER** has sharp coffee flavours, with a mild characteristic not unlike Latakia tobacco (3.5).

SHACKLANDS BREWING COMPANY

📍 100 Symes Road, Unit 101, Toronto
📞 (416) 763-2424
🐦 @Shacklands
🌐 shacklands.com

The road to a physical location is often a long one for contract brewers that attempt to make a go of it. This has certainly been the case with Shacklands, which began producing beer in 2012 and then underwent a brief hiatus in production in 2015 while weighing options. Brewer Jason Tremblay has a wealth of experience as a home brewer and was involved with Bar Volo's onsite House Ales brand before producing his own beer at Junction Brewing.

With the addition of partner Dave Watts, Shacklands has moved into a new home in the newly crowded Stockyards neighbourhood. As always, the focus will be on Belgian- and saison-style beers, but the transformation to physical brewery is nowhere near complete. Upgrades will continue for the foreseeable future, with an expansion from the current, partially improvised 2-hL brewhouse to a larger and more conventional set of equipment. In the meantime, the taproom has borrowed its aesthetic from the sense of found materials and ramshackle construction of the area's industrial past. Plans exist for live music, and the seating area is graced with a *Twilight Zone* pinball machine.

———

FARMHOUSE IPA develops peppery character from its Belgian yeast strain and aromas of lemon pith, peach, and lychee on the palate (3.5).

SHAWN & ED
BREWING COMPANY

📍 65 Hatt Street, Dundas
📞 (289) 238-9979
🐦 @lagershed
🌐 lagershed.com
🕐 Daily 11a.m.–7p.m.

Housed in an enormous Victorian skating rink from the 1860s, Shawn & Ed is the result of a partnership between Shawn Till and Ed Madronich. While the partners dreamed about opening a brewery a quarter century ago, it has taken this long to bring that dream to fruition. It is not as though that time has been idly spent. Madronich is one of the founders of Flat Rock Cellars in Jordan, which has just celebrated its tenth anniversary. Rob Creighton has had a long career as a brewer within Ontario, stretching back to the early days of craft beer in the province at Upper Canada in Toronto, although many newer drinkers will recall his tenure at Grand River.

Shawn & Ed focus on two separate production streams for their beer. The Lagershed series focuses on the creation of fairly easy drinking German-style lagers. The Barrelshed series is where the brewery's relationship with Flat Rock

Cellars comes to the fore; beers in this series are aged in pinot noir barrels, taking on some of that fruity, lightly acidic character during the aging process.

———

LIGHTER is an interesting new world lager featuring a tropical pineapple hop character over a body not unlike the crumb of a whole wheat loaf (3.5). **ORIGINAL** sits somewhere between helles and pilsner, with a baking dough body of honey and cracker and a mild hint of floral spice (3.5). **DARKER** is closest in style to a dunkel, with a reasonably nutty toasted–grain body that briefly features coffee and caramel notes (3.5).

BARRELSHED NO. 1, the first in a series of pinot noir barrel–aged beers, begins with a whiff of matchstick complemented by pine, orange, and light orchard fruit, which fight for dominance (2).

SHILLOW BEER COMPANY

 @ShillowBeer

🌐 shillowbeer.com

Founded in 2014 by Ben and Jamie Shillow, the real strength of this contract brewery is the amount of experience brought to the table by the husband-and-wife team. Ben Shillow spent four years as a sommelier at Toronto's Oliver and Bonacini group of restaurants, while Jamie Shillow gained experience at Bar Volo and beerbistro prior to attending Niagara College's brewing program. While their first beer was exclusive to beerbistro, they are now contracting three beers out of Niagara, Cameron's, and Common Good and have made some of those offerings available at the LCBO and selected pubs. Plans for their own physical space will begin sometime this year.

———

The beerbistro exclusive, **SASS ON THE SIDE** is an American brown ale with a lightly sweet body that is reminiscent of a chocolate chip cookie, with biscuit and cocoa notes (3). **BITTER WAITRESS** is a black IPA that lives up to its name, running from spruce branch down to the pine-tar roast of an export stout in a creamy mouthfeel (3.5). Shillow's latest offering, **BEER SNOB**, is a Belgian rye saison with plenty of spicy rye in the aroma and taste, balanced well by the twirl of Belgian candi, honey, cloves, and figs (3).

SIDE LAUNCH BREWING COMPANY

📍 200 Mountain Road, Unit 1, Collingwood

📞 (705) 293-5511

🐦 @sidelaunch

🌐 sidelaunchbrewing.com

🕐 Mon—Wed 12p.m.—6p.m., Thu—Fri 12p.m.—7p.m.,
   Sat 10a.m.—6p.m., Sun 12p.m.—5 p.m.

Despite the fact that Side Launch entered the market in May 2014, many of the beers on offer have been on the market since the early 1990s. Brewer Michael Hancock was the prime mover and shaker behind Denison's Brewing Company in downtown Toronto. The quality at Denison's was never in doubt; Prince Luitpold of Bavaria was one of their principal investors. In fact, the quality of Denison's range of beers was such that, despite the brewery being shuttered in 2003, the beer remained in high demand in Toronto and gained a cult reputation internationally. For a not insignificant period of time, Denison's Weissbier enjoyed the position of the highest-rated wheat beer in the world. Despite this, the brand bounced around as a contracted product from Mill Street to Black Oak to Cool.

The genius of Side Launch is having provided an excellent brewer with a platform to bring his products to market. If the ubiquity of Side Launch's tap handles and the number of awards received in 2016 (Best Brewery in Ontario in our first edition and Canadian Brewery of the Year at the Canadian Brewing Awards) are any indication, it is a strategy that has paid off. As of 2016, production has expanded in their glass-walled Collingwood brewery, nearly doubling the amount of fermentation space available. While the core four brands make up a significant majority of the brewery's production and will continue to do so for the foreseeable future, the rapidly expanding brewing team seem to have lent a touch of creativity to the company. Occasional seasonal releases now emerge from the brewery, nearly all of which have lived up to the quality Ontario's beer drinkers have come to expect from the brand. Some of them have been named for ships launched in the town's heyday.

————

WHEAT is a fine example of a hefeweizen that manages to balance three different yeast esters (banana, clove, and bubble gum) with a creamy mouthfeel and effervescent carbonation on the way to a tangy wheat finish (4.5). **DARK LAGER** lives in a malt mid-range where there's chocolate, but without its rich intensity; dark, dried fruit without assertive sweetness; and nutty grain verging on woodiness. A fine choice paired with barbecue (4.5). **MOUNTAIN LAGER** may be billed as a simple lager, but it's actually Ontario's finest example of a Munich helles. The soft mouthfeel and lightly bready cereal is balanced perfectly by spicy, herbal hops, creating a drinking experience that is at once both quenching and moreish (5). **PALE ALE** is on the maltier side of the American pale ale spectrum, displaying a typically English mild caramel influence to balance the resinous, citrus hop character (4).

HURONIC is a Belgian-style tripel with aromas of lemon and wildflower over a sweet, creamy body with a bitterness that is perhaps a little outsize for the style (4). **GERMANIC** is a dunkler bock that celebrates a deeply toasted spicy rye bread with gentle dried fruit notes playing through the full body (4.5).

SILVERSMITH BREWING

📍 1523 Niagara Stone Road, Niagara-on-the-Lake

📞 (905) 468-8447

🐦 @SilversmithBrew

🌐 silversmithbrewing.com

🕐 Mon–Wed 11a.m.–9p.m., Thu–Fri 11a.m.–11p.m.,
Sat 10a.m.–11p.m., Sun 10a.m.–9p.m.

Opened in 2011, Silversmith Brewing is an early figure in the current explosion of small-town breweries in Ontario. Located in a hundred-year-old church on the Niagara Stone Road and covered with ivy, Silversmith Brewing is deceptively small and picturesque. Brewing is actually carried out in an extension just off the taproom, and external fermenters stretch in a row adjoining the parking lot beside the brewery. The bar dominates the church's converted nave. Communal seating, frequent live entertainment, and a food menu curated and prepared by the Tide and Vine Oyster House mean that there is no less a congregation than there was before the conversion. The result of the clever incorporation of the building is a restful space not unlike a traditional English pub that has become equally popular with locals and tourist groups.

ONTARIO CRAFT BREWERIES

BLACK LAGER is a schwarzbier and the brewery's specialty. The espresso roast character is rounded out on the palate by a touch of brown sugar sweetness and a waft of tar (3.5). **BAVARIAN BREAKFAST WHEAT** is a banana and graham cracker affair and rather like a banoffee pie in a glass (3). **HILL 145 GOLDEN ALE** is suggestive of orchard fruit; apple and peach character lingers over sweet malt and an appropriate bitterness (3.5). **DAM BUSTER ENGLISH PALE ALE** leans into ESB territory with a touch of dank woodiness to go along with light stone fruit and nutty malt (3.5).

SKELETON PARK BREWERY

 @SkeletonPrkBeer

 skeletonpark.ca

Named for local landmark McBurney Park, which was a cemetery for the people of Kingston up until 1864, Skeleton Park's branding incorporates the theme of mortality in a playful way: a skeletal dog running, perhaps to catch a spectral Frisbee. Brewer Trevor Lehoux hopes eventually to open a physical brewery in Kingston but is temporarily producing his beer on a contract basis in Ottawa at Broadhead Brewing.

———

Their first brand, **AMBER 6.6**, is inspired partially by beers that would have been brewed in Ontario in the early nineteenth century, but at the same time reminiscent of early eighties microbrew. Malt-forward, this beer is toffee- and toast-dominant, with some small red fruit and a spicy English hop character in the mid-palate before a small, bitter finish (3).

ONTARIO CRAFT BREWERIES

465

SLEEPING GIANT BREWING COMPANY

📍 712 MacDonell Street, Thunder Bay

📞 (807) 344-5225

🐦 @sleepgiantbrew

🌐 sleepinggiantbrewing.ca

🕐 Mon—Wed 11a.m.–6p.m., Thu—Fri 11a.m.–7p.m.,
Sat 10a.m.–6p.m., Sun 12p.m.–5p.m.

Perhaps the fastest to succeed of northern Ontario's breweries, Sleeping Giant was founded in 2012 by two couples who wanted to bring better beer to the area. While the ownership structure has changed during the brewery's lifespan, Sleeping Giant has done a remarkable job in building its fiercely loyal audience, in part by instilling a sense of local pride through its use of ingredients sourced right in Thunder Bay. Owner Matt Pearson has also led the charge over the years on a much-needed expansion to match local demand. While 2015 saw the integration of an in-house canning line and merchandise such as beer-cured beef jerky, the brewery's most significant development came when they moved to a much larger location in the fall of 2016, with plans to further expand distribution.

Along with making beer, Sleeping Giant does its best to make sure that they deserve the praise of their local fan base by taking part in the Thunder Bay community. Perhaps most notable was the selling of their Northern Logger shirt, made famous by a photo shoot with typically shirtless Prime Minister Justin Trudeau, with proceeds going to the Boys & Girls Clubs of Thunder Bay.

———

NORTHERN LOGGER is billed as a kölsch-style beer, but the grassy burst of bitterness in the mid-palate, along with the distinct honeyed biscuit flavour in the finish, suggests it may be a bit bigger for the style (3.5). **360 PALE ALE** is juicy clementine marmalade with basil and bay leaf balanced out by the English-style caramel malts (3.5). **BEAVER DUCK** American pale ale has an irresistible aroma of lemon, pine, and tangerine that makes its way into the taste, followed by a crackery middle and a surprisingly neat finish (4). **SKULL ROCK STOUT** is not unlike a milk-chocolate-covered raisin, with warming cocoa notes that find its way into the finish (3.5).

SMITHAVENS BREWING COMPANY

📍 687 Rye Street, Unit 6, Peterborough

📞 (705) 743-4747

🐦 @SmithavensBrew

🌐 smithavensbrewing.ca

🕐 Mon–Wed 11a.m.–5:30p.m., Thu 11a.m.–6:30p.m.,
Fri 11a.m.–8p.m., Sat 11a.m.–7p.m.

🛒 Mon–Wed 10a.m.–5:30p.m., Thu 10a.m.–6:30p.m.,
Fri 10a.m.–8p.m., Sat 10a.m.–7p.m.

Located on the site of the old Kawartha Lakes Brewery (which was moved to Toronto after being purchased by Amsterdam in 2003), Smithavens, founded in 2014, is the most recent addition to Peterborough's brewing scene. Trained in Germany, brewer Graham Smith works in traditional European styles in order to set his brewery apart from the crowd. Special attention is given to authentic brewing techniques, which means that the wheat beers are produced in a special room with open fermenters and that all of the beers from the brewery are bottle conditioned for carbonation. The brewery's taproom and tank-view rooms lean heavily into the German alpine feel, emulating the wooden beam structure of a hunting lodge in a tasteful and under-stated way. Plans are already underway to expand the volume of the brewery to allow for additional production.

———

DUNKELWEIZEN has the aroma of moist banana bread, the dark malts cutting through wheat trailing a touch of ripe cherry and cherry stone (3.5). **HEFEWEIZEN** develops an extremely creamy texture behind an aroma of clove and mashed banana with a refreshing wheat tang (4). **KELLERBIER** is an unfiltered pale lager with a full bready malt presence and a heavier than usual lime and herbal thyme bite (3.5). **AMBER SOLACE** is somewhere between a festbier and a Vienna style, with sweet, almost-candied malt with a light bitter sting that redemptively plays through the finish (3). **BLONDE ALE**, the only ale Smithavens produces, is 7.5% and hides it well behind a swell of black pepper and orange peel on the aroma (3.5).

SOUTHPAW BEVERAGE COMPANY

📍 9 Glenellen Drive E, Toronto

📞 (416) 232-1542

🐦 @southpawbevco

🌐 southpawbev.com

Founded in late 2015, the Southpaw Beverage Company is a sinister organization, but only in the sense that it celebrates left-handedness. Both of its owners, Murray Milthorpe and Greg Valentyne, are left-handed, and that fact has come to define this contract brewery's identity. Their first (and, to date, only) offering is Heroes Blonde Lager, proceeds from which go to help charities like Wounded Warriors, which offers assistance to members of the military and first responders. The beer enjoys popularity among branches of the Royal Canadian Legion.

———

Brewed at Cool and designed by brewmaster Adrian Popowycz, **HEROES BLONDE LAGER** has a deeply nutty grain character for the style, which never quite comes together with the floral hop presence, resulting in a slightly inharmonious beer (2.5).

SPEARHEAD BREWING COMPANY

📞 (416) 907-6952

🐦 @SpearheadBeer

🌐 spearheadbeer.com

Founded in 2011, Spearhead was one of the first in a series of contract breweries, a system that has become popular in Ontario. They were also one of the first to brew out of Cool in Etobicoke on a regular basis. The factor that set Spearhead apart from the other breweries in the genre initially was the inclusion of a talented brewer. Ex-Labatt brewer Tomas Schmidt's involvement means that there are frequently experimental and one–off batches available on tap at festivals, if not at retail. Spearhead's beers are noted for their inclusion of whimsical ingredients and geographic inspiration, making a sample flight something like a world cruise.

The year 2016 was a tumultuous one for the Spearhead Brewing Company and saw the departure of founder Dimitri Van Kampen and the instatement of Josh Hayter as CEO. With that change in personnel, the company has taken a different direction. A change in packaging means that the number of available products has dwindled as Spearhead switches from six-packs of custom glass bottles to cans. This change in direction means that one of the pioneers of the contract trend will finally become a physical brewery in their own right at some point in 2017.

———

HAWAIIAN STYLE PALE ALE was the first offering from the brewery in 2011 and uses pineapple juice to emphasize the tropical fruit and citrus character that comes through on the aroma (4). **MOROCCAN BROWN ALE** is brewed with figs, dates, raisins, and cinnamon, which reinforce the dried fruit malt character that comes through in a brown ale but also creates a very sweet finish (3).

SPLIT RAIL BREWING COMPANY

MANITOULIN ISLAND

SPLIT RAIL
BREWING CO

📍 31 Water Street, Gore Bay

📞 (705) 370-8284

🐦 @SplitRailBrew

🌐 splitrailmanitoulin.com

🕐 Hours vary. Check website for updated information.

The small Manitoulin-based brewery with big ambition, Split Rail Brewing first gained notoriety in 2014 when owners Eleanor Charlton and Andrea (Andy) Smith launched a successful crowdfunding campaign to help them cover some of the costs that occur when starting up a new brewery, a dream the pair had held since 2009.

Even with their opening in 2015, Split Rail has definitely come a long way since their days of making small batches of beer in a garage with brewmaster Glen Fobes of Lakeport Brewing fame. Thanks to successful initial sales, local help, and a relationship with the famous Manitoulin Transport, Charlton and Smith have seen their dream fully realized. Their massive building is a literal stone's throw away from the Gore Bay harbour and

ONTARIO CRAFT BREWERIES

473

features a retail shop, taproom, and front door patio for a nice sit-down with a pint.

———

COPPER LAGER is rather crisp on the palate with a light to medium body. Deep, biscuity grain character dominates briefly before a short, berry-like sweetness hits at the end (3.5). **AMBER ALE** features molasses acting as a prelude to rich caramel and light earthy characteristics (3). The **HAWBERRY ALE** makes the ultimate Manitoulin beer, using the locally based hawberry as the key ingredient. Huge toffee and silky caramel notes make this beer an almost warming treat, but as the beer warms the subtle, slightly tart and earthy notes from the hawberry balance it out into a nice finish (4).

SQUARE TIMBER BREWING COMPANY

📍 800 Woito Station Road, Pembroke

📞 (613) 312-9474

🐦 @squaretimber

🌐 squaretimber.com

🕐 Fri 3p.m.–6p.m., Sat 1p.m.–4p.m.

Located in the Ottawa Valley, Square Timber was founded by Marc Bru, an avid home brewer with a family history in the beer industry. Bru has also been an active member of his local community and has helped to promote the rise of craft beer in the valley, having co-hosted the first-ever Ottawa Valley Craft Beer Festival in the autumn of 2015. His brewery, named for the square-timber industry that was instrumental in making the Ottawa Valley what it is today, officially opened its doors in the fall of 2014. The small taproom is open two days a week.

———

TIMBER CRIB PALE ALE is an American pale ale with notes of caramel and a distinctive floral hop note (NR). **BIG PINE IPA** presents heavy pine notes followed by jammy fruit sweetness (NR). **DEACON SEAT HEFEWEIZEN** features the classic notes of banana and clove familiar in the style (NR). **BELGIAN WAFFLE MAPLE QUAD** is brewed with local maple sap (NR). **CAMBOOSE DOUBLE IPA** has a large citrus character with a strong malt backbone that carries into the end (NR).

ST. MARY AXE BEER COMPANY

 @smxbeer

🌐 stmaryaxe.ca

Named after the medieval church in London, England, St. Mary Axe was founded in Toronto by two people from financial services backgrounds, former CEO of Echelon Insurance Steve Dobronyi and Manulife executive Christine Haselmayer. Breaking free from the financial world to start their own brewery, the two have enlisted the consulting help and expertise of world-renowned brewer Alan Pugsley, who got his start in 1982 at the legendary Ringwood Brewery in Hampshire and has been a driving force in the American brewing scene. Most notably, Pugsley was co-founder and brewmaster of Shipyard Brewing Company in Portland, Maine.

Having launched at the start of 2016, St. Mary Axe currently brews under contract at London's Forked River Brewing, with plans to expand to their own facility sometime in the future. In the meantime, beer is available on tap at select bars and in cans at a number of Beer Store locations.

———

The brewery's flagship, **CANADIAN BEST BITTER**, is a contemporary take on a traditional English bitter. It contains earthy herbal notes followed nicely with biscuity grain and light caramel, going in for a bitter, coppery finish (3.5).

STACK BREWING

📍 1350 Kelly Lake Road, Sudbury
📞 (705) 586-7822
🐦 @StackBrewing
🌐 stackbrewing.ca
🕐 Mon–Sat 9a.m.–9p.m.,
    Sun 12p.m.–5p.m.

Sudbury's first craft brewery, Stack has enjoyed a large amount of success locally since starting in July 2013. Its beer proved so popular in northern Ontario that, with the help of the Northern Ontario Entrepreneur Program, it was able to increase production by 1,500 percent after only three months of operation. Stack has become a significant part of the community, hosting fundraisers for breast cancer research and "beer and yoga" events.

Stack has been undergoing a significant expansion thanks to being awarded $281,538 from the Northern Ontario Heritage Fund in the summer of 2016. The funds have gone toward new equipment and a second location.

——

SATURDAY NIGHT has a Cap'n Crunch cereal sweetness with light fruit notes following (2.5). **IMPACT ALTBIER** is a lighter take on the style, with earthy malt and Boston brown bread blanketed by toffee and chocolate (4). **STACK '72** brings candied grapefruit and pine to a 9% imperial IPA and manages to balance the bitterness admirably (3). **VANILLA CHAI** is a restrained and subtle take on a spiced brown ale that tastes exactly like its name. Delicate chai tea notes blend well with vanilla with an almost gingerbread character to it (4). **LA CLOCHE** is a Belgian blonde ale that starts off quite sweet and then develops into a bitter biscuit number as it finishes (2.5). **LES PORTES DE L'ENFER** is a Bière de Garde that has no shortage of notes of figs, sticky toffee pudding, plum, and chocolate with excellent earthy character and an infernally warm finish (4). **BLACK ROCK** black IPA has a surprisingly light body for such a dark beer, with notes of orange peel and pine asserting themselves over cocoa and coffee flavours (3).

STALWART BREWING COMPANY

📍 10 High Street, Carleton Place

📞 (613) 253-2307

🐦 @stalwartbrewing

🌐 stalwartbrewing.ca

🕐 Tue–Wed 12p.m.–6:30p.m., Thu–Sat 12p.m.–8p.m.,
Sun 12p.m.–6p.m.

While the name of Stalwart isn't that old, folks might remember the brewery better as Stock Pot Ales, the short-lived Ottawa nanobrewery that operated from the kitchen of the Wellington Gastropub from 2013 to autumn 2014. Nathan Corey, Adam Newlands, and Edwin McKinley, all three staff members at the Wellington, initially bonded over home-brewing and worked alongside Shane Clark from Beyond the Pale Brewing to learn the ropes. After that extensive and informative work experience, and even collaborating with Beau's on the beer Walloon Dragon Belgian Black IPA, the trio began concocting primarily small-batch beers from the Wellington's kitchen every Sunday.

Almost a year after the announcement of Stock Pot Ales' closure, the popular nano was reincarnated as Stalwart

Brewing, with a sizeable location of their own located a short walk away from the Mississippi River in downtown Carleton Place. With a system over seven times larger than their original capacity at the Wellington, Stalwart has significantly grown their distribution and is making a number of beers, both old favourites from the Stock Pot days and new offerings.

———

DOWN BY THE RIVER is an American wheat ale with notes of sweet grapefruit that make it different for the typical wheat style (3.5). **BIG PAPA** is a peach and apricot ale, with notes of both covered well and featuring a strong malt backbone supporting the flavours (3). **DR. FEELGOOD** is a nice and juicy IPA, with grapefruit and orange peel bitterness (3.5). **BAD MOON RYE STOUT** has heavy notes of cocoa and spiced coffee, with a slightly creamy finish (3.5).

STEAM WHISTLE BREWING

📍 The Roundhouse, 255 Bremner
Boulevard, Toronto

📞 (416) 362-2337

🐦 @steamwhistle

🌐 steamwhistle.ca

🕐 Tours run every thirty minutes Mon–Sat 11:30a.m.–5p.m.,
Sun 11:30a.m.–4p.m. For groups of ten or more,
please book in advance.

🛒 Mon–Sat 11a.m.–6p.m., Sun 11a.m.–5p.m.

When Frank Heaps's Upper Canada Brewing Company was acquired by Sleeman in the late 1990s, Steam Whistle Brewing was an unintended consequence. Steam Whistle was founded in 2000 by Greg Taylor, Cam Heaps, and Greg Cromwell, all of whom had been fired by Upper Canada after the takeover. Having learned the problems that can result from over-diversification during their days at Upper Canada, the owners of Steam Whistle made a pact to do things differently. As a result, Steam Whistle operates under the motto "Do one thing really, really well."

While Steam Whistle continues to produce a single beer out of the Bremner Boulevard roundhouse, many of their accomplishments in recent years have to do with their responsible ecological choices. The brewery runs on renewable energy and uses bottles with significantly longer lifespans than the industry standard. Steam Whistle has managed to flawlessly combine this green ethos with an instantly recognizable 1950s aesthetic. As a result, they have long occupied a position as an ambassador for craft beer in Ontario.

———

STEAM WHISTLE PREMIUM PILSNER is a Czech-style pilsner with a pleasingly grassy aroma and a lightly grainy malt character (3.5). For maximum enjoyment, it is best drunk as fresh as possible. During the brewery tour, which is one of the best brewery tours on offer to the public in Ontario, if you're lucky, you may be able to try the **UNFILTERED PILSNER**, which has an enhanced hop aroma and a slight doughy yeastiness (4).

STONE CITY ALES

 275 Princess Street, Kingston

 (613) 542-4222

 @stonecityales

 stonecityales.com

🕐 Daily 11 a.m.–12 a.m.

🛒 Daily 11 a.m.–11 p.m.

Located in downtown Kingston, Stone City Ales has managed to develop a significant following in their first year of operation. Taking into account the calibre of the breweries they have collaborated with and the number of awards they have won, Stone City was likely the best brewery of the many that opened in the province in 2014. Stone City managed to brew twenty-four separate one-off batches in their first year of operation. Despite this, they have not at any time lost focus on their four core brands. The bottle shop mostly features growlers, but some specialty one-offs are sold by the bottle.

Stone City is scheduling a small expansion in early 2017 into an adjacent space that will provide more room for barreling and storage. Given the popularity that the taproom has developed among students and young residents of Kingston,

ONTARIO CRAFT BREWERIES

extra space is sorely needed. In addition to the beer that they are brewing, the taproom features a patio that juts onto Princess Street and a full menu of light modern pub fare that will appeal to vegetarians and omnivores alike. It has become one of the busiest spots on the strip, and with good reason.

———

WINDWARD BELGIAN WHEAT features chamomile, grains of paradise, and orange peel, which support a pleasantly smooth, wheaty body and a freshly squeezed orange juice character (4). **12 STAR SESSION ALE** is a completely balanced pale ale with an orange zest aroma that includes a hint of chalkiness somewhat akin to orange pith (4). **UNCHARTED IPA** presents aromas of grapefruit and peach balanced by lightly sweet caramel malt throughout (4), while **SHIPS IN THE NIGHT OATMEAL STOUT** has gentle, dry leafy hops poking through nutty chocolate and coffee roastiness (4.5).

   PEACH DON'T KILL MY VIBE is a low-alcohol take on a Berliner weisse that uses Ontario peaches to accent the sourness and provide some aromatic interest (3.5). **RATHLIN GAEL** is a red rye pale ale with big pine aromas, a medium-full body, and a balanced bitterness playing off rye spice. It was originally brewed at the request of the author's mother, who believes it should be half a point higher (4). **CHLOE** is a French-accented saison with Brettanomyces that uses the Alsatian Barbe Rouge hop to good effect, creating a strawberry pie and lime character with a massively effervescent, bone-dry body (4.5). **JUGGERNAUT** is a bourbon barrel–aged imperial stout that runs toward being thin bodied even as it complements traditional roast, coffee, and semi-sweet chocolate character with dried fruit and a mid-palate punch of caramel (4).

STONE HOUSE BREWING COMPANY

📍 76050 Parr Line, Varna

📞 (519) 281-1167

🌐 stonehousebrewing.ca

🕐 Mon 11a.m.–6p.m., Wed–Thu 11a.m.–6p.m.,
Fri–Sat 10a.m.–7p.m., Sun 10a.m.–5p.m.

Opened in June 2016, Stone House is not the first professional brewing project from owner Mike Corrie. For fifteen years, he operated a brew-on-premises business in London, Ontario. For the opening of his new brewery in Varna, just down the Parr Line adjacent to Lake Huron, he recruited his brewer from the original business, Stefan Riedelsheimer. While the potential exists for Stone House to brew beers in a number of styles, their Czech pilsner enjoyed significant popularity over the course of the summer, moving six thousand bottles in the first three weeks of operation. They are experiencing a great deal of success expanding sales to licensees in Huron County.

―――

Their first offering, **STONE HOUSE PILSNER**, falls into the Czech style. A robust bread crust barley character combines with peppery bitterness and an appropriate hint of diacetyl to do justice to its old-world inspiration (3.5).

STONEHAMMER BREWING

📍 355 Elmira Road N, Unit 135, Guelph

📞 (519) 824-1194

🐦 @StoneHammerBeer

🌐 stonehammer.ca

🕐 Tours are available Saturdays at 12:30p.m., 2p.m., and 3:30p.m., call to book.

🛒 Mon—Wed 10a.m.—5p.m., Thu—Fri 10a.m.—6 p.m., Sat 12p.m.—5p.m.

Founded in 1995 by Rick Fortnum and Charles MacLean, F&M Brewery was a late casualty of the Ontario craft beer market contraction of the mid-1990s. It reopened in 1997, but the branding became somewhat confused as a result of the introduction of the StoneHammer brands. Despite the presence of a widely respected and universally beloved brewer, George Eagleson, the brewery languished over the years.

Jump forward to 2015. The brewery's new owners, Phil and Lesley Woodhouse, have reinvigorated the business. The F&M name has been dropped completely in favour of StoneHammer, and the packaging has shifted entirely to tall-boy cans. The staff has been retained, and the brewery is now frequently producing one-offs, allowing for some creativity and an increased presence in the LCBO.

———

LIGHT features a healthy cereal character with light floral notes and a hint of banana from the yeast esters (2.5). **PILSNER** leans toward toasted grain, with a fresh minty and grassy hop character (3.5). The darker beers benefit from caramelization from the direct-fired kettle. **PALE** is a toasty, sweet interpretation of early West Coast pine and citrus pale ales (3.5). **DARK ALE** is toffee in a glass, with hints of dried berries as it warms through (4). **OATMEAL COFFEE STOUT** uses coffee from local roasters Planet Bean to great effect. While full bodied, the roast never overtakes the cocoa and tobacco notes on the palate (4). **CONTINUITY BALTIC PORTER** is massively complex, with notes of roast, smoke, red currant and dark fruit, pumpernickel, rye whisky, and chocolate syrup in immaculate balance (4.5).

STRANGE BREWING COMPANY

📍 371 Chase Road, Hillier

📞 (613) 885-3135

f The-Strange-Brewing-Company-521725648004032

Strange Brewing is the beer half of veteran winemaker Dave Frederick's life. Frederick, a co-winemaker with Vida Zalnieriunas at the now-for-sale By Chadsey's Cairns Winery & Vineyard in Wellington, fell in love with brewing when he realized some of the parallels between it and winemaking. Working out of his home setup, Strange Brewing hopes to make a number of brews that are accessible with a very clear artisanal bent. Those wishing to try the beer have a good chance of catching them being poured at the Kin Café in Bloomfield, which incidentally is where the brewery's launch was held in the fall of 2016.

———

Strange's first beer, **HORNTRIP JUNIPER PALE ALE**, carries with it a controversial name, as *horntrip* is a Prince Edward County term meaning to drive through a particular county route while consuming mass quantities of liquor and beer. The beer itself is malt-forward, with juniper berries making a small appearance, providing a slight gin note in the middle. It then shifts into a sweet, dry, biscuity finish and leaves a slight spice kick in the aftertaste (3).

STRATFORD BREWING COMPANY

📍 114 Erie Street, Stratford
📞 (519) 273-6691
🐦 @stratfordbrew
🌐 stratfordbrewing.com

Founded in 2004 by Joseph Tuer, the Stratford Brewing Company occupies an unassuming repurposed auto mechanic shop near the market square. Dedicated largely to brewing lager-style beers for the Ontario market, Stratford has had some success selling their products at the LCBO, and their pilsner currently represents one of the best values in the category. Their beers are best enjoyed fresh in one of Stratford's many bars and restaurants.

————

COMMON is a take on a pre-Prohibition California common, a hybrid-style lager fermented at higher temperatures. The toasted grain and roasted nutty-malt character is complemented by an aroma with a touch of pear and grassy, floral hops in a rather smooth body (3.5). The **PILSNER**'s aroma is that of saddle soap and meadow grasses. The body is, perhaps, slightly heavy for the Czech style that it purports to emulate (2).

STRATHROY BREWING COMPANY

📍 62 Albert Street, Strathroy

📞 (226) 238-1815

🐦 @StrathroyBrewCo

🌐 strathroybrewingcompany.ca

🕐 Thu—Fri 12p.m.–6p.m., Sat 11a.m.–4p.m.

Opened by brothers Alex and Matt Martin in 2014, Strathroy Brewing is based in a former flour mill that has been converted to purpose by Alex, an experienced home brewer with a background in chemical engineering. The brewery's running theme is deeply history-based, paying tribute to the Canadian men and women who protected their land from invasion during the War of 1812. Although initially operating out of a tiny, one-room retail space, renovations for a larger taproom are currently in the works.

———

Strathroy's core brand is their **1812 INDEPENDENCE PALE ALE**, a bottle-conditioned product that features notes of banana and caramel, with a harsh bitterness in the middle that dries out toward a crackery finish (2). **1815 LONGWOODS LAGER** runs on the German side of the premium lager style, slightly sweet with nice biscuit notes surrounded by a caramel body (3). The **1815 LONGWOODS LAGER LIGHT** has a rather astringent note to it before diving into a subtle Saaz crackery flavour with a slightly peppery finish (2). The **1815 HOP-HAPPY HAYMAKER**, also known as the "Double Independence Ale," is a bit of a monster, made with seven different varieties of hops. Citrus plays heavily in here, accompanied by freshly cracked black pepper with earthy and citrus undertones (2.5). **1815 PEACE WHEAT** is a Belgian-style wit that has a doughy sweetness with light caramel, toffee, and a slight lime citrus note, ending in a biscuit dry finish (2). **1815 SMOKIN' CANNON STOUT** is referred to as a dry oyster stout, though the oyster aspect is a suggested pairing rather than an ingredient. For a light-bodied stout it has some heavy flavours, with light roast coffee and bittersweet chocolate chips in a creamy, somewhat dry finish (3).

A point of pride for Strathroy is their brewing of gluten-free products. **1815 LOCKSTOCK ALE** might perhaps be one of the better gluten-free beers in Ontario. It's very light bodied with a delicate jab of ginger and lime and a slight tropical Australian hop punch, finishing very quickly (3). **1815 FREEDOM FRAMBOISE** is a delightful blend of raspberries, blackberries, and wild blueberries. While it is wonderful consumed cold, as it warms the fruit character shows itself even more (4).

STRAY DOG BREWING CO.

 501 Lacolle Way, Orléans

 @StrayDogBeer

🌐 straydogbrewing.ca

After a fair amount of time actively daydreaming about starting their own brewery, Justin MacNeill and Marc Plante, two experienced and award-winning home brewers, met with Gen Benay, whose entrepreneurial spirit proved to be the drive that the pair needed to make their dream into a reality. While the trio are currently contracting their beer out of Forked River in London, plans to open their own location in the Taylor Creek business park are scheduled for late spring/early summer 2017.

———

THIS ONE is a California common based on a beer that won best of show and gold in the style's category at the 2015 Because Beer Homebrew Competition in Hamilton. Significant malt backing with light grassy notes lead into a biscuity finish (2.5).

SWEETGRASS BREWING COMPANY

 @sweetgrassbeer

 sweetgrassbeer.com

Founded in 2013, Sweetgrass Brewing is a Toronto brewery started by the owners of the Auld Spot Pub on the Danforth, Nathan Hynes and Nicole Crozier. After contracting through a number of different breweries over the course of their existence, they have finally settled on brewing their duo with Brick in Waterloo.

Sweetgrass's owners enjoy playing around with flavour in their beer, and this has helped them become involved in other projects and collaborations. As part of the Local 7 group of pubs, Sweetgrass has acted as the brewery of record (with guest brewmaster Sam Corbeil) for a series of beers for Session Toronto Craft Beer Festival, including a lemon-verbena saison, a gose, and a dry-hopped West Coast pilsner. At this point, the releases are a highly anticipated annual event.

———

SWEETGRASS GOLDEN ALE is a different beast than it has been in previous years. Described by the owners as a Munich helles style fermented with an ale yeast, the beer is now better integrated with noble hops coming through in the aroma and on the finish (3.5). **SHAGBARK STOUT** is a rare bird: a foreign export stout. As such, it is highly carbonated, with pronounced roast character, Brio and cola notes, and a woody character from hickory honeycombs used in conditioning (3.5). **MIDLANDS BUTTER TART ALE** does precisely what it says on the tin, managing to fold the sweet caramel, raisin, and crust character of one of Canada's iconic desserts into a glass (4).

ONTARIO CRAFT BREWERIES

SYNDICATE RESTAURANT AND BREWERY

 syndicaterestaurant.ca

SYNDICATE GRIMSBY

📍 13 Mountain Street, Grimsby

📞 (289) 447-1122

🕐 Sun—Thu 11:30a.m.—10p.m., Fri—Sat 11:30a.m.—11p.m.

SYNDICATE NIAGARA FALLS

📍 6863 Lundy's Lane, Niagara Falls

📞 (289) 477-1022

🕐 Daily 11:30a.m.—11p.m.

🛒 Daily 11:30a.m.—11p.m.

The initial location of the Syndicate restaurant has a storied brewing history in Niagara Falls. The Lundy's Lane location was at one time home to Niagara Falls Brewing, before the brewery was purchased by Moosehead. Filling the void after that was Niagara's Best, which itself moved to Niagara Falls in 2009. While the Niagara's Best brands still exist (and are still available at a small number of Beer Store locations), the brewery location became the Syndicate brewpub in 2010, adopting a Prohibition-era, Mafioso-themed branding with a twist. Focusing on a food menu that includes simplified bistro fare with locally sourced ingredients and an accessible three-course, prix fixe menu, the Syndicate and its second location in Grimsby both pour beer from their home brewery in Niagara Falls. Further adding to the prohibition theme, Niagara Falls Craft Distillers have also set up shop in the Syndicate, producing a range of small batch gins, vodkas, and other spirits. Since the same family owns Taps On Queen in Niagara Falls, it is common to see their beer on tap at all of the locations.

––––

NIAGARA'S BEST BLONDE is a straightforward blonde ale, with a medium body and biscuit grain and honey flavours (3). **NIAGARA'S BEST LOGGER LAGER** is a thin, lightly bready pale lager with light grassy notes and a swirl of caramel in a dry finish (3).

TAPS ON QUEEN BREWHOUSE & GRILL

📍 4680 Queen Street, Niagara Falls

📞 (289) 477-1010

🐦 @TapsOnQueen

🌐 tapsbeer.ca

🕐 Daily 12p.m.–1a.m.

🛒 Daily 12p.m.–11p.m.

Although Taps On Queen began brewing in 2004, it has since changed locations, leaving behind its original premises in Niagara-on-the-Lake for its current home on Queen Street in Niagara Falls. The brewpub operates in a bright-yellow converted garage, which houses a large, open brewhouse and bar area with ample seating. In the summer, a large and well-appointed patio provides a relaxed venue for lounging in the sun. Throughout the year the bar features live music twice a week and nightly food specials. Taps has become very popular locally; its special Growler Club provides members the opportunity to try new small-batch projects and interact with the brewers, and they offer contracting services to new brewers in the area. Taps also serves Niagara's Best beers because of their shared ownership.

SINISTER SAM'S INSANE IPA doesn't quite need a straight-jacket. Mandarin oranges are prominent throughout with hints of lemon, belittling somewhat the malt core (2). **RED CREAM ALE** is smooth and coppery with sweet fruit and caramel (2.5).

THORNBURY VILLAGE CIDERY & BREWERY

 5645 King Road, Nobleton

 (905) 859-5464

 @thornburybevco

🌐 thornbury.co

Until this year, the fate of the brand once known as King Brewery was very much in flux. The King branding provided an instantly recognizable logo and a mantle under which the original brewer, Phil DiFonzo, had won dozens of awards. The acquisition of the King brand by Provincial Beverages of Canada proved confusing after the company half-scrapped the original branding in favour of that of a popular cidery, Thornbury, which they also owned. Adding to this confusion was the fact that pubs tended to reject the change in brand, with "King Pilsner" remaining on the menu of a number of licensees, a fact that frequently called the age of the product into question. A subsidiary company referred to as Barn Door Beverage Company complicated matters further as they released additional seasonal beers throughout much of 2014.

The year 2016 saw the takeover of the Thornbury brand by Colio Winery, based out of Harrow, and this can only be seen as a positive step. Thornbury is a brand with a great deal of potential, possessing as it does one of very few decoction brewhouses in Canada and, therefore, capable of producing authentic German lagers in the right hands. This year has seen something of a return to form, with Pickup Truck Pilsner winning World's Best Czech-Style Pale Lager at the World Beer Awards.

———

PICKUP TRUCK PILSNER develops a depth of bread crust malt due to the decoction mash and retains significant Maillard character through the mid-palate. The hop character has ticked up lightly, with a more assertive floral and pepper bite (4). **DARK HORSE LAGER** toys with the palate, with dark malt and roast notes dancing around the outside of a sweet grain core with an effervescent body (3.5). **JUBILEE AMBER LAGER** has toasted bready malt with a hint of brown sugar and a touch of vinous fruit (3). **BLUE MOUNTAIN LAGER** is a newer beer; in the German helles style, it complements a full cereal body with hints of thyme, mint, and long grasses (4).

THE 3 BREWERS

 @3brasseursca

 les3brasseurs.ca

THE 3 BREWERS KANATA

📍 565 Kanata Avenue, Kanata

📞 (613) 380-8190

🕐 Mon–Wed 11:30a.m.–12a.m., Thu 11:30a.m.–1a.m.,
Fri–Sat 11:30a.m.–2a.m., Sun 11:30a.m.–12a.m.

THE 3 BREWERS HEARTLAND

📍 5860 Mavis Road, Mississauga

📞 (289) 643-1888

🕐 Mon–Wed 11a.m.–12a.m., Thu 11a.m.–1a.m.,
Fri–Sat 11a.m.–2a.m., Sun 11a.m.–12a.m.

THE 3 BREWERS OAKVILLE

📍 2041 Winston Park Drive, Oakville

📞 (289) 813-2239

🕐 Mon–Thu 11:30a.m.–12a.m., Fri–Sat 11:30a.m.–1a.m.,
Sun 11:30a.m.–12a.m.

THE 3 BREWERS SPARKS

📍 240 Sparks Street, Ottawa

📞 (613) 380-8140

🕐 Mon–Wed 11:30a.m.–12a.m., Thu 11:30a.m.–1a.m.,
Fri–Sat 11:30a.m.–2a.m., Sun 11:30a.m.–12a.m.

THE 3 BREWERS RICHMOND HILL

📍 125 York Boulevard, Richmond Hill

📞 (289) 637-2637

🕐 Mon–Wed 11a.m.–12a.m., Thu–Sat 11a.m.–2a.m.,
Sun 11a.m.–12a.m.

THE 3 BREWERS ADELAIDE

📍 120 Adelaide Street W, Unit 100, Toronto

📞 (647) 689-2898

🕐 Mon–Wed 11a.m.–12a.m., Thu–Sat 11a.m.–1 a.m.,
Sun 11a.m.–11p.m.

THE 3 BREWERS YONGE STREET

📍 275 Yonge Street, Toronto

📞 (647) 347-6286

🕐 Mon–Wed 11a.m.–12a.m., Thu 11a.m.–1a.m.,
Fri–Sat 11a.m.–2a.m., Sun 11a.m.–12a.m.

THE 3 BREWERS LIBERTY VILLAGE

📍 2 Liberty Street, Toronto

📞 (416) 477-2619

🕐 Mon—Wed 11a.m.—12a.m., Thu—Sat 11a.m.—1a.m.,
   Sun 11a.m.—12 a.m.

The 3 Brewers chain of brewpubs was started in France in 1985. Perhaps because of the commonality in language, the chain succeeded in Quebec in the first decade of the twenty-first century. The expansion into Ontario has been more rapid than anyone would have predicted when the first location opened at Yonge and Dundas in 2009. Now with eight locations spread across Ontario, the chain succeeds by bringing a level of standardization to its brewing and a focus on healthy portions of Alsatian and German food at very reasonable prices. How many pub menus feature cassoulet and flammekuchen?

————

The core lineup of beers shares a house character due to the spicy character of the proprietary yeast strain. The **BLONDE** is a touch full bodied for the style, with floral and peppery notes (2.5), while the **AMBER** touches simply on caramel and brown sugar in aroma and body (2). The North American–style **BROWN** ale is remarkably complex, with notes of toasted grain, chocolate, and molasses (3). The more contemporary offerings are more successful. The **IPA** is heavy on citrus and tropical fruit and packs a solid bitterness (3).

On a location-to-location basis, the main attractions are the neighbourhood beers, each tied to its specific location. The most recent version, in Toronto's Liberty Village, has named their neighbourhood beer **HI-FIDELITY PALE ALE** after a phonograph company that once operated in the district (NR).

Additionally, brewers at the different locations compete frequently for the prestige of creating a seasonal offering to be brewed across the chain, resulting in a textbook **BLACK IPA** (3.5).

TOBERMORY BREWING CO. & GRILL

📍 28 Bay Street, Tobermory

📞 (519) 596-8181

🐦 @tobermorybrew

🌐 tobermorybrewingco.ca

🕐 Daily 12p.m.–11p.m.

Overlooking the harbour in the small tourist-heavy community at the northern tip of the Bruce Peninsula, Tobermory Brewing is the work of husband and wife Matt and Kristin Buckley, who also own the Crowsnest Pub located less than a minute's walk away. Tobermory's brewmaster is Niagara College brewing program grad Morag Kloeze, who drove up to the Tub shortly after writing her final exam just in time for the opening on the May 24 weekend in 2015. In charge of the food side of Tobermory is executive chef Robert Larochelle, who takes a one-hundred-mile market approach to his ingredients, underlining the importance of fresh and local (the authors suggest the rainbow trout). When you arrive at Tobermory Brewing, be sure to say hi to manager Chris McCoy, a former London police officer who had rank over the Buckleys back in the day.

The beauty of Tobermory Brewing is that the space is small and Kloeze has been given free reign to produce a number of approachable one-offs and experimentations, though there are several mainstays. The **BRUCE TRAIL BLONDE ALE** is somewhat light in body, with delicate grapefruit and berry notes and a pleasant copper-like tang brought on by the local water (3.5). The **FATHOM FIVE PORTER** is a medium-bodied beer with cocoa, caramel, and plum notes along with a slight tobacco flavour toward the end (3). **SAILOR'S DELIGHT RASPBERRY WHEAT** has enormous amounts of raspberry combining with a light vanilla biscuit character ending in a dry finish (3). **SINGING SANDS SAISON** has a lot of banana compounded by a gradually climbing bitterness and a peppery, dry finish (2.5). **ANGRY LOGGER MARZEN**, while featuring some warming bready notes, tastes predominantly of chocolate and toffee with a touch of berry sweetness, which suggests it doesn't quite match the style (2.5). **TILTED WINDMILL IPA** is a grapefruit and pine affair, with a low caramel note leading toward a bitter, dry finish (3).

TOBOGGAN BREWING COMPANY

📍 585 Richmond Street, London

📞 (519) 433-2337

🐦 @TobogganBrewery

🌐 tobogganbrewing.com

🕐 Mon—Wed 11:30a.m.–1a.m., Thu—Sat 11:30a.m.–2a.m., Sun 11:30a.m.–1a.m.

🛒 Daily 11a.m.–11p.m.

Located in the space that used to house popular student bar Jim Bob Ray's, Toboggan is a well-appointed modern brewpub, one that seems poised to cater to a wider audience in London's downtown core. The wood-accented dining room is large and comfortable, subtly tied together by the massive sled that acts as ceiling and lighting feature. The contemporary pub menu has something for everyone, with vegetarian and gluten-free options featured alongside house-smoked meats and topping-heavy customizable pizzas. In summer, a large outdoor patio allows patrons to work on their tans while hoisting a pint.

In the short amount of years since the brewpub's opening, Toboggan has proven to be a destination. This may be accounted for in equal parts by the talent of brewer Tomas Schmidt and the great enthusiasm for the place among London's craft beer drinkers. Screens behind the bar display the taplist, which features beers from a number of breweries throughout the province in addition to their own in-house selection.

————

MR. INSURANCE MAN BLONDE takes its name from one of London's most successful industries. The beer itself derives the majority of its character from earthy hops and a biscuit body (3). **AMBER** has a creamy caramel mouthfeel with a low-roasted earthy character acting as balance (3). **LAGER** is an award-winning German kellerbier, with sweet malt presence hitting fast and leaving a lingering, earthy warmth (3.5). **DOUBLE IPA** is surprisingly light bodied for the style, which starts out rich in caramel notes before the Cascade and Simcoe hops give it that citrus and pine kick at the end (3.5). **BLACKFRIARS BRIDGE STOUT** is a particular highlight, with semi-sweet chocolate and cream blending with light roast coffee to form a flavour combination not unlike a coffee truffle (4). An alteration of the stout, **BLACKFRIARS BRIDGE VANILLA STOUT** contains a healthy dose of vanilla beans added onto the original beer (4).

TOGETHER WE'RE BITTER CO-OPERATIVE BREWING

📍 300 Mill Street, Unit 1, Kitchener

📞 (519) 954-4433

🐦 @twbcoop

🌐 brewing.coop

🕐 Wed–Sat 11a.m.–9p.m., Sun 11a.m.–5p.m.

Together We're Bitter (more commonly known by the acronym TWB) is a multi-stakeholder co-operative brewery with six worker-owners and eighteen community supporters who have a say in how the brewery is operated. The brewery opened in Kitchener in June 2015 and features a small but well-appointed taproom with a bar made out of bowling alley lanes. TWB's primary focus is on creating a vibrant community for beer lovers in Kitchener, although the model limits immediate expansion to some extent. In the meantime, the brewery has a neighbourhood feel because of the ownership structure, location in a residential neighbourhood, and live music on Sundays.

TWB possesses the single most iconoclastic brewing system in Ontario. The brewhouse, nicknamed Sputnik, is an extremely rare single vessel unit of German design not typically seen west of Prague or, in general, since 1996. TWB uses converted Czech pilsner tankova as brite tanks and a modified Cadbury chocolate liquor vessel as a hot liquor tank. Despite the somewhat odd combination of repurposed steel, all of the equipment has been converted to the purpose of brewing North American craft beer under brewer Culum Canally.

TWB produces a number of different beers at once and the selection rotates. At time of writing there are a small number of consistently available choices, mostly the ones named with union references. **HE AIN'T GOT A CLUE BLONDE** is a lightly peppery blonde ale with a clean honey and cracker malt body (4). **WIT THE HELL** is a witbier fermented with hefeweizen yeast and brewed with lemon grass, lemon zest, coriander, and black pepper, creating a banana nose with a thin, wheaty body (3). **MAGGIE'S FARM PALE ALE** is a straightforward southern California APA with a lemon and orange hop character (3.5). **WOBBLY WHEEL** is a big West Coast IPA with seven hops that comes across full bodied with candied orange and light pine bitterness (3.5). **AMERICAN BROWN** develops clementine from Amarillo hops and bready malt with chocolate character throughout a medium body (3.5).

PUMPKIN RYE ALE soaks pie spices in rye whisky prior to brewing, creating a poppy seed cake effect rather than pumpkin pie — a welcome change (4). **PULLMAN PORTER** has a small amount of chocolate and raspberry on the nose, followed by a whiff of smoke on the finish (3). **BLACK JACK IPA** is brewed entirely with Zeus hops creating a lemon and licorice profile in a dry, roasty body with a pine sap finish (3).

TOOTH AND NAIL BREWING COMPANY

📍 3 Irving Avenue, Ottawa

📞 (613) 695-4677

🐦 @toothnailbeer

🌐 toothandnailbeer.com

🕐 Mon–Wed 4p.m.–11p.m., Thu 3p.m.–12a.m., Fri 3p.m.–1a.m., Sat 1p.m.–1a.m., Sun 1p.m.–6p.m.

🛒 Mon–Sat 12p.m.–11p.m., Sun 12p.m.–6p.m.

Opened in September 2015 in Ottawa's Hintonburg neighbourhood, Tooth and Nail is the first brewing project from husband-and-wife team Matt Tweedy and Dayna Guy. Both are professionals in their own right. Tweedy has spent the last six years brewing in various locales around North America, including King Brewery and Beau's in Ontario. Guy worked as bar manager for nearly a decade at Toronto's beerbistro, an influential beer destination. Tooth and Nail benefits from their collection of skills, experience, and context of international beers; the result is a brewery producing high-quality, complex offerings out of the gate. The brewpub menu offers a selection of beer-friendly snacks including sandwiches, charcuterie, and

ONTARIO CRAFT BREWERIES

Korean BBQ salmon that pair well with an excellent assortment of North American–style craft beers.

———

VALOR is a complex saison with a multitude of grains in the grist. Barley, oats, wheat, and rye combine to create a ballooning mid-palate that fades to nothing on the swallow (4). **TENACITY** is an English pale ale with an aroma of lightly toasted raisin bread because of the inclusion of crystal malt and Crystal hops (4). **BRAVADO** is a straight ahead American pale ale that develops Simcoe and Amarillo hops into a pine and lemon aroma that persists through the palate and makes for an extremely balanced example of the style (4.5). **RABBLE-ROUSER IPA** uses El Dorado and Azacca hops and derives its peach, ground-cherry, and mango character from them. There is a persistence of fruit that helps to lessen somewhat the bitter finish (4). **SUCKER PUNCH** is an enormous Double IPA (theoretically 165 IBU) that not only retains its balance, but also displays a wide variety of orchard, citrus, and tropical fruits over a solid malt backbone (5).

VIM AND VIGOR is a bracing pilsner in the current American craft style, with assertive, peppery mown hay and wildflower aromas and a stinging mouthfeel (5). The stout, **FORTITUDE**, is in the sweeter American style and aims for the impression of a chocolate chip cookie (4). **FORTIFIED** is the exaggerated version, twice the size of its baby brother with enormous depths of coffee, chocolate, and lactose (4.5).

TRACKS BREW PUB

📍 60 Queen Street E, Brampton

📞 (905) 453-3063

🐦 @tracksbrewpub

🌐 tracksbrewpub.com

🕐 Mon–Thu 11a.m.–11p.m., Fri–Sat 11a.m.–1a.m.,
Sun 11a.m.–11p.m.

Tucked away on a pedestrian lane off of Union Street, Tracks is a tastefully appointed cross between a traditional pub and a sports bar occupying the building that was once the Brampton Knitting Mill. The bar is popular among the younger citizens of Brampton and stocks, for the most part, mainstream beer and cider. The glassed-in brewery onsite is a holdover from the late 1980s, a time when extract brews were immensely popular in brewpubs and Continental Supplies furnished equipment out of Mississauga.

———

The house beer on offer at Tracks currently is their take on an **ESB** and designed specifically for the system. Very mild dark fruit and a whisper of roast underpin a very light body, leaving a faint impression of copper and cucumber (1.5).

ONTARIO CRAFT BREWERIES

TRAFALGAR ALES & MEADS

📍 1156 Speers Road, Oakville

📞 (905) 337-0133

🐦 @allornothingbh

🌐 allornothing.beer

🕐 Daily 10a.m.–5p.m.

Founded during the last gasp of the first wave of Ontario's brewing renaissance, Trafalgar has proved to be one of the most durable of Ontario's breweries since. An initial site in Oakville, founded in 1993, and the Old Mill Brewery in Elora, established in 1997, were eventually consolidated on the current site in 2003.

Trafalgar has rightly suffered in the estimation of beer enthusiasts over the last decade because of severe inconsistencies in packaging, quality, and execution. However, a change in ownership in early 2016 and massive upgrades to the brewery equipment are likely to mean that many of the problems drinkers had experienced previously will be rectified. Now under the ownership of All or Nothing Brewhouse, Trafalgar exists in practice more or less as a contract brand within the facility they once inhabited. What this means is that many brands that were previously available are likely to disappear as selections are streamlined. Owners Eric and Jeff Dornan intend to focus increasingly on Trafalgar's mead brands.

———

APA is a straightforward American pale ale with a buttered cracker nose and a pine and caramel finish that lingers bitterly (2.5). **STINGER IPA** is similar in flavour profile, although slightly larger in aromatic presence because of its increased size (2.5).

Trafalgar has a number of meads, including a **MASALA CHAI MEAD** and a **MEAD BRAGGOT** available year-round for those of you who wish to channel your inner Viking.

TRIPLE BOGEY BREWING & GOLF CO.

 (416) 844-7702

 @Triplebogey

 triplebogey.com

As is evidenced by the name of the company, the primary thrust of Triple Bogey is to appeal to those golfers completing a quick pause for refreshment on the way to the back nine. Contracted out of Great Lakes Brewing in Etobicoke, Triple Bogey is simply interested in selling beer to thirsty duffers who are focused on not slicing the ball into the rough. In 2015, Triple Bogey launched a second brand called Hurry Hard, which has found its way into curling clubs across the province, aided by the pedigree of champion curlers Brent Laing, Glenn Howard, and Jennifer Jones as investors. While both brands are primarily focused on marketing rather than brewing, one must admit that they are at least very successful at it.

―――

TRIPLE BOGEY PREMIUM LAGER has a light cereal body with a hint of green apple and a barely detectable noble hop character (2). **HURRY HARD AMBER LAGER** is a clean, lightly bready Vienna lager (3).

TUQUE DE BROUE

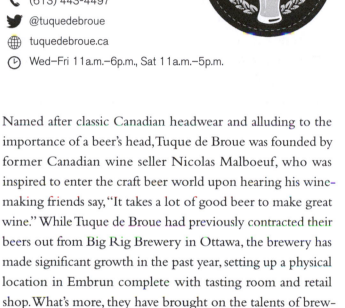

📍 189 Bay Street, Embrun

📞 (613) 443-4497

🐦 @tuquedebroue

🌐 tuquedebroue.ca

🕐 Wed–Fri 11a.m.–6p.m., Sat 11a.m.–5p.m.

Named after classic Canadian headwear and alluding to the importance of a beer's head, Tuque de Broue was founded by former Canadian wine seller Nicolas Malboeuf, who was inspired to enter the craft beer world upon hearing his wine-making friends say, "It takes a lot of good beer to make great wine." While Tuque de Broue had previously contracted their beers out from Big Rig Brewery in Ottawa, the brewery has made significant growth in the past year, setting up a physical location in Embrun complete with tasting room and retail shop. What's more, they have brought on the talents of brew-master Zach Trynda, formally of Railway City Brewing and one of the first students to come out of Niagara College's brewmaster program. Since this significant development, Tuque de Broue has expanded on their year-round offerings and frequently release seasonal beers in their store.

The brewery's flagship beer, **TUQUE DORÉE CANADIAN PALE ALE**, has prominent biscuit grain character and caramel notes, with a bitter grassiness toward the end (3). **BARBE BLANCHE** has a wonderful sweet Belgian influence paired with a very light body and notes of clove, making it the Ontario answer to Unibroue's Blanche de Chambly (3.5). **GOUGOUNES ROUSSES RED ALE** has a smooth mouthfeel with deep toffee and mild coffee notes, going into a biscuity finish (3.5). **LA CAVALERIE** stands as a very unique IPA, with notes of pineapple, freshly cracked black pepper, and apricot (4).

UNION JACK BREWING COMPANY

📍 9 Queen Street E, Sault Ste. Marie

📞 (705) 575-8991

🐦 @UnionJackBrewin

🌐 unionjackbrewing.ca

🕐 Mon–Sat 12p.m.–8p.m.

Right next door to the well-known Ernie's Coffee Shop on Queen Street in Sault Ste. Marie, Union Jack Brewing Company has been open for business since May 2015. It is run by two brothers, Jeff and Jordan Jack, who both work in the medical profession when not making beer for the good people of the Soo and breathing new life into the city's west end. While its beers are primarily sold in bars, restaurants, and Beer Stores in and around the area, growlers, cans, kegs, and even draft balls of head brewer Jeff's offerings can be found within the brewery itself.

———

Offerings from Union Jack include the **ALGOMA PALE ALE**, which goes heavy on the ginger notes throughout the taste, finishing with a sharp jab of pine (1.5), and **RAPID RIVER CREAM ALE**, which features light caramel throughout the body, with a honey and cracker note leading into an abrupt finish, leaving a slight dryness on the tongue (2). The **1870 ALGOMA AMBER ALE** is very much a crunchy chocolate bar, with heavy toffee notes and a light coating of cocoa (2).

UPPER THAMES BREWING COMPANY

📍 225 Bysham Park Drive, Woodstock

📞 (519) 290-0053

🐦 @upperthamesbrew

🌐 upperthamesbrewing.ca

🕐 Tue–Sat 11a.m.–7p.m., Sun 11a.m.–4p.m.

Upper Thames Brewing is the result of five friends, Carl Bloomfield, Moe Morris, Frank Raso, Chad Paton, and brewmaster Josh Bowes, who wanted to form a brewery right in the heart of their home of Oxford County. As it turns out, it was just what the area needed. Right from their announcement, all the way through to their opening in summer 2016, the brewery has seen an outpouring of support from the community, with folks even stopping by daily for a status update while the facility was still under construction. Since opening, the five friends have had a time keeping up with demand, but the beers, complete with well-designed branding, are regularly offered in nearby restaurants and their beautifully spacious bar and event space, with LCBO offerings currently in the works.

Some of the more regular offerings from Upper Thames include **DEAD RECKONING AMERICAN PALE ALE**, which has a light crackery mouthfeel and a crisp, drying finish (3); **MAD RIVER FARM HOUSE WHEAT**, a Belgian wit with a berry sweetness that moves into orange peel and a light coriander finish (3); **TIMBER BEAST BROWN ALE**, which has a rather light colour to it, but don't let that fool you; it drinks like a cup of cold brew light roast coffee (4); and **PORTAGE INDIA PALE ALE**, which has a whole lot of grapefruit and orange citrus with a distinct note of caramel (3).

WALKERVILLE BREWERY

📍 525 Argyle Road, Windsor

📞 (519) 254-6067

🐦 @WalkervilleBrew

🌐 walkervillebrewery.com

🕐 Tours are available for $7 Saturdays at 12:30p.m., 3:30p.m., and
5p.m. Tours are available for groups of fifteen or more by
advance appointment.

🛒 Mon–Wed 11a.m.–6p.m., Thu 11a.m.–7p.m., Fri 11a.m.–9p.m.,
Sat 11a.m.–7p.m., Sun 11a.m.–6p.m.

Located in the Walkerville neighbourhood of Windsor, this brewery borrows from the pedigree of two previous incarnations under the Walkerville name. The first, distiller Hiram Walker's own brewery, was founded in 1890 and survived until 1956. The next, a second-wave brewery, was ahead of its time and survived from 1998 until 2007, garnering a number of accolades. The current version is housed in a repurposed tank-storage warehouse that was itself originally part of Hiram Walker's distilling empire.

Walkerville differentiates itself from a number of recently founded breweries in that they are set up to produce both ales and lagers, rather than focusing solely on quicker-to-turn-over ales. The brewery is also able to produce specialty barrel-aged beers thanks to their relationship with the adjacent Hiram Walker plant — a relationship that ensures the brewery has ready access to aged oak barrels.

Walkerville prides itself on being a neighbourhood brewery and has a spacious taproom that has become popular for events locally. Their recent expansion into the LCBO stands them in good stead for the near future, and 2016 has seen them expand their basic number of offerings and their production capacity to nearly 7,000 hL.

——

HONEST LAGER is a light-bodied, bready, Oktoberfest-style beer that ranks among the best brewery flagships in the province, with a spicy, late-palate bitter pop that fades into a clean finish (4.5). **EASY STOUT** is a flavourful milk stout with coffee character — specifically cream and two sugars (3.5). **GERONIMO IPA** possesses restrained bitterness with a grapefruit character leaning toward blood orange (3.5). **PURITY PILSENER** is an excellent representation of a properly conditioned Northern German pilsner, with crackery malt body and a spicy, floral hop character from Herkules and Hallertauer Mittelfruh hops (4.5).

LOOPHOLE ALE is a crystal-clear, filtered, kölsch-style beer whose fruity character leans toward peach with a black pepper sting (4). **WATERFRONT WIT** is a light summery affair flavoured with organic Florida-orange peel (3.5). **COLLABORATION PALE ALE** is made in conjunction with local restaurants The Willistead and Snackbar-B-Q in Windsor. Featuring tropical fruit aromas from Mosaic hops, the body is bready and packed with light caramel flavour (3.5). **BARREL AGED SCOTCH ALE** is a recurring annual release. A larger version of their regular scotch ale, it spends eight months in fresh Jim Beam barrels from the distillery across the road, which adds vanilla and a smooth texture to a robust, deeply caramelized body (4.5).

WALLER ST. BREWING

📍 14 Waller Street, Ottawa

📞 (613) 860-1515

🐦 @WallerStBrewing

🌐 wallerst.ca

🕐 Hours vary seasonally. Check website for details.

Located in the basement of the Loft Board Game Lounge, an 1868 Ottawa heritage building, Waller St. Brewing's image has been inspired by the romanticism of the Prohibition era since its opening in 2015. The brewery is very much the product of its founders' dreams; indeed, much of the brewing equipment was designed by brewmaster and co-founder Marc-Andre Chainey himself, pulling from his background in engineering.

———

While the brewery has a number of rotating beers, including different variations of a house sour and a new hop variant IPA, Waller St.'s primary offerings include the **BOOTLEG BLONDE**, with a refreshingly thin mouthfeel, distinct grain characteristics, and a dry finish that gives off the taste of lemon zest (2.5). The quite smooth **MOONLIGHT PORTER** offers intense roasted-coffee flavours and a lingering, bitter-sweet finish (3), and the **SPEAKEASY RED**, a dry-hopped, red rye session IPA, has a lot of peppery notes accompanied by passion fruit and a quite bitter finish (2.5).

WASAGA BEACH BREWING COMPANY

 @wasagabeer

 wasaga.beer

With the Piping Plover shorebird marking the logo, it's evident that Wasaga Beach Brewing Company is devoted to their home situated on the longest freshwater beach in the world. Headed up by David Cubitt, the founder of the CD Plus retail stores, Wasaga Beach Brewing hopes to add to the area's identity as a destination for summer. Currently contracting from Etobicoke while they look for their own physical space, Wasaga Beach's flagship beer is available in LCBOs and at their own beach bar during the summer.

———

BEACH 1 CERVEZA is rather suitable for a sunny day on the sandy shores, quite light in body but with a pronounced grain character and a crisp, dry finish (3).

WELLINGTON BREWERY

📍 950 Woodlawn Road W, Guelph

📞 (519) 837-2337

🐦 @WellingtonBrew

🌐 wellingtonbrewery.ca

🕐 The brewery hosts guided samplings on Fridays between 12 p.m. and 7 p.m. and Saturdays between 12 p.m. and 6 p.m.

🛒 Mon–Wed 9 a.m.–6 p.m., Fri 9 a.m.–8 p.m., Sat 10 a.m.–8 p.m., Sun 11 a.m.–6 p.m.

Founded in 1985, Wellington occupies the spot of Ontario's oldest independent microbrewery, and its character highlights the gist of the early brewing renaissance in Ontario. The beers that Wellington brews are mostly English in style and influenced by time the company's earliest brewers spent in England — then one of the only remaining bastions of diversity in brewing. As such, the brewery's early adoption of cask-conditioned ales makes perfect sense. Less successful was the initial plastic retail packaging, which may also be put down to English influence.

Thirty years later, Wellington has been expanding their volume while diversifying both their own portfolio and their business practices. A not inconsiderable part of their business is made up of producing brands for contract breweries.

That said, the core lineup remains nearly identical to the way it was during the 1980s. Wellington is one of a very few breweries in Ontario that has a house yeast character, a traditionally English strain that imparts a light savouriness not unlike Marmite across their entire range. It is a flavour profile that lends itself to service on cask and you should enjoy their beer from that source if possible.

——

ARKELL BEST BITTER is lightly coppery in body with an almost cruciferous leafy bitterness, and is mildly tea-like with a hint of caramel (3). **SPECIAL PALE ALE** deepens the caramel flavour and the impression of orange pekoe and a hint of vanilla on the finish (3). **COUNTY DARK** forges ahead into nutty crystal malts with hints of raisin, licorice, and chocolate (3.5). **IMPERIAL RUSSIAN STOUT** is a well of complexity with leather and peat smoke emerging from the bittersweet depths of its roasty body (4.5).

TRAILHEAD is the brewery's take on a Vienna lager and for many years the best value in the Beer Store's discount section: a light, doughy caramel body with gentle noble-hop accents (3).

KICKIN' BACK is a dry-hopped session ale using local Ontario hops in order to impart a gentle orange peel and field grass characteristic that is a little more contemporary than most of the lineup (3.5).

WHIPRSNAPR BREWING COMPANY

📍 14 Bexley Place, Unit 106, Nepean

📞 (613) 596-9882

🐦 @whiprsnaprbrew

🌐 whiprsnaprbrewingco.com

🕐 Summer: Wed—Fri 12p.m.—8p.m., Sat 12p.m.—6p.m.,
Sun 12p.m.—4p.m.
Winter: Wed 12p.m.—6p.m., Thu—Fri 12p.m.—8p.m.,
Sat 12p.m.—6p.m., Sun 12p.m.—4p.m.

Located in Bells Corners, a suburb of Ottawa, Whiprsnapr is one of the more ambitious breweries in the Ottawa craft beer scene. While the majority of the brewing at Whiprsnapr is done on a 1.5-BBL system that allows for a large amount of experimentation in recipes and a large amount of choice for their customers, they also have a 20-BBL brewhouse on site that is able to produce large batches for distribution through the LCBO. There is some difference in character between the small and large batches because of differences in fermentation technology; the small system relies on fermentation within plastic bags in large food-grade drums, while the large system uses steel conical fermenters.

ONTARIO CRAFT BREWERIES

This experimentation truly separates Whiprsnapr from the rest of the Ottawa market. Their tendency is not to abide by conventional stylistic distinctions or guidelines. Rather than emulating beers from particular regions or historical designations, the focus is on a recipe-development and marketing process that appears largely autobiographical. This results in interesting products, some of which are more successful than others. Rather than attempting to slot each beer into a pre-existing style for ratings, we have used the brewery's descriptions.

———

ROOT OF EVIL is a pre-Prohibition lager with a whiff of matchstick on the nose and a lightly peachy corn aroma. Reminiscent of Vermont smoked ham, the beer has a surprisingly crisp finish (2.5). **CAROL ANNE** is an Irish blonde ale hopped with East Kent Goldings for a touch of spicy orange peel; it is full-bodied because of the use of an Irish ale yeast (3). **OK LAH!** is a cream ale flavoured with ginger and coriander, producing a certain amount of zippy citrus and aromatic fresh ginger in a light, refreshing body. Drink it, steam mussels with it, or pair it with pad Thai (3.5). **INUKSHUK** is a "Canadian IPA," with a nose of pine and juniper berries ending in a full, bitter finish (3).

WRECKING CREW is a single-hop pale ale brewed with El Dorado hops that develops peach and tangerine skin in the aroma (3). **BACKBEET WHEAT**, made with roasted beets, develops a slight tang on the way to a root vegetable sweetness (3.5). **TROUBLMAKR**, brewed every year on the brewery's anniversary, is an imperial black IPA with an enormous scrub pine hop character and massive depth of roast (4). **GTFO** is a double IPA with aromas of kiwi, cape gooseberry, and passionfruit (3.5).

WHITEWATER BREWING COMPANY

 @WhitewaterBrew

 whitewaterbeer.ca

📍 22 Fletcher Road, Foresters Falls

📞 (613) 582-7227

🕐 Summer: Mon–Thu 10a.m.–6p.m., Fri 10a.m.–8p.m.,
Sat 12p.m.–8p.m., Sun 12p.m.–6p.m.

📍 78 Pembroke Street, Cobden

📞 (613) 646-0101

🕐 Mon–Thu 11:30a.m.–9p.m., Fri 11:30a.m.–11p.m.,
Sat 10a.m.–11p.m., Sun 10a.m.–9p.m.

Inspired by their adventures on the mighty Ottawa River, professional whitewater rafting guides Chris Thompson, Chris Thompson (yes, there are two of them), and James Innes started the brewery in 2013. After a year during which the brewery experienced considerable growth, the founders decided to expand by opening a three-thousand-square-foot brewpub near popular tourist destination Wilderness Tours

Rafting in Foresters Falls, opening seven days a week during the peak summer months. While larger-scale brewing operations for bars and the LCBO are handled through Big Rig Brewery in Ottawa, Whitewater still provides brewpub patrons with regular and seasonal beers brewed in-house.

———

CLASS V is a standard North American IPA, with caramel notes accompanied by hints of orange peel and grapefruit zest lightly bitter for its 78 IBUs (3). **FARMER'S DAUGHTER** is a very malt-forward blonde ale that features clean cereal-grain notes followed up with flavours of honey and lemon (3). **WHISTLING PADDLER** is an English-style pale ale that includes toffee and citrus character with a grassy bitterness (2.5). **MIDNIGHT STOUT** is a very sessionable offering, with cocoa and brown sugar coming together with a smooth mouthfeel brought to bear by oatmeal (3.5).

WILD CARD BREWING COMPANY

📍 38 Gotha Street, Trenton

📞 (613) 394-1010

🐦 @wildcardbeer

🌐 wildcardbrewco.com

🕐 Mon–Sat 11a.m.–6p.m.

Wild Card is a new development in Trenton's small brewing scene. The brewery displaces Gateway Brewing (itself opened in 2011), which has become the name for the brew-on-premises business in the unit next door. Owned by Nathan and Zack Card, and located just across the Trent River from the Fraser Park Marina, Wild Card is named for the boat the Card family owned during Nathan and Zack's childhood. The brewery's branding is largely inspired by card games, specifically poker.

The range of beer on offer at Wild Card has diversified somewhat since the handover from Gateway Brewing, with more complex flavours and specialty ingredients being used. Fermentation still takes place in the type of equipment that one might find in a brew-on-premises facility, but as the brewery upgrades, plastic fermenters are being swapped out for steel and specialized ingredients from nearby Barn Owl Malt are being used to give the proceedings a local feel.

———

ACE OF DIAMONDS is a heavily raspberry-focused saison that obscures somewhat the Belgian yeast character with a tart juice presence and the pronounced bitterness of berry seeds (2.5). **BLONDE BARISTA** is ostensibly a blonde stout but uses coffee and lactose to produce a beer that tastes like a combination of a hoppy pale ale and a Tim Hortons double-double (3.5). **THE FLOP** is a blonde ale with a sweetly malty nose, accented by drying herbs in a medium body (2.5). **BUSTED FLUSH** is a gently roasty milk stout with lactose sweetness that creates a relatively velvety body (3). **RIDE THE BRAKE** is the brewery's India pale ale, a hybrid of the English and American styles using mostly West Coast hops to promote an orange-peel and mango-pulp aroma with a lurking pine bitterness (3). **SAVED BY THE DUNK** is a dunkelweizen with a banana bread character and a mildly spicy hop aroma (3).

TRAP KING is a Belgian-style abbey beer that is highlighted by a red licorice character in the aroma and in the sweet body (3). **GOOD THINGS ALL ONTARIO SAISON** develops a creamy texture with high notes of eucalyptus, clover honey, and roadside wildflowers in a fully textured body (4).

WILLIAM STREET BEER COMPANY

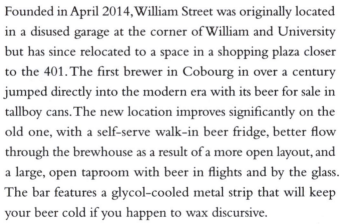

📍 975 Elgin Street W, Cobourg

📞 (888) 524-2337

🐦 @CobourgBeer

🌐 williamstreetbeer.com

🕐 Wed–Sat 11a.m.–7p.m., Sun 12p.m.–4p.m.

Founded in April 2014, William Street was originally located in a disused garage at the corner of William and University but has since relocated to a space in a shopping plaza closer to the 401. The first brewer in Cobourg in over a century jumped directly into the modern era with its beer for sale in tallboy cans. The new location improves significantly on the old one, with a self-serve walk-in beer fridge, better flow through the brewhouse as a result of a more open layout, and a large, open taproom with beer in flights and by the glass. The bar features a glycol-cooled metal strip that will keep your beer cold if you happen to wax discursive.

Owner Sean Walpole has taken the relocation as an opportunity to improve the skill levels of the staff, hiring brewers Karen Belfry and Corey Fairs out of the Niagara College brewing program. Additionally, on top of the expanded equipment, William Street is now exclusively using hops from the Bickle Farm in Northumberland County, managing to display some local character.

———

The year-round offering, **CLIFF TOP PALE ALE**, leans slightly toward the English golden ale in style, contrasting some light caramel malt with candied pineapple character from locally grown Chinook hops (3.5). **BOCK VON KRAMPUS**, a Christmas season specialty, displays brown bread crust, raisin, and a spicy hop character in the mid-palate with a mild yeast sourness (3). **MONKEY MOUNTAIN** is apparently an export India porter, filling that brown body with robust toasted malt, roasted grain, and the power of local, piney Cascade (3).

WINDMILL BREWERY

📍 5 Newport Drive, Johnstown

📞 (613) 704-0154

🌐 windmillbrewery.ca

🕐 Wed–Fri 3p.m.–7p.m., Sat 11a.m.–7p.m., Sun 12p.m.–5p.m.

Located across the road from a national historic site and Windmill Point Lighthouse, Windmill Brewery is housed in a purpose-built facility that serves double duty not only as a brewery but also as the home of King's Lock Craft Distillery (makers of 1000 Islands Moonshine). The Lucey family are the owners of the property, and Sean Lucey is Windmill's brewer. Having spent years as a homebrewer, his first venture into commercial territory is this lager production facility, with its ample space for lagering and conditioning. The brewery features a small bottle shop with a view of the brewery and distillery, which holds a tasting room licence so customers can enjoy glasses of pilsner. Plans for the future include a small outdoor patio, a hop garden, and, potentially, an onsite bakery.

____

Windmill's single beer is **1838 PILSNER**, named not for the year in which the style of beer was invented but to commemorate the Battle of the Windmill in the Patriot War. A Czech-style pilsner single hopped with Sterling, 1838 has a floral, spicy hop character and a bready, lightly sweet body that finishes with a clean yet assertive bitterness (4).

WOODHOUSE BREWING CO.

 @woodhousebeer

 woodhousebrewing.com

Founded in 2014, Woodhouse Brewing is the first independent venture from Graham Woodhouse, a brewer with a Labatt pedigree who decided to test the waters of the craft market. The initial offering from Woodhouse Brewing was a lager developed in collaboration with Charles MacLean and currently brewed in Etobicoke at Cool Brewing. It has since been joined by a more fully flavoured stout. Woodhouse's beers have enjoyed a great deal of popularity in bars and restaurants in Toronto because of the simple, recognizable log trademark on the label, and both have earned spots on LCBO shelves.

———

WOODHOUSE LAGER is an amber lager leaning toward the Vienna style that features significant crystal malt fruitiness and a lightly floral hop aroma (3). **WOODHOUSE STOUT** is somewhere between Irish and Scandinavian in character, with dry roast barley and a touch of salinity expanding the mouthfeel to a fuller body (3.5).

INTRODUCTION

Some of the best places to drink craft beer in Ontario are the local pubs and bars that make up an integral part of the province's beer scene. To help you find such places, we have assembled a list of over one hundred bars, pubs, and restaurants from around the province that we think are great places to drink beer.

This is by no means an exhaustive list. In the case of chains like Beertown in western Ontario, we have not included all locations. A number of pubs listed are included based on the recommendations of brewers who have vouched for them. We think there's no better recommendation for a place to drink beer than one that comes from the person who made that beer.

Tip your server! Try the special! Most importantly, drink responsibly. If you find that you have been overserved, we recommend taking a taxi or public transit, or possibly just walking. It's what we do.

WESTERN ONTARIO

THE BLACK DOG, BAYFIELD

- 📍 5 Main Street N
- 📞 (519) 565-2326
- 🐦 @BlackDogDish
- 🌐 blackdogpubbistro.ca

A fine pub on a gentle stretch in downtown Bayfield, the Black Dog sports a number of Ontario craft brews, including some from the emergent Huron coast scene.

THE KING EDWARD, ILDERTON

- 📍 13239 Ilderton Road
- 📞 (519) 666-1991
- 🐦 @KingEddyPub
- 🌐 thekingedward.com

This pub not only features rotating taps of Ontario, but highlights the impact that a pub can have in a small community.

In the Christmas season it features a choir night and festive singalong. Ding dong merrily three pints deep.

HAWGS BREATH SALOON & DELI, KINCARDINE

📍 896 Queen Street

📞 (519) 396-6565

Thankfully it does not smell like its name, but instead this is a wonderful place, noted for a well-put-together taplist and some superb sandwiches.

THE EARLY BIRD, LONDON

📍 355 Talbot Street

📞 (519) 439-6483

🐦 @TheEarlyBirdLdn

🌐 theearlybird.ca

This tiki-inspired breakfast spot does double duty during the day, serving a selection of cocktails and local beers alongside their largely portioned food.

MILOS' CRAFT BEER EMPORIUM, LONDON

📍 420 Talbot Street N

📞 (519) 601-4447

🐦 @PubMilos

🌐 pubmilos.com

Featuring a selection of Ontario craft beers and the house's Beer Lab products, Milos' is a favourite in London, and Milos himself is one of the few remaining examples of a real publican.

THE MORRISSEY HOUSE, LONDON

📍 359 Dundas Street

📞 (519) 204-9220

🐦 @morrisseyhouse

🌐 themorrisseyhouse.wordpress.com

The Morrissey House features seventeen taps of Ontario craft beer and cider. The converted mansion provides an interesting ambience and a pleasant patio with a courtyard feel in the summer.

THE POACHER'S ARMS, LONDON

📍 171 Queens Avenue

📞 (519) 432-7888

🐦 @Poachers_Arms

🌐 www.poachersarms.ca

The Poacher's Arms is just diversifying into craft beer but provides a number of options both on tap and in bottles.

MERCER HALL INN, STRATFORD

📍 104-108 Ontario Street

📞 (519) 271-9202

🐦 @MercerHallInn

🌐 mercerhall.ca

This kitchen, beer hall, and heritage hotel in the heart of historical downtown Stratford features a number of excellent beers both familiar and obscure.

THE BARREL HOUSE, WINDSOR

📍 3199 Sandwich Street

📞 (519) 977-5334

📘 barrelhousedraughtco

The Barrel House serves a variety of Ontario beers on tap and is a contender for the hotly contested title of best burger in Windsor.

RINO'S KITCHEN AND ALE HOUSE, WINDSOR

📍 131 Elliott Street W

📞 (519) 962-8843

🐦 @rinoskitchen

🌐 rinoskitchen.com

Located in a converted one-hundred–year-old house, Rino's carries only Ontario beers, and the menu is dedicated to showcasing Essex County on a farm-to-table basis.

ROCK BOTTOM BAR AND GRILL, WINDSOR

📍 3236 Sandwich Street

📞 (519) 258-7553

🌐 rockbottom.ca

Rock Bottom has Windsor's best selection of Ontario beers on tap (thirty-one) and a total lack of pretense. It is the kind of bar in which peanut shells crunch underfoot, which can be a refreshing change in an age of unnecessary refinements.

SNACK BAR-B-Q, WINDSOR

📍 39 Chatham Street E

📞 (519) 977-6227

🌐 snackbarbq.ca

Snack Bar-B-Q has the distinction of having not only good barbecue but also excellent vegetarian dishes and shareable plates. A carefully curated list of local offerings and a collaboration tap with Walkerville, not to mention a shockingly affordable selection of bourbons, make this downtown spot a real winner.

THE WALKERVILLE TAVERN, WINDSOR

📍 1850 Wyandotte Street E

📞 (519) 252-9661

🐦 @WalkervilleTav

🌐 thewalkervilletavern.com

Although the menu is fairly small in this popular Windsor haunt, it is distinctive. In addition to a selection of wok dishes, dessert is a Brownie Spring Roll, an idea whose time has apparently come.

GUELPH/ KITCHENER-WATERLOO

BEERTOWN PUBLIC HOUSE, CAMBRIDGE

📍 561 Hespeler Road, Unit 1A

📞 (519) 629-0288

🐦 @beertownph

🌐 beertown.ca

This three-location chain of pubs features a mix of Ontario craft products, imports, and macro beers. The modern decor and eclectic pub food menu make for a good destination for those new to craft beers or for craft beer drinkers with friends who haven't made the switch yet.

KIWI GASTROPUB, CAMBRIDGE

📍 47 Dickson Street

📞 (519) 622-3722

🐦 @KiwiCambridge

This little spot keeps busy with constant live performances, open mic nights, comedy nights, and trivia nights. It goes without saying that you probably need a good beer to go with trying to remember Grace Jones's first single.

BAKER STREET STATION, GUELPH

📍 76 Baker Street

📞 (519) 265-7960

🐦 @bakerststation

🌐 bakerstreetstation.ca

This well-known pub's menu features a number of truly interesting fusion items in addition to a series of brewery-dedicated taps that frequently rotate. The second floor balcony patio is a real drawing feature in summer.

THE FAT DUCK, GUELPH

📍 210 Kortright W

📞 (519) 827-0533

🐦 @thefatduckpub

🌐 fatduck.ca

This gastropub features a number of local craft beers, but the real attraction is the menu, which features a variety of influences from India, North Africa, and traditional British pubs. The curry chicken pie with housemade puff pastry is the result of such fusion.

RED BRICK CAFE, GUELPH

📍 8 Douglas Street

📞 (519) 836-1126

🐦 @redbrickguelph

🌐 redbrickcafe.ca

The Red Brick Cafe is a European-focused spot with light breakfast and lunch menus, shareables after 5p.m., and the rotational Welly one-off on tap. It is also a regular host of art shows and live performances.

WOOLWICH ARROW, GUELPH

📍 176 Woolwich Street

📞 (519) 836-2875

🐦 @WoolwichArrow

🌐 woolwicharrow.ca

A legendary Guelph pub and formerly part of the Neighbourhood Pub Group, the Wooly is a great place to try beers from the Guelph and Kitchener-Waterloo region, and it periodically hosts interesting tap takeovers from out-of-town breweries.

ARABELLA PARK, KITCHENER

📍 740 Belmont Avenue W

📞 (226) 220-6374

🐦 @ArabellaParkBar

🌐 arabellaparkbar.com

In the relatively short time it's been open, Arabella Park has become the talk of Kitchener, and for good reason. They offer an incredible selection of exciting craft beers and ciders on tap, as well as a truly enviable bottle list.

THE BENT ELBOW, KITCHENER

- 2880 King Street E
- (519) 208-0202
- @HaroldKroeker
- thebentelbow.ca

The Bent Elbow features thirty-nine taps, the vast majority of which are full of Ontario craft beer. While the rest of the selections are from other countries, they're still really good. The pub menu has a daily burger that changes according to the chef's whim.

KICKOFF SPORTS BAR AND CAFE, WATERLOO

- 170 University Avenue W
- (519) 888-9699
- @kickoffwaterloo

Supporting a diverse lineup of beer from across the province and across its borders, Kickoff is a laid-back sports bar with great beer. A perfect place to watch the footie and probably also the football.

THE JANE BOND, WATERLOO

- 📍 5 Princess Street W
- 📞 (519) 886-1689
- 🐦 @jane_bond005
- 🌐 janebond.ca

Do you like beer and hate meat? Man, veganism hit a home run with this place and its beer-friendly menu. Home of the WHOPPIE!

THE GOLDEN HORSESHOE

SOCIABLE KITCHEN AND TAVERN, BRANTFORD

- 📍 45 King George Road
- 📞 (519) 751-4042
- 🐦 @SociableTavern
- 🌐 sociabletavern.ca

Sociable has a nice 90s mixtape vibe, but one of the big treats of this dining spot is their From the Vault series, which features a highly coveted bottle selection.

ZANDER'S FIRE GRILL & BREW LOUNGE, BRANTFORD

📍 190 King George Road

📞 (519) 304-7625

🐦 @ZANDERS_BTFD

🌐 zanders.ca

Featuring a rock 'n' roll highway Americana aesthetic, live music, and a few surprising beers on draft, Zander's is Brantford's place to get a whole mess o' wings with a pint of something tasty.

RIB EYE JACK'S, BURLINGTON

📍 4045 Harvester Road

📞 (905) 633-9929

🐦 @ribeyejacks

🌐 ribeyejacksalehouse.com

Rib Eye Jack's has a healthy taplist featuring a number of Ontario beers and a bottle list longer than your arm. Macro beers seem to be priced at a premium and require you to order from the "Beginner's List." Nice.

IGGY'S PUB AND GRUB, FONTHILL

📍 115 Highway 20 E

📞 (905) 892-6667

🐦 @Iggyspub

🌐 iggyspub.com

THE ONTARIO CRAFT BEER GUIDE

With its myriad craft beers listed in bright colours on a chalk-board and updated frequently, Iggy's is a favourite of the brew-master students from Niagara College. If that's not a ringing endorsement, I'm not sure what would be. The menu focuses on bringing farm-to-table cuisine to a traditional pub menu.

COPPER KETTLE PUB, GLEN WILLIAMS

- 517 Main Street
- (905) 877-5551
- @CopperKettleGW
- copperkettle.ca

With a small, carefully chosen number of local craft beer and cider taps, this may well be one of the province's best-looking pubs, with its large windows and handsome stained glass transom. I will not apologize for that terrible rhyme or for sending you to this excellent pub.

AUGUSTA'S WINKING JUDGE, HAMILTON

- 25 Augusta Street
- (905) 524-5626
- @WinkingJudge
- winkingjudge.com

The Winking Judge is a holdover from the first wave of microbreweries in Ontario and feels not unlike an English front room. The selection of beers on offer is purely Ontario craft and in most cases very local to Hamilton.

BRUX HOUSE, HAMILTON

📍 137 Locke Street S

📞 (905) 527-2789

🐦 @BruxHouse

🌐 bruxhouse.com

This is something of a destination in Hamilton. The two-floor space features a well-curated beer selection and excellent food by executive chef Fraser Macfarlane.

DEMOCRACY*, HAMILTON

📍 202 Locke Street S

📞 (289) 389-2466

🐦 @DemocracyCoffee

🌐 democracyonlocke.com

This spacious and hip coffee shop has a number of vegan dishes, baked treats, and a respectable beer list.

THE SHIP, HAMILTON

📍 23 Augusta Street

📞 (905) 526-0792

🐦 @ShipTwits

🌐 theship.ca

The Ship features a well-curated thirteen-tap lineup of craft beers and ciders in addition to a limited number of cans. The late night eats menu makes it a natural choice for an evening out on the lash in Hamilton.

THE GARRISON HOUSE, NIAGARA-ON-THE-LAKE

- 111C, Unit 2, Garrison Village Drive
- (905) 468-4000
- @TGHNOTL
- thegarrisonhouse.ca

A gastro-style tavern, the Garrison House has six taps with Ontario beer. The real attraction here is chef David Watt's menu, which features his take on modern Canadian pub fare, including a fun Black Lager Beer-a-misu for dessert.

THE OLDE ANGEL INN, NIAGARA-ON-THE-LAKE

- 224 Regent Street
- (905) 468-3411
- @oldeangelinn
- angel-inn.com

Standing since 1789, the main draw of the Olde Angel Inn is the ambience. Low ceiling beams and a pub that has seen four separate centuries make for a nice place to enjoy a craft beer and a ploughman's.

BRÜ RESTAURANT, OAKVILLE

- 📍 138 Lakeshore Road E
- 📞 (905) 844-4400
- 🐦 @BruResto
- 🌐 brurestaurant.ca

Brü sports up to fifteen taps of Ontario beer, making for one of the better beer spots in Oakville. When it's paired with modern takes on classic pub food, you can't go wrong.

RISE ABOVE RESTAURANT, ST. CATHARINES

- 📍 120 St. Paul Street
- 📞 (289) 362-2636
- 🐦 @riseabovefoods
- 🌐 riseaboverestaurant.com

Niagara's first and only vegan restaurant and bakery, Rise Above has regular community events, a rotational art exhibition, and an all–Ontario beer and cider selection.

THE GTA

CROOKED CUE, MISSISSAUGA

📍 75 Lakeshore Road E

📞 (905) 271-7665

🐦 @crookedcue

🌐 crookedcue.ca

The Crooked Cue is a great place to play pool and catch an Ontario craft beer.

GROUND BURGER BAR, NEWMARKET

📍 #2-352 Doug Duncan Drive

📞 (905) 235-6328

🐦 @groundburgerbar

🌐 groundburgerbar.ca

Featuring a number of local craft offerings and a couple of rotational taps, this basement burger bar provides a comfortable environment and beer pairing suggestions for each of the burgers on their menu.

HUNGRY BREW HOPS, NEWMARKET

📍 211 Main Street S

📞 (905) 235-8277

🐦 @HungryBrewHops

🌐 hungrybrewhops.com

Hungry Brew Hops features thirty-three taps that include a number of Ontario choices along with quality international selections. The rustic industrial feel of the bar area and the contemporary menu make this pub on Newmarket's main street a destination. The authors recommend the pork rinds.

BUSTER RHINO'S, OSHAWA

📍 28 King Street E

📞 (905) 436-6986

🐦 @busterrhinosbbq

🌐 busterrhinos.com

Buster Rhino's features completely legit southern BBQ, chicken and waffles, an extensive selection of craft beers, and a whisky menu longer than many grade school primers.

PORT RESTAURANT, PICKERING

📍 1289 Wharf Street

📞 (905) 839-7678

🐦 @PORTrestaurant

Housed right on the dock, PORT is a bistro/bar with a number of modern takes on comforting foods and an excellent wine and beer list, with growlers occasionally on offer for sharing. It's also the sibling of east end Toronto's Maple Leaf Tavern.

KING HENRY'S ARMS, RICHMOND HILL

📍 9301 Yonge Street

📞 (905) 787-0900

🐦 @KingHenrysArms1

King Henry's Arms is a comfortable English-style pub with appropriate pub grub and an excellent local focus on beer. The annual craft beer tasting festival is always a local favourite.

BAR HOP, TORONTO

📍 391 King Street W

📞 (647) 352-7476

🐦 @barhopbar

🌐 barhoptoronto.com

Bar Hop's original location continues to be a bastion of craft beer in Toronto's entertainment district, pouring only the best of Ontario craft and bottles from all over the place. The daily savoury pie is an excellent choice on the food menu, but you'd best come hungry.

BEERBISTRO, TORONTO

📍 18 King Street E

📞 (416) 861-9872

🐦 @beerbistroTO

🌐 beerbistro.com

Started by chef Brian Morin and beer writer Stephen Beaumont, Beerbistro remains a sundown destination for the Bay Street crowd. While the bottle selection may have lost a step since the change in ownership, the taps are still well curated and include the house beer from Shillow Beer Co. The Belgian frites are a favourite of the clientele.

THE BELSIZE PUBLIC HOUSE, TORONTO

535 Mt. Pleasant Road

(416) 487-6468

thebelsize.pub

The Belsize Public House, from the same ownership as Toronto pub stalwart Harbord House, features a solid menu of inventive pub fare, thanks to chef Jimmy Fu, and an eclectic selection of craft offerings. A popular patio is a real draw in the summer months.

BIRRERIA VOLO, TORONTO

612 College Street

@barVolo

birreriavolo.com

Bar Volo isn't dead. It's just that both the focus and the bar room are narrower. The Morana family have concentrated on bringing in specialty offerings to this College Street hot spot and have so far featured some truly incredible imports on tap. The future is bright.

BRYDEN'S, TORONTO

📍 2455 Bloor Street W

📞 (416) 760-8069

🌐 brydens.ca

Bryden's occupies a special place in Bloor West Village and in the hearts of the staff of Great Lakes Brewing, who have been known to use it as a clubhouse. The upside of this affiliation is that it is frequently possible to find Great Lakes one-offs on tap before they're available elsewhere. The comfortable seating doesn't hurt either.

CASTRO'S LOUNGE, TORONTO

📍 2116 Queen Street E

📞 (416) 699-8272

🐦 @CastrosLounge

🌐 castroslounge.com

Castro's features a selection of Ontario craft beers on tap, on cask, and in bottles and cans. The menu is vegetarian and vegan friendly. The decor is of the Communist-Socialist persuasion in this cozy little pub.

CEILI COTTAGE, TORONTO

📍 1301 Queen Street E

📞 (416) 406-1301

🐦 @TheCeiliCottage

🌐 ceilicottage.com

As properly Irish a pub as one can fit into a modified garage, the Ceili features oysters and daily dinner specials in addition to a selection of Ontario beers, a whisky selection worthy of Brendan Behan.

THE CRAFT BRASSERIE AND GRILL, TORONTO

📍 107 Atlantic Avenue

📞 (416) 535-2337

🐦 @CraftBrasserie

🌐 thecraftbrasserie.com

Catering to the Liberty Village condo crowd, the Craft features 120 different taps, many of which feature Ontario's craft breweries. The eclectic menu features upscale takes on pub classics and interesting bistro fare.

DUKE'S REFRESHER, TORONTO

📍 382 Yonge Street, Unit 8

📞 (416) 979-8529

🐦 @DukesRefresher

🌐 dukesrefresher.ca

THE ONTARIO CRAFT BEER GUIDE

Duke's is an odd duck: it is basically a test kitchen for SIR Corp's Jack Astor's chain of pubs. The fact that the beer selection is good and that it has a frequently updated chalkboard with feature taps bodes well for the beer selection at that chain in the future.

GET WELL, TORONTO

- 1181 Dundas Street W
- (647) 351-2337
- @GetWellBar
- getwellbar.com

Get Well features a variety of craft and import beers on tap and an enormous selection of reasonably priced bottles. Plus, they've got Tetris. Those L-shaped ones always screw me up.

LANSDOWNE BREWERY, TORONTO

- 303 Lansdowne Avenue
- (416) 588-1641
- @LansdowneBrew
- lansdownebrewery.com

Lansdowne is one of the best places in the west end of Toronto to keep up with the developments in the city's craft beer scene. With a full brewhouse in the back of the pub, it's only a matter of time until their own beers join the guest taps at their bar.

LOOSE MOOSE, TORONTO

📍 146 Front Street W

📞 (416) 977-8840

🐦 @LooseMooseTO

🌐 theloosemoose.ca

The Loose Moose features something for everyone, with a significant number of craft beers on offer, in addition to macro lagers for the pre-sports crowd in downtown Toronto.

MORGANS ON THE DANFORTH, TORONTO

📍 1282 Danforth Avenue

📞 (416) 461-3020

🐦 @morgansonthedan

🌐 morgansonthedanforth.com

Morgans has a small but dependable selection of Ontario beers with rotating taps and an interesting bottle selection. Try the hoisin chicken wings.

THE OLD NICK, TORONTO

📍 123 Danforth Avenue

📞 (416) 461-5546

🐦 @oldnickpub

🌐 old-nick.com

A cozy, comfortable LGBTQ-friendly pub, the Old Nick has fourteen beers on tap and an exquisite brunch menu. Regular open mic nights and friendly conversation with the locals are a bonus. Robin likes going there for a nice, quiet pint. When visiting, tell the staff she said hi.

THE ONLY CAFE, TORONTO

📍 972 Danforth Avenue
📞 (416) 463-7843
🐦 @TheOnlyCafe
🌐 theonlycafe.com

The Only's frequently rotating taps and 70s–rec-room feel make it a comfortable hangout on the Danforth. Bonuses include the spacious patio and the fact that it's stumbling distance to Donlands station.

THE QUEEN AND BEAVER, TORONTO

📍 35 Elm Street
📞 (647) 347-2712
🐦 @QueenBeaverPub
🌐 queenandbeaverpub.ca

The Queen and Beaver serves pub fare of the extremely olde school. British fare includes excellent curries, deviled kidneys, and Scotch eggs. A good place to catch Ontario ales on cask.

THE REBEL HOUSE, TORONTO

📍 1068 Yonge Street

📞 (416) 927-0704

🐦 @rebelhouse_ca

🌐 rebelhouse.ca

A Rosedale institution, the Rebel House isn't just for the rich folks. The selection of beer on tap is not just restricted to Ontario but to brewers with bricks-and-mortar facilities. There is also a limited selection of cans. In summer, the patio is an excellent hideaway from the real world.

THE RHINO, TORONTO

📍 1249 Queen Street W

📞 (416) 535-8089

🐦 @TheRhinoBar

🌐 therhinobartoronto.com

The Rhino is a Parkdale institution featuring a great selection of Ontario craft beers and ciders on tap, in addition to an interesting cellar. The patio is an excellent place to people watch in summer.

STOUT IRISH PUB, TORONTO

📍 221 Carlton Street

📞 (647) 344-7676

🐦 @StoutIrishPubTO

🌐 stoutirishpub.ca

Situated in Cabbagetown, Stout has all the trappings of a traditional Irish pub, but with a vast beer list of both standards and seasonal taps. In summer, the alley patio is a popular spot for a beer in the shade.

TALL BOYS, TORONTO

- 838 Bloor Street W
- (416) 535-7486
- @tallboysbar
- tallboyscraft.com

Tall Boys likely features the largest number of Ontario craft beers available in a single location. While the taps rotate periodically, the real attraction here is the vast number of different canned beers, many of which aren't available anywhere else in the GTA.

TEQUILA BOOKWORM, TORONTO

- 512 Queen Street W
- (416) 504-2334
- @tequilabookworm
- tequilabookworm.com

Tequila Bookworm is a popular destination for Ontario-made beer and cider, using its "upshtairs" event space to host tap takeovers and allow breweries to show off their new products. A patio on the second floor at the rear is a quiet sanctuary from bustling Queen Street.

TRINITY COMMON, TORONTO

📍 303 Augusta Avenue

📞 (647) 346-3030

🐦 @Trinity_Common

🌐 trinitycommon.com

A staple of Kensington's gentrifying pub scene, this pub is located next to the Kensington Brewery and has one of the most bleeding-edge beer lists in the city of Toronto. While all the food is recommended, the authors suggest brunch in the market to up your hipster cred. Try the Cajun roasted sweet potatoes.

THE WALLACE GASTROPUB, TORONTO

📍 1954 Yonge Street

📞 (416) 489-3500

🐦 @wallacegastro

🌐 thewallacegastropub.ca

Located just north of Toronto's Davisville station, this pub has a storied history in craft beer circles and a taplist that features both Ontario and American craft beers. Friday is curry night. Jordan, who has been drinking there since he was eighteen, recommends the Malaysian fish curry. He may at some point get cask back on the drinks menu, having ensured a handpull survived the last renovation.

WISE BAR, TORONTO

📍 1007 Bloor Street W

📞 (416) 519-3139

🐦 @WiseBarToronto

🌐 wisebar.ca

With a masterfully curated beer list courtesy of owner Tamara Wise, Wise Bar is a small and relaxed hangout with simple, unpretentious snacks for grazing. There's something for everyone to enjoy.

WVRST, TORONTO

📍 609 King Street W

📞 (416) 703-7775

🐦 @WVRSTbeerhall

🌐 wvrst.com

Specializing in duck fat fries and a variety of sausages from different parts of the world, Wvrst is a good place for communal dining and stein hoisting. Their cellaring program will eventually produce interesting results. The authors recommend the Boerewors from the sausage menu.

THE TAP AND TANKARD, WHITBY

- 📍 224 Brock Street S
- 📞 (905) 666-8090
- 🐦 @tapandtankard
- 🌐 thetapandtankard.com

In addition to a permanent selection of several mainstream taps, this bar features sixteen rotating taps of Ontario and American craft beer. The food menu is similarly deep, making this an all-things-to-everyone kind of night out.

EASTERN ONTARIO

KIN CAFE, BLOOMFIELD

- 📍 254 Main Street
- 📞 (613) 393-3332
- 🐦 @KinCafePEC
- 🌐 kincafe.ca

When you're daytripping in Prince Edward County, this little spot that specializes in bento makes for a lovely lunchtime break, serving a few of the county's beers alongside some Ontario offerings.

SCHNITZELS EUROPEAN FLAVOURS, CORNWALL

📍 158 Pitt Street

📞 (613) 938-8844

🐦 @Schnitzels

🌐 schnitzels.ca

It's pretty safe to assume what the food region of choice is for this Cornwall spot, though it should be said the menu is rather eclectically European, serving everything from goulash to wood oven pizza along with seventeen beers on tap.

THE SOCIALIST PIG, GANANOQUE

📍 21 King Street E

📞 (613) 463-8800

🐦 @socpigcoffee

🌐 thesocialistpiggananoque.com

Sporting a front counter made of books and a patio that overlooks Gananoque Brewing Company, this locally focused cafe and dining spot might be the best place to break out your unread copy of Ferdinand Lassalle's *What is Capital?*

THE ALIBI, KINGSTON

📍 293 Princess Street

📞 (613) 767-1312

🐦 @AlibiKingston

🌐 thealibikingston.com

The Alibi has a relaxed atmosphere suited to trivia nights and tap takeovers. With beers from east and west of Kingston, it might have one of the most diverse tap lineups in the province geographically.

BARCADIA KINGSTON, KINGSTON

📍 347 Princess Street

🌐 barcadia.ca

Barcadia is an arcade and bar with a number of excellent options both on tap and available for play. Just remember to put your beer down when the space invaders increase speed and reverse direction, provoking you to shoot through your own defences to reach them, you wild card.

THE BROOKLYN, KINGSTON

📍 14 Garrett Street

🐦 @brooklynktown

🌐 brooklynktown.com

The Brooklyn features a taplist best encapsulated by their motto "No crap on tap." They feature American selections as well as Ontario craft. The pub functions as a live music venue and on some nights has a busy dance floor.

RED HOUSE, KINGSTON

- 369 King Street E
- (613) 767-2558
- @RedHouseKtown
- redhousekingston.com

Red House has a small number of craft taps available, but the selection is rock solid. In terms of food, the variety might be best categorized as down-home bistro.

ASHBURNHAM ALE HOUSE, PETERBOROUGH

- 128 Hunter Street E
- (705) 874-0333
- ashburnhamalehouse.ca

Billed as a "craft beer cafe," this contemporary spot features both coffee and beer and is planning on three to four rotational taps that will complement their menu of thin crust pizzas.

THE OTTAWA REGION

CHESHIRE CAT PUB, CARP

- 2193 Richardson Side Road
- (613) 831-2183
- @cheshirecatpub
- cheshirecatpub.com

Rising like a phoenix from the ashes is this Ontario craft beer institution that features constantly rotating taps and casks. Absolutely everyone is glad to have them back.

THE ARROW & LOON, OTTAWA

📍 99 Fifth Avenue

📞 (613) 237-0448

🐦 @ArrowandLoon

🌐 arrowandloon.com

Originally a part of the Neighbourhood Pub Group, the Arrow & Loon continues to supply Ontario-made beer to the people of Ottawa. The authors heartily recommend the bison chili.

BLACK TOMATO, OTTAWA

📍 11 George Street

📞 (613) 789-8123

🐦 @theblacktomato1

🌐 theblacktomato.ca

This staple of Ottawa's ByWard market scene has been in operation since 1995 and features twenty-one rotating taps of Ontario and Quebec craft beers. A serious draw not only for the attractive red brick interior, but also for their jambalaya.

BROTHERS BEER BISTRO, OTTAWA

📍 366 Dalhousie Street

📞 (613) 695-6300

🐦 @brosbeerbistro

🌐 brothersbeerbistro.ca

Located in the ByWard Market, Brothers features a selection of European beers in addition to the local brewery choices that are exploding onto the Ottawa scene. The cheese and charcuterie boards offer fantastic customization.

HINTONBURG PUBLIC HOUSE, OTTAWA

📍 1020 Wellington Street W

📞 (613) 421-5087

🐦 @theHPH

🌐 hintonburgpublichouse.ca

Hintonburg has a very comfortable and cozy atmosphere that matches well with their comforting food and beer options, with an excellent selection of cans and bottles available. Watch out for the pub's mascot, a SUPER creepy doll named Susan. Seriously, it freaks me out.

HOUSE OF TARG, OTTAWA

📍 1077 Bank Street

📞 (613) 680-8274

🐦 @HouseofTarg

🌐 houseoftarg.com

Look, sometimes you just want to go to a place where you can eat some house-made pierogies, drink from a modest selection of craft beer, and play some pinball. This is the place in Ottawa to do that. Robin suggests the *Ghostbusters* machine if it's still there, but then she always does.

PROHIBITION PUBLIC HOUSE, OTTAWA

📍 337 Somerset Street W

📞 (613) 565-2704

🐦 @prohibition337

🌐 prohibitionhouse.com

Prohibition Public House has a fun, Chicago speakeasy vibe, with over twenty local beers on tap and a modest but delectable mix of shareables and entrees.

PUB ITALIA, OTTAWA

📍 434 1/2 Preston Street

📞 (613) 232-2326

🐦 @pubitalia

🌐 pubitalia.ca

A combination of Italian restaurant and Irish pub has resulted in a beer bar that provides an excellent selection of craft and imports and the ability to order them in a 38-ounce pint. The can and bottle list is extensive.

WELLINGTON GASTROPUB, OTTAWA

- 1325 Wellington Street W
- (613) 729-1315
- @thegastropub
- thewellingtongastropub.com

The Wellington specializes in delicious bistro fare, with a large selection of wine and beer to pair it with. This gastropub was also the birthplace of what is now known as Stalwart Brewing.

NORTHERN ONTARIO

KENZINGTON BURGER BAR, BARRIE

- 40 Dunlop Street E
- (705) 725-1667
- @kenzburgerbar
- kenzington.ca

This famous Barrie-based burger joint sports four locations and a food truck, serving a number of Ontario craft beers alongside their exceptional burgers.

THE LOCAL GASTROPUB, BARRIE

📍 37 Dunlop Street W

📞 (705) 252-9220

🐦 @thelocalgastro

🌐 thelocalgastropub.com

The Local boasts sixteen Ontario craft taps and one cask tap in addition to monthly beer dinners, a vegetarian-friendly menu, and a deep-fried Mars bar just in case you thought that thistle was on the website for decoration only.

GRIFFIN GASTROPUB, BRACEBRIDGE

📍 9 Chancery Lane

📞 (705) 646-0438

🐦 @griffingastro

🌐 thegriffinpub.ca

Run by Curt Dunlop and Jed Corbeil, who are in charge of Toronto's annual Session beer festival, the Griffin's twelve taps rotate but frequently feature Sawdust City.

THE OLD STATION RESTAURANT, BRACEBRIDGE

📍 88 Manitoba Street

📞 (705) 645-9776

🌐 oldstation.ca

Nestled in the heart of Bracebridge, this spacious, cabin-like restaurant has long been a favourite for visitors and locals alike, serving excellent pub grub and beers from the Muskoka region.

THE HURON CLUB, COLLINGWOOD

📍 94 Pine Street

📞 (705) 293-6677

🐦 @thehuronclub

🌐 thehuronclub.ca

A popular Collingwood lunch spot with a wide selection of local beers, the Huron Club really comes into its own during the summer months, when a spacious patio results in lunch guests becoming lazy-afternoon guests.

THE IRON SKILLET, COLLINGWOOD

📍 20 Balsam Street

📞 (705) 444-5804

🌐 theironskillet.ca

The folks of Collingwood are rather serious when it comes to good schnitzel, and the Iron Skillet is purported to be the best in town, featuring a modest selection of craft to wash it down.

BUOYS EATERY AND TAKEOUT, GORE BAY

📍 1 Purvis Drive

📞 (705) 282-2869

🐦 @BuoysEatery

🌐 buoyseatery.com

Situated right on the bay and a stone's throw from Split Rail Brewing, Buoys makes for a great place to sip on a beer, have some of their famous pizza, and watch the ships come and go.

LAVIGNE TAVERN, LAVIGNE

📍 10521 Highway 64

📞 (705) 594-2301

🐦 @lavignetavern

🌐 lavignetavern.com

Mostly featuring northern Ontario craft taps from breweries like Stack and Lake of Bays, this pub claims to have the best wings in West Nipissing. With a little advance notice, they'll whip up a pig roast with all the fixins for you and your friends.

THE RAVEN AND REPUBLIC, NORTH BAY

📍 246 First Avenue W

📞 (705) 478-6110

🐦 @ravenandrepubli

🌐 ravenandrepublic.ca

The Raven and Republic has sixteen taps focused on local breweries and serves upscale pub food. The owner runs a beer 101 course the first Wednesday and Thursday of each month. Delicious, but also educational.

WHITE OWL BISTRO, NORTH BAY

- 639 Lakeshore Drive
- (705) 472-2662
- @whiteowlbistro
- thewhiteowlbistro.ca

The White Owl Bistro's main focus, through and through, is local. Using a farm-to-table approach for the food and featuring a number of beers from the breweries of the region, this notable spot also features a decent wine selection and a truly breathtaking view of the lake.

CASERO KITCHEN TABLE, OWEN SOUND

- 946 3rd Avenue E
- (519) 416-8226
- @casero_bus
- caserofood.ca

Who doesn't love tacos? Seriously. While Casero also has a taco bus on Sauble Beach, the main location on 3rd Avenue East features a modest but commendable bottle and can offering. Also, c'mon, some of the best tacos in town, including vegetarian, vegan, and gluten-free options.

LOPLOPS LOUNGE & GALLERY, SAULT STE. MARIE

📍 651 Queen Street E

📞 (705) 945-0754

🐦 @LopLopLounge

🌐 loplops.com

Loplops features local craft taps and live music and is instrumental in the production of Sault Ste. Marie's Festival of Beer. Go and check out Bad Idea Thursday. You won't regret it, unless you do!

HARDROCK 42, SUDBURY

📍 117 Elm Street

📞 (705) 586-3303

🐦 @hardrock42G

🌐 hardrock42.com

It's easy to see why Hardrock 42 is Sudbury's beer destination. With its whopping sixty-five taps featuring both Ontario and international beers, you'd be a sucker not to go check it out. While there, try the famous Sudbury Hangover burger and be sure to bring your own headache.

LAUGHING BUDDHA, SUDBURY

📍 194 Elgin Street

📞 (705) 673-2112

🐦 @buddhasudbury

🌐 laughingbuddhasudbury.com

In addition to a carefully chosen list of Ontario beers in cans and bottles, Laughing Buddha has beer from all over the world. It may be the only pub in the world with a sandwich named after the star of *The Hilarious House of Frightenstein*.

THE FOUNDRY, THUNDER BAY

📍 242 Red River Road

📞 (807) 285-3188

🐦 @TheFoundryPub

🌐 thefoundrypub.com

This spacious, Irish–influenced pub is a Thunder Bay institution, with a wide selection of craft beer on tap, mouthwatering pub grub, and, best of all, folks of all ages stopping in for something local.

RED LION SMOKEHOUSE, THUNDER BAY

📍 28 Cumberland Street S

📞 (807) 286-0045

🌐 redlionsmokehouse.ca

With a selection of over one hundred beers and ciders from Ontario and around the world, this Thunder Bay spot is a local go-to. While there, try the brisket!

TOMLIN RESTAURANT, THUNDER BAY

📍 202 1/2 Red River Road

📞 (807) 346-4447

🌐 tomlinrestaurant.com

While supplying an excellent range of local beers, Tomlin's real attraction is its food, which has helped the Thunder Bay dining scene step up its game. Most notable dishes to try are the house-cured charcuterie board and the biggest steak you've ever laid eyes on.

GLOSSARY

ACETALDEHYDE An organic compound that presents as a flaw in beer above certain concentrations and is notable for its pungent green-apple aroma. Typically a sign of young beer that has been rushed through production.

AMERICAN FARMHOUSE ALE A North American derivation of the Belgian saison style of beer. Typically made with some percentage of wheat and fermented with a Belgian yeast strain, and frequently finished with Brettanomyces for a dry mouthfeel.

AMERICAN IPA An invention of the North American brewing renaissance, American IPA borrows the structure of the heavily hopped India pale ale from England and substitutes American hop varieties for English ones. The beer is usually quite bitter (between 40 and 70 IBU) and features notes of pine and citrus from C-hop varieties.

AMERICAN WHEAT BEER American wheat beers are defined largely by the inclusion of wheat in their grist rather than the yeast esters prevalent in their German counterparts. The American version is frequently filtered, resulting in a light-coloured, clear beer with more hop than yeast character.

ALT (BIER)   A hybrid style of beer from Dusseldorf that is fermented with ale yeast and then conditioned as though it were a lager. Typically coloured between amber and chestnut, alts tend to be earthy in character and lean toward malt-dominance.

BARREL (BBL)   One of two commonly used brewery volume measurements. In America, a barrel represents 31.5 U.S. gallons, which is approximately 119 litres of beer.

BITTER   Referring to a range of styles of English beers from the early decades of the twentieth century, *bitter* is something of a catch-all term for lower-alcohol English ales served on cask and featuring biscuit malts and mild hop bitterness.

BLONDE ALE   A light ale, typically offered by breweries as an alternative to a pale lager. Although lightness in body and in flavour is of primary concern, the blonde ale can be a good showcase for fruit and hop flavours.

BOCK   Properly a family of lager styles that has its origin in the town of Einbeck in northern Germany, bocks tend to enjoy a complex, malty character, although their primary commonality is their above-average strength. Since *bock* means *ram* in German, labels are frequently festooned with goats.

BOTTLE CONDITIONING   Instead of being bottled at the desired carbonation level, beer is packaged in bottles with a small amount of unfermented wort or priming sugar and left to carbonate naturally. This is popular in Belgian styles and may include a number of different yeast strains.

BRETTANOMYCES   A strain of wild yeast most commonly found on the skin of fruit. The specific strain *bruxellensis* is a defining characteristic of sour beers made in Brussels. Brettanomyces typically dries out beers by eating sugars other yeast strains can't. Frequently used descriptors of the resultant aroma include "horse blanket," "sheep pen," and the more general "funky."

BREWHOUSE — A general term for the equipment used in the first half of the brewing process, including but not limited to the mash tun, lauter tun, and kettle.

BREWMASTER — Properly, a professional designation afforded to the most senior member of staff at a large brewery after years of experience have been gained. Commonly, whoever is doing the brewing at a brewery.

BREWPUB — Typically a restaurant that has its own in-house brewery and largely features its own beers on tap. Usually brewpubs sell their beers only on their own premises, but there are exceptions.

BROWN ALE — Full-strength English ales that tend toward deep caramel and malt character; predictably coloured. American versions retain the colour but frequently have a cleaner yeast profile and substitute American hop varieties.

BUTYRIC ACID — In beer, an off-flavour. At low concentrations it may present as vaguely cheesy, reminiscent of Parmesan. At high concentrations it is similar to baby vomit and therefore to be avoided.

CAMPAIGN FOR REAL ALE (CAMRA) — An English consumer-advocacy group concerned about the dwindling diversity of traditional beers on draft.

CANDI SUGAR — A specialty invert sugar typically used in stronger Belgian-style beers. The simple sugars (fructose and glucose) are more easily digestible by yeast and result in a quick and characteristic boost in alcohol.

CREAM ALE — A North American hybrid-style beer that is fermented like an ale but conditioned like a lager. Developed as a response to the popularity of pale lagers, cream ale may contain adjuncts for lightness of body.

CZECH PILSNER   The originator and most hop-forward version of the pilsner style, Czech pilsner tends to feature Saaz hops and a low level of diacetyl among its notable characteristics. Pilsner Urquell is a prime example.

DIACETYL   A flavour compound in beer that is typically noted as a brewing flaw. At low levels it may help define a style, such as Czech pilsner or some English ales. At high concentrations it is detectable as butterscotch or imitation-butter flavouring and creates an unpleasant, slick mouthfeel.

DIMETHYL SULFIDE   A brewing flaw that typically presents as cooked or canned vegetables. In home-brewing it is frequently the result of an insufficiently vigorous boil or a covered kettle.

DOUBLE IPA   An outsize version of the American IPA, double IPA tends to be higher in alcohol and bitterness, frequently surpassing the human threshold for detection (110 BU). Vibrant hop aromas define the style.

DRY HOPPING   A technique whereby fermented beer is dosed with hops in order to produce a more vibrant aroma in the finished beer.

EXPORT STOUT   Historically, a version of stout brewed for international markets that is stronger and sweeter than usual in order to survive transport.

FESTBIER   A modern version of the traditional marzen style usually served at Oktoberfest celebrations in Germany. This lager is typically just above 5% alcohol and is characterized by heavier malt sweetness than a typical lager.

GOLDEN ALE   Typically, golden ale refers to a style of beer developed in England in the 1980s as a response to the prevalence of lagers in the market. Often includes North American hop varieties in some quantity.

GOSE

A nearly forgotten style of beer originating in Leipzig, which has risen to prominence in North America in recent years. Typically consisting of 50 percent wheat, gose's main attraction is that it is salted and dosed with coriander. It's an acquired taste on the road to triumph, despite its oddity.

GRISETTE

A low-alcohol Belgian ale in the style of a saison, designed for refreshment. Typically includes a significant portion of wheat and very low bitterness. Popular with miners, historically speaking.

HALLERTAUER

A family of German landrace hops that typically produces spicy herbal notes, but in sufficient concentration can create a lime aroma.

HECTOLITRE (HL)

The more prevalent metric measurement of brewery volumes, a hectolitre is 100 litres. One hectolitre is approximately 0.85 barrels.

HEFEWEIZEN

A German style of wheat beer typically redolent of banana, clove, or bubble gum yeast esters and featuring a creamy body. Often open-fermented. Asking for it with a slice of orange will get you hooted at in beer bars.

HELLES

A style of lager developed in Munich in the late nineteenth century that is the culmination of a century of lightening malt character in the city's beer. Typically finds a balance between a simple grain character and a herbal, floral hop aroma.

HOPS

The flowers of the rhizomatous plant *Humulus lupulus*, hops are to beer what spices are to cooking. Hops provide bitterness if used early in the boil and aroma and flavour if used later in the brewing process.

IMPERIAL STOUT	A type of export stout originally brewed in England for export to the court of Catherine II of Russia. It is typically high in alcohol with pronounced roasted- and dark-malt characters and a significant amount of sweetness due to residual sugars.
INDIA PALE ALE	An English style of higher-alcohol, heavily hopped ale that acquired the name as a result of being shipped from England to India during the nineteenth century, surviving because of the preservative nature of the hops. An inspiration for North American craft beer due to its assertive bitterness and pronounced flavour.
INTERNATIONAL BITTERING UNIT (IBU)	The standard unit of measurement for bitterness in a beer, the IBU scale runs from 0 (no bitterness) to 100 (very bitter indeed). It is theoretically possible to exceed the scale, but the perception threshold in humans sits at around 100, raising the question, "Who are you brewing that for? Robots?"
KÖLSCH	A style of beer from Cologne in Germany, kölsch is a hybrid style of beer fermented at ale temperatures and then lagered. It is noted for being lightly fruity and spicy, golden in colour and coming in 200 millilitre glasses in its native city.
KOYT	A Dutch style of gruit recently in resurgence, featuring wheat and oats as significant percentages of the malt bill. Traditionally the style does not use hops, preferring instead sweet gale.
LAGER	Beer produced with bottom-fermenting yeast strains and cold conditioned in storage. Typically central European in origin, lager styles are diverse and are frequently given a bad rap because of the prevalence of relatively bland pale lagers on the world stage.
MALT	Any germinated cereal grain that has had its sprouting process arrested. In brewing, *malt* usually refers to barley that has been kilned to some extent, resulting in different treatments and flavour profiles.

MICROBREWERY In normal usage, the term *microbrewery* connotes a brewery that is independently owned and produces less than 15,000 BBL of beer annually. In general parlance, it's what craft breweries were called before the term caught on.

MILD A low-alcohol English beer with regional variants (lighter in colour in the south U.K., darker in Wales and the north). Typically below 4% alcohol, mild is a sessionable option for refreshment.

MILK STOUT Named for the use of lactose as a sweetening agent, milk stout tends to take on a sweeter body and creamier texture than regular stouts. A good choice if you like the sweetness of an imperial stout but not the alcohol.

MOUTHFEEL The texture of a beverage in your mouth. It might be sparkling and fizzy, or slick and coating, or bone dry. Texture is an important sensory element to take into account

NANOBREWERY A very small brewhouse capable of producing an extremely limited amount of beer. If it could fit in your garage, it's a nanobrewery.

PALE ALE A popular style of English beer brewed mostly with pale malt and usually moderately hopped, meaning that it can vary in flavour immensely. Pale ale has spawned a number of regional and international variants.

PHENOL A group of aromatic organic compounds that make up aromas in beer. In low concentrations they are appropriate, spicy, and pleasant. In high concentrations they're a little like melting plastic or a dirty Band-Aid, and are therefore a brewing flaw.

PILSNER A style of lager developed in the Czech town of Plzeň in 1842, which has spawned regional variants including a more lightly hopped German variety. Possibly the most influential beer style in history.

PORTER   A style of dark English ale brewed in London since the beginning of the eighteenth century, sometimes catastrophically as in the case of the London Beer Flood of 1814. Typically it includes a nutty malt presence in addition to dark malt flavours and roast. Historical recreations frequently include a souring note.

REAL ALE   Cask conditioned rather than artificially carbonated, real ale still contains live yeast at time of service and is frequently a better treatment for subtle flavours and certain English styles like bitter and mild.

REINHEITSGEBOT A law enacted in Bavaria in 1516 that limited the ingredients to be used in beer to barley, hops, and water. The law was as much about crop management and ensuring food supply as it was about beer quality, but it did result in some nice lager, which we're all grateful for.

SAISON   A Belgian style of farmhouse ale historically brewed for farmhands to drink during the summer planting and harvest seasons. It usually contains a significant amount of wheat and relatively few hops.

SCHWARZBIER   A dark lager made in Germany that typically has a light roast quality with hints of coffee or chocolate, which fade away into the body and a clean finish. Currently growing in popularity in North America.

SESSION IPA   A low-alcohol variant of the American IPA, which usually features large amounts of late and dry hopping in order to place the aromas of a regular IPA in a beer that you can drink all day. If you attempt to drink full-strength IPA all day, it's going to be a short day.

STOUT   A dark style of ale that is usually defined by the presence of roasted barley, which gives the beer a lightly burnt character in addition to other features. Extremely popular on St. Patrick's Day.

STRONG ALE	More than merely an ale with increased alcohol, strong ale tends to connote increased malt complexity and assertive flavour, regardless of national genre. In the case of England, it denotes a specific genre of bottled beer. In the case of American and Belgian styles, the descriptor is something of a catch-all.
TABLE BEER	A Belgian style of ale noted for its extremely low alcohol content, managed without sacrificing flavour. Until the 1980s it was served to schoolchildren at lunchtime. Belgian children are less belligerent now but no happier.
VIENNA-STYLE LAGER	An early style of lager developed in the 1830s whose hallmark is its reddish tint and malt-forward, caramel-accented body. Popular as a gateway craft beer style for those acclimatizing to flavourful beer.
VLB BERLIN	Versuchs–und Lehranstalt für Brauerei, a German institute that provides beer-making training and education.
WEISSE	The German word for "white," not for "wheat." The name has to do with the light colour of wheat beers more than the content of their grist.
WEST COAST IPA	Referring to the West Coast of the U.S., this IPA variant features American hops.
WHEAT BEER	A catch–all term for a number of styles featuring wheat as a significant part of their makeup. If you can use a more specific term, you're wise to do so.
WITBIER	A Belgian ale made with a significant portion of wheat and featuring orange peel and coriander seeds as flavouring additions. The style nearly disappeared in the middle of the twentieth century but was revived by brewer Pierre Celis.
WORT	A technical brewing term for unfermented beer. Beer is wort right up until the yeast starts eating it, at which point you still want to wait a couple of weeks before drinking it.

BREWERIES BY REGION

WESTERN ONTARIO

Anderson Craft Ales	London
Bad Apple Brewing	Zurich
Banded Goose Brewing Co.	Kingsville
Bayside Brewing Co.	Erieau
Beer Lab London	London
Black Swan Brewing	Stratford
Blue Elephant Craft Brew House	Simcoe
Brew Windsor	Windsor
CEEPS	London
Cowbell Brewing Co.	Blyth
Craft Heads Brewing Co.	Windsor
Forked River Brewing Co.	London
Frank Brewing Co.	Tecumseh
Half Hours on Earth	Seaforth
Last Castle Brewing Co.	Port Stanley
London Brewing Co-op	London
Lonsbery Farms Brewing Co.	Harrow
Midian Brewing	Windsor
Motor Craft Ales	Windsor
Neustadt Springs Brewery	Neustadt
New Limburg Brewery	Simcoe
Pint Pursuits Brewing Co.	St. Thomas
Railway City Brewing Co.	St. Thomas
Ramblin' Road Brewery Farm	La Salette

THE ONTARIO CRAFT BEER GUIDE

Refined Fool Brewing Co.	Sarnia
Sandwich Brewing Co.	Windsor
Stone House Brewing Co.	Varna
Stratford Brewing Co.	Stratford
Strathroy Brewing Co.	Strathroy
Toboggan Brewing Co.	London
Upper Thames Brewing Co.	Woodstock
Walkerville Brewery	Windsor

GUELPH/KITCHENER-WATERLOO

Abe Erb Brewery and Restaurant	Waterloo
Barncat Artisan Ales	Cambridge
Bitte Schön Brauhaus	New Hamburg
Block Three Brewing Co.	St. Jacobs
Brick Brewing Co.	Kitchener
Brothers Brewing Co.	Guelph
Caledon Hills Brewing Co.	Caledon
Descendants Beer & Beverage Co.	Kitchener
Elora Brewing	Elora
Four Fathers Brewing Co.	Rockwood
Grand River Brewing	Cambridge
Hockley Valley Brewing Co.	Orangeville
Innocente Brewing Co.	Waterloo
Lion Brewery Restaurant	Waterloo
Royal City Brewing Co.	Guelph
StoneHammer Brewing	Guelph
Together We're Bitter Co-operative Brewing	Kitchener
Wellington Brewing Co.	Guelph

THE GOLDEN HORSESHOE

All or Nothing Brewhouse	Oakville
Bamboo Beer Ltd.	Hamilton
Bell City Brewing Co.	Brantford
Bench Brewing Co.	Beamsville

BREWERIES BY REGION

605

Brimstone Brewing Co.	Ridgeway
Bush Pilot Brewing Co.	Burlington
Cameron's Brewing Co.	Oakville
Clifford Brewing Co.	Hamilton
Collective Arts Brewing	Hamilton
Crazy Beard	Oakville
Exchange Brewery, The	Niagara-on-the-Lake
Hamilton Brewery, The	Hamilton
High Road Brewing Co.	Niagara-on-the-Lake
Kame & Kettle Beer Works	Fonthill
Lock Street Brewing	St. Catharines
Mash Paddle Brewing Co.	Brantford
Merchant Ale House	St. Catharines
Niagara Brewing Co.	Niagara Falls
Niagara College Teaching Brewery	Niagara-on-the-Lake
Niagara Oast House Brewers	Niagara-on-the-Lake
Nickel Brook Brewing Co.	Burlington
Old Credit Brewing Co.	Port Credit
Orange Snail Brewers	Milton
Pepperwood Brewery & Catering	Burlington
Plan B Beer Works	St. Catharines
Shawn & Ed Brewing Co.	Dundas
Silversmith Brewing	Niagar-on-the-Lake
Syndicate Restaurant and Brewery	Niagara Falls
Syndicate Restaurant and Brewery (Grimsby)	Grimsby
Taps On Queen Brewhouse & Grill	Niagara Falls
3 Brewers, The (Oakville)	Oakville
Trafalgar Ales and Meads	Oakville

THE GTA

Ace Hill Beer	Toronto
Amber Brewery	Markham
Amsterdam Brewing Co.	Toronto
Arch Brewing	Newmarket
Bandit Brewery	Toronto

Bar Hop Brewco	Toronto
Batch (by Creemore)	Toronto
Bellwoods Brewery	Toronto
Big Rock Brewery	Toronto
Black Creek Historic Brewery	Toronto
Black Oak Brewing Co.	Toronto
Blood Brothers Brewing	Toronto
Brock Street Brewing	Whitby
Brunswick Bierworks	Toronto
Burdock Brewery	Toronto
C'est What?	Toronto
Cheetah International Brewers Inc.	Toronto
Cheshire Valley Brewing Co.	Toronto
Common Good Beer Co.	Toronto
Cool Beer Brewing Co.	Toronto
County Durham Brewing Co.	Pickering
Danforth Brewery	Toronto
Double Trouble Brewing Co.	Toronto
Draught Dodger Brewery	Toronto
Duggan's Brewery	Toronto
Falcon Brewing Co.	Ajax
5 Paddles Brewing Co.	Whitby
Folly Brewpub	Toronto
Granite Brewery & Tied House	Toronto
Great Lakes Brewery	Toronto
Halo Brewery	Toronto
Henderson Brewing Co.	Toronto
High Park Brewery	Toronto
Hogtown Brewers	Toronto
Hop City Brewing Co.	Brampton
Indie Ale House Brewing	Toronto
Junction Craft Brewing Co.	Toronto
Katalyst Brewing Co.	Toronto
Kensington Brewing Co.	Toronto
Lake Wilcox Brewing Co.	Vaughan
Laylow Beer Bar & Eatery	Toronto

Left Field Brewery	Toronto
Liberty Village Brewing Co.	Toronto
Longslice Brewery	Toronto
Lost Craft Beer	Toronto
Louis Cifer Brew Works	Toronto
Magnotta Brewery	Vaughan
Mascot Brewery	Toronto
Mill Street Brewery (production)	Toronto
Mill Street Brewpub	Toronto
Muddy York Brewing Co.	Toronto
Old Tomorrow Beer	Toronto
Pitschfork Brewing Co.	Toronto
Radical Road Brewing Co.	Toronto
Rainhard Brewing Co.	Toronto
Rhythm & Brews Brewing Co.	Toronto
Rouge River Brewing Co.	Markham
Saint Andre	Toronto
Shacklands Brewing Co.	Toronto
Shillow Beer Co.	Toronto
Southpaw Beverage Co.	Toronto
Spearhead Brewing Co.	Toronto
St. Mary Axe Beer Co.	Toronto
Steam Whistle Brewing	Toronto
Sweetgrass Brewing Co.	Toronto
3 Brewers, The (Adelaide)	Toronto
3 Brewers, The (Liberty Village)	Toronto
3 Brewers, The (Mississauga)	Mississauga
3 Brewers, The (Richmond Hill)	Richmond Hill
3 Brewers, The (Yonge St.)	Toronto
Tracks Brew Pub	Brampton
Triple Bogey Brewing	Toronto
Woodhouse Brewing Co.	Toronto

EASTERN ONTARIO

Bancroft Brewing Co.	Bancroft
Barley Days Brewery	Picton
Beau's All Natural Brewing Co.	Vankleek Hill
Bobcaygeon Brewing Co.	Bobcaygeon
Calabogie Brewing Co.	Calabogie
Cartwright Springs Brewery	Pakenham
Cassel Brewery	Casselman
County Canteen, The	Picton
County Road Beer Co.	Prince Edward County
Crooked Mile Brewing Co.	Almonte
4 Degrees Brewing	Smith Falls
Gananoque Brewing Co.	Gananoque
King's Town Beer Company	Kingston
Kingston Brewing Co.	Kingston
Lake on the Mountain Brewing Co.	Prince Edward County
MacKinnon Brothers Brewing Co.	Bath
Manantler Craft Brewery	Bowmanville
Napanee Beer Co.	Napanee
Northumberland Hills Brewery	Cobourg
Old Flame Brewing Co.	Port Perry
Olde Stone Brewing Co., The	Peterborough
Parsons Brewing Co.	Picton
Perth Brewery	Perth
Publican House Brewery, The	Peterborough
Rurban Brewing	Cornwall
Second Wedge Brewing Co.	Uxbridge
Skeleton Park Brewery	Kingston
Smithavens Brewing Co.	Peterborough
Square Timber Brewing Co.	Pembroke
Stone City Ales	Kingston
Strange Brewing Co.	Prince Edward County
Whitewater Brewing Co.	Foresters Falls, Cobden
Wild Card Brewing Co.	Trenton
William Street Beer Co.	Cobourg
Windmill Brewing	Johnstown

BREWERIES BY REGION

609

THE OTTAWA REGION

Ashton Brewing Co.	Ashton
Beyond the Pale Brewing Co.	Ottawa
Bicycle Craft Brewery	Ottawa
Big Rig Brewery & Taproom	Kanata
Big Rig Kitchen & Brewery	Gloucester
Big Rig Kitchen & Brewery	Ottawa
Brasserie Étienne Brûlé	Embrun
Broadhead Brewing Co.	Nepean
Broken Stick Brewing Co.	Ottawa
Brown Van Brewing	Ottawa
Clocktower Brewpubs (various locations)	Ottawa
Covered Bridge Brewing Co.	Ottawa
Dog and Pony Brewlab	Ottawa
Dominion City Brewing Co.	Ottawa
Evergreen Craft Ales	Nepean
Hogsback Brewing Co.	Ottawa
Kichesippi Beer Co.	Ottawa
Lowertown Brewery	Ottawa
Mill Street Brewpub (Ottawa)	Ottawa
Nita Beer Co.	Ottawa
Stalwart Brewing Co.	Carleton Place
Stray Dog Brewing	Orléans
3 Brewers, The (Kanata)	Kanata
3 Brewers, The (Ottawa)	Ottawa
Tooth and Nail Brewing Co.	Ottawa
Tuque De Broue	Embrun
Waller St. Brewing	Ottawa
Whiprsnapr Brewing Co.	Nepean

NORTHERN ONTARIO

Barnstormer Brewing Co.	Barrie
Belmont Lake Brewery	Havelock
Big Water Brewing Co.	North Bay

Black Bellows Brewing Co.	Collingwood
Boshkung Brewing Co.	Minden Hills
Cecil's Brewhouse & Kitchen	North Bay
Collingwood Brewery	Collingwood
Creemore Springs Brewery	Creemore
Dawson Trail Craft Brewery	Thunder Bay
Flying Monkeys Craft Brewery	Barrie
Full Beard Brewing Co.	Timmins
Haliburton Highlands Brewing	Haliburton
Highlander Brew Co.	South River
Horseshoe Valley Brewing Co.	Oro-Medonte
Kilannan Brewing Co.	Owen Sound
Lake of Bays Brewing Co.	Baysville
Lake of the Woods Brewing Co.	Kenora
MacLean's Ales	Hanover
Manitoulin Brewing Co.	Little Current
Muskoka Brewery	Bracebridge
New Ontario Brewing Co.	North Bay
Norse Brewery	Nobel
Northern Superior Brewing Co.	Sault Ste. Marie
Northwinds Brew Ltd.	Collingwood
Outlaw Brew Co.	Southampton
Outspoken Brewing	Sault Ste. Marie
Redline Brewhouse	Barrie
Sawdust City Brewing Co.	Gravenhurst
Side Launch Brewing Co.	Collingwood
Sleeping Giant Brewing Co.	Thunder Bay
Split Rail Brewing Co.	Gore Bay
Stack Brewing	Sudbury
Thornbury Village Cidery & Brewery	Nobleton
Tobermory Brewing Co. & Grill	Tobermory
Union Jack Brewing Co.	Sault Ste. Marie
Wasaga Beach Brewing Co.	Wasaga Beach

INDEX OF BEERS

INDEX OF BEERS

Hearsay Entire Porter, 222
Hearts Collide, 430
Hefeweizen (Smithavens
  Brewing Co.), 469
Heller Highwater, 302
Henderson's Best, 276
Hennepin Stout, 378
Henry's Irish Ale, 423
Heroes Blonde Lager, 470
Hibiscus Saison, 443
Hi-Fidelity Pale Ale, 509
High Noon, 423
Highland Hillwalker, 211
Highlander Stout, 281
Hill 145 Golden Ale, 464
Hockley Amber, 283
Hockley Classic, 283
Hockley Dark, 282–83
Hogtown Ale, 285
Holiday Honey, 399
Home Sweet Home, 239
Homegrown Hemp Ale, 179
Honest Lager, 530
Honey Badger, 252
Honey Brown Ale, 271
Honey Cream Ale, 95
Honey Elixir, 427
Honey Ginger Shandy, 403
Honey Habanero, 254

Honeymoon Peach Radler,
  378
Hop Addict, 197
Hop Cone Syndrome, 429–30
Hopbot, 287
Hopping Mad, 262
Hops & Bolts, 210
Hops & Robbers, 223
Hopside IPA, 417
Hopsta La Vista, 330
Hopstravaganza, 74
Hoptical Illusion Almost Pale
  Ale, 241
Horntrip Juniper Pale Ale,
  492–93
Huron Street Hefeweizen,
  124
Huronic, 462
Hurry Hard Amber Lager,
  522

Iconoclast, 291
Illiterate Librarians, 436–37
Impact Altbier, 480
Imperial Coffee Stout, 206
Imperial Russian Stout, 536
Imperial Super Guy, 111
Imposter Syndrome
  Farmhouse IPA, 244

ACKNOWLEDGEMENTS

This book was a combined effort, and we couldn't have done it without a little help, both direct and indirect, from the following. Thanks to Stephen Beaumont for the wise advice and moral support, and to fellow beer scribes Jamie MacKinnon, Josh Rubin, Crystal Luxmore, Ben Johnson, Alan McLeod, Dan Grant, Chris Schryer, Robert and Kathryn Arsenault, Kole McRae, Katy Watts, and Brian Papineau. Deserving of special mention is Chris Burek, who we routinely talk to about listings on the excellent Ontario Beverage Network, and Greg Clow, whose wonderful site Canadian Beer News is an excellent source of past and current news.

We would also like to thank the nice people who helped us organize the logistics of dealing with nearly 250 separate breweries, for the most part without recompense, making them nearly as crazy as we are. For this edition of the book, that group includes David Lee, Jill Currie, Brian Yeo, Jenn Donovan, April Tremblay-Thibert, Chuck Thibert, André Proulx, and Renee Navarro.

Thanks also to Tourism Thunder Bay, the Manitoulin Tourism Association (especially Lori), Ottawa Tourism (especially Jantine), Southwest Ontario Tourism Corporation (especially Jatinder), and Norfolk County Tourism (especially Ted). If you're reading this section, why not check out their websites and find fun things to do in those regions? You can't drink all the time.

Writing a book of this kind is nearly impossible without the assistance of brewers and brewery employees who help each other out by ferrying us back and forth even when it doesn't benefit them. Thanks to Ken Woods, Chuck Galea, Dennis Talon, Tomas Baldasaro, and Lon Ladell for understanding that the road is long, the budget for cabs is small, and the time dwindles fearsome.

Additional thanks goes to the Ontario Craft Brewers; our tenacious and brilliant agent, Clare F. Pelino; Milos Kral; the team at Dundurn — Michelle Melski, Beth Bruder, Carrie Gleason, Margaret Bryant, and Kirk Howard; and our fantastic editors Kathryn Lane, Jenny Govier, and Emma Warnken Johnson.

Finally, thanks to the Ontario breweries for being yourselves. Keep brewing, keep refining, keep evolving, and, of course, keep drinking.

FROM ROBIN LEBLANC:

Special thanks to my parents, Anya and Larry LeBlanc, for their constant support. Thanks also to Cheryl Weatherill, Candice Donovan, Michael Millan, and the Whitechapel crew for being completely unwavering in your friendship and encouragement. It means more to me than you will ever know. Additional thanks goes to the region of northern Ontario. I saw a lot more of you this time round, and you never cease to take my breath away.

I know they were thanked in the general acknowledgements, but I can't overstate how grateful I am to Jill Currie, Jenn Donovan, April Tremblay-Thibert, Chuck Thibert, and fellow drinks columnist André Proulx for agreeing to drive me places without hesitation. The trips were infinitely more enjoyable with your world-class company.

Finally, thanks goes to Life Without Buildings for their song "The Leanover," which got me through the final two weeks of writing. And to Matt Berry for "One Track Lover," proving he actually is more attractive like Dagless.

FROM JORDAN ST. JOHN:

Special thanks to my parents, who both muled beer for this edition: Neil St.John, who cannot believe there are two breweries in Bayfield, and Laurel Dempsey, who actually convinced Stone City to make a beer for her (she thinks

Rathlin Gael should be rated higher than I do). Thanks also to Chris Mayo for the ride to Waterloo.

Thanks go to Lorne Michaels, my bad impression of whom got us through several hours of boring countryside on the way to Ottawa. Then again, it may only have seemed like several hours. Thanks also to James McMurtry, whose excellent song "Choctaw Bingo" propelled some of the mayhem.

JORDAN ST. JOHN

Jordan St. John has been writing about beer since 2010, and in that time he has published five books, over two hundred syndicated newspaper columns as Canada's only nationally syndicated beer columnist, three hundred blog posts at saintjohnswort.ca, and several dozen magazine articles. If he had to guess, he'd say that puts him just over a million words on beer in total. He has appeared on *Storage Wars Canada*, CBC Radio One, Global News, and a number of other media outlets as a beer expert. He holds the ranks of Certified Cicerone and Certified BJCP. Periodically he even considers writing about things that aren't beer. When no one is watching, he drinks club soda instead of beer and enjoys a quiet night in. Shhh. Don't tell anyone.

———

JORDAN is best described as an acquired taste: somewhat acerbic, although lighter in body than previous years, redolent of spicy salad greens and coffee, and undergoing a continuous packaging redesign (4).

ROBIN LEBLANC

Robin LeBlanc began writing about beer in 2011, shortly after being captivated with the deep complexities of the beverage. Her website, thethirstywench.com, has won multiple awards, including the *Saveur* Best Food Blog Award in the Best Wine or Beer Blog category (the first Canadian-based site to do so). She is the former beer columnist for *Torontoist* and currently writes the syndicated "On Tap" for Metroland North Media. She has appeared regularly as a beer expert and Cicerone Certified Beer Server at various events and on media outlets such as Rogers Daytime Toronto and 680 News Radio. When not writing, she works as a photographer and publicist. She lives in Toronto and takes her coffee black with two sugars, thanks.

———

ROBIN is a fine example of an English/North American hybrid that has gotten a touch more complex in the past year. While there is an initial jab of bitterness upfront, a gentle, sweet character balances things out before moving in for a somewhat looming, dry finish (4).

THE ONTARIO CRAFT BEER GUIDE